ADVANCE PRAISE FOR
Dispatches from the Threshold

"The authors of *Dispatches from the Threshold* remind us that housing crises are one of many routinized catastrophes of capital, and yet reading this book is not to drown in crisis but to rise with the power of tenants. Read it, and get organized."

—**ASTRA TAYLOR**, author of *The Age of Insecurity: Coming Together As Things Fall Apart*

"This book is an essential document for this dystopian century, a powerful account of collective resistance, imagination, and thinking that can provide hope and illuminate possible futures."

—**RAQUEL ROLNIK**, former UN Special Rapporteur on adequate housing

"A multi-point perspective like this is exactly what we've needed to understand the struggle for adequate housing. This work is a rich, collectively woven tapestry. It is not just a record of a unique and useful moment of crisis, but it is crammed with wisdom and experience. It is full of hope, insight, and vital lessons in how to have each other's backs."

—**NICK BANO**, barrister and author of *Against Landlords: How to Solve the Housing Crisis*

"This book merges the energy of a housing protest with the analytic insights of critical social science. It offers a clear perspective on our current crisis and a much-needed picture of what tenant power looks like."

—**DAVID MADDEN**, co-author of *In Defense of Housing: The Politics of Crisis*

"This collection illustrates the audacity of collective action in the face of our most difficult obstacle: insecurity. It captures the struggle for immediate relief and the gift these movements and their participants provide us all — a glimpse of more just, humane, and radical urban futures and the imagination, language, and tools to realize it."

—**JOSH AKERS**, researcher, Urban Praxis

"The fight for housing justice is gaining momentum, but individual battles are geographically dispersed, immersed in local dynamics, and not always visibly related. This volume compiles rich accounts of many of these battles. Unrestricted by theoretical or political frameworks, the authors describe housing struggles as they happen on the frontline. Each story is unique. Yet, the forces behind tenant exploitation and displacement are the same everywhere, and the political responses of organized tenants share many similarities. If capital is an international force, tenant power is pushing new boundaries. This book documents this process and helps advance it."

—RICARDO TRANJAN, Canadian Centre for Policy Alternatives and author of *The Tenant Class*

DISPATCHES
FROM THE
THRESHOLD

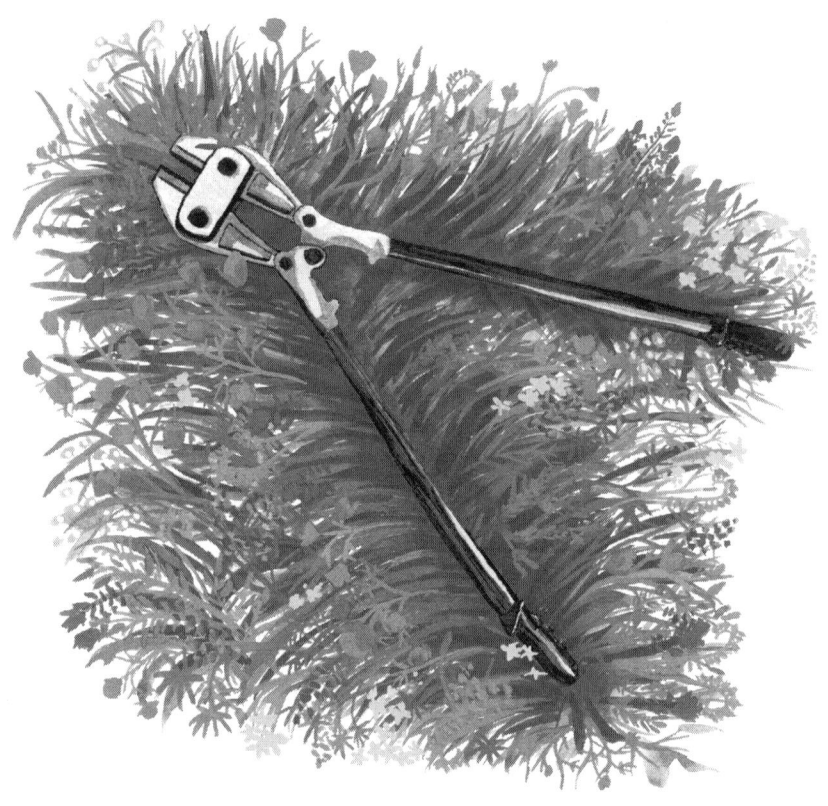

Created as a promotional image for the 2021 Annual Assembly of the Los Angeles Tenants Union (LATU), the bolt cutters are a reference to the many illegal evictions LATU has prevented, which sometimes involves breaking back into apartments when landlords illegally change the locks. The flowers refer to the seeds of revolution being sown by tenant organizers in the fight for housing justice.

DISPATCHES FROM THE THRESHOLD

TENANT POWER IN TIMES OF CRISIS

EDITED BY
Rae Baker & Alexander Ferrer
FOREWORD BY
Samuel Stein

FERNWOOD PUBLISHING
HALIFAX & WINNIPEG

Copyright 2025 © Rae Baker and Alexander Ferrer

All rights reserved. No part of this book may be reproduced or transmitted in any form by any means without permission in writing from the publisher, except by a reviewer, who may quote brief passages in a review.

Development editor: Tanya Andrusieczko
Copyediting: Brenda Conroy
Text design: Lauren Jeanneau
Cover design: Evan Marnoch
Printed and bound in the UK

Published by Fernwood Publishing
Halifax and Winnipeg
2970 Oxford Street, Halifax, Nova Scotia, B3L 2W4
www.fernwoodpublishing.ca

Fernwood Publishing Company Limited gratefully acknowledges the financial support of the Government of Canada through the Canada Book Fund and the Canada Council for the Arts. We acknowledge the Province of Manitoba for support through the Manitoba Publishers Marketing Assistance Program and the Book Publishing Tax Credit. We acknowledge the Nova Scotia Department of Communities, Culture and Heritage for support through the Publishers Assistance Fund. We also acknowledge the Urban Studies Foundation for publishing support.

Library and Archives Canada Cataloguing in Publication
Title: Dispatches from the threshold : tenant power in times of crisis / edited by Rae Baker & Alexander Ferrer ; foreword by Samuel Stein.
Names: Baker, Rae, editor. | Ferrer, Alexander, editor. | Stein, Samuel, writer of foreword
Description: Includes bibliographical references and index.
Identifiers: Canadiana 20240535065 | ISBN 9781773637273 (softcover)
Subjects: LCSH: Housing—Case studies. | LCSH: Housing policy—Case studies. | LCSH: Landlord and tenant—Case studies. | LCSH: Apartment dwellers—Case studies. | LCGFT: Case studies.
Classification: LCC HD7287 .D57 2025 | DDC 307.3/36—dc23

This book is for everyone who has struggled with housing insecurity, which together we will make a thing of the past.

CONTENTS

Contributors x

Acknowledgements xiv

Foreword... 1

Introduction: The Struggle for Housing Justice 3
   DETROIT, MICHIGAN, UNITED STATES
   Rae Baker

1   Tenant-Centred Public Health in Vancouver's Downtown Eastside 14
    VANCOUVER, BRITISH COLUMBIA, CANADA
    Aaron Bailey, Dani Aiello, Bryan Jacobs & the Right to Remain Research Collective

2   Community Control of Public Housing...24
    NEWARK, NEW JERSEY, UNITED STATES
    Ari McCaskill & Peter Blackmer

3   Rehabilitative Capitalism in Winnipeg's Rental Market 34
    WINNIPEG, MANITOBA, CANADA
    Stefan Hodges

4   Leveraging Land and Housing Occupations 45
    PHILADELPHIA, PENNSYLVANIA, UNITED STATES
    Amanda Ricketts & Claire Herbert

5   Housing and Home as Key Sites of Struggle 54
    MINNEAPOLIS, MINNESOTA, UNITED STATES
    Nina Medvedeva

6   Building Tenant Power out of Crises 64
    ATLANTA, GEORGIA, UNITED STATES
    Natalie McLaughlin, Dani Aiello, Karimah Dillard-Mickey &
    the Housing Justice League

7   Contradictions in Infra-Commoning Networks in Serbia.....................73
    BELGRADE, SERBIA
    Ana Vilenica & Vladimir Mentus

8   Detroit Renter City 82
    DETROIT, MICHIGAN, UNITED STATES
    Rae Baker

9	Against Landlord Technology in San Francisco 95
	SAN FRANCISCO, CALIFORNIA, UNITED STATES
	Erin McElroy, Matthew Martignoni, Jeantelle Laberinto, Joseph Smooke & Priya Prabhakar
10	Tenant-Organized Eviction Court Watch 108
	PORTLAND, OREGON, UNITED STATES
	Colleen Carroll (Don't Evict PDX)
11	Lawyers in the Housing Justice Movement 114
	LOS ANGELES, CALIFORNIA, UNITED STATES
	Greg Bonett, Faizah Malik, Katie McKeon & Doug Smith
12	Housing Justice in the Bluegrass State 129
	LEXINGTON, KENTUCKY, UNITED STATES
	Lukas Bullock
13	Envisioning Collective Bargaining Rights for Renters 139
	VANCOUVER AND VICTORIA, BRITISH COLUMBIA, CANADA
	Pierce Nettling, Rebecca Kantwerg, Anna Gabriela Doebeli, Ben Ger, Ryan Hong, Alex J. Kiczales & Alex McLean
14	The Political Renter Class in So-Called Australia................................. 148
	MELBOURNE, VICTORIA, AUSTRALIA
	David Kelly, Prashanti Mayfield, Eirene Tsolidis Noyce, Traça DeBarra, Zachary Doney & Jordan Adams
15	Mapping Conviction-Based Housing Restrictions in Chicago 157
	CHICAGO, ILLINOIS, UNITED STATES
	Celia Magnone
16	Organizing during Forced Eviction in Khori Gaon 167
	DELHI, INDIA
	Ishita Chatterjee
17	The Public Park as a Commons 179
	TORONTO, ONTARIO, CANADA
	Anna Kramer & Jesse Upton Crowe
18	Encampment Evictions in Washington, DC 187
	WASHINGTON, DC, UNITED STATES
	Aaron Howe & Shannon Clark
19	Unhoused Tenants and the Struggle for Housing Liberation 196
	LOS ANGELES, CALIFORNIA, UNITED STATES
	Annie Powers & Ashley Bennett
20	Housing Should Not Be a Luxury 206
	VANCOUVER, BRITISH COLUMBIA, CANADA
	Marena Skinner

Afterword: Ours to Shape 207
LOS ANGELES, CALIFORNIA, UNITED STATES
Alexander Ferrer

Index 211

CONTRIBUTORS

Anti-Eviction Mapping Project is a data visualization, digital media, and counter-mapping collective that produces maps, stories, analyses, tools, murals, zines, and more to support housing organizing in the San Francisco Bay Area, New York City, and Los Angeles. **Erin McElroy** (they/them) and **Matthew Martignoni** (they/he) are members of AEMP.

After Echo Park Lake Research Collective brings together university-based and movement-based scholars along with unhoused comrades to undertake research towards housing justice that operates in the UCLA Luskin Institute on Inequality and Democracy. **Annie Powers** and **Ashley Bennett** are collective members.

Rae Baker is a critical geographer and assistant professor who lives and organizes in Detroit. They were a member of Detroit Renter City during the organization's operation and continue to organize against evictions, displacement, and police surveillance. They contribute research to Urban Praxis Workshop (urbanpraxis.org).

Peter Blackmer is an assistant professor of Africology and African American studies at Eastern Michigan University. He is a scholar of the Black Freedom Movement and lead researcher of Rise Up North (riseupnorth.com).

Lukas Bullock (he/they) is an organizer with **Lexington Housing Justice Collective** and a PhD candidate and instructor in the Gender & Women's Studies Department at the University of Kentucky. His research engages state feminism, knowledge politics, and social movements.

Colleen Carroll is an anti-eviction organizer and researcher, particularly interested in examining power dynamics in the eviction system and participating in participatory action research and direct action towards collective liberation.

Ishita Chatterjee is an early career researcher who studied the Khori Gaon settlement on the Delhi-Haryana border. She has been an integral part of the settlement's struggle for justice and assists in community empowerment workshops, legal processes, and advocacy.

Alexander Ferrer is a PhD student and movement-based researcher in Los Angeles. He works with Strategic Actions for a Just Economy, The Debt Collective, and the UCLA Institute on Inequality and Democracy.

Stefan Hodges has worked as a tenant organizer and a housing support worker in Winnipeg's West Broadway neighbourhood. His master's thesis studied a burgeoning movement of recovery landlordism in Winnipeg's private rental market.

Housing Justice League is a grassroots, community-led non-profit in Atlanta that organizes at the building level to build racial and class consciousness, train new organizers, and realize our collective power. **Dani Aiello**, **Natalie McLaughlin**, and **Karimah Dillard-Mickey** are researchers, organizers, and members within HJL.

Anna Kramer is an urban planner and a volunteer with the **Encampment Support Network**. **Jesse Upton Crowe** is a co-founder of the **Parkdale neighbourhood committee** and a volunteer with Encampment Support Network in Toronto.

Los Angeles Tenants Union is a member-funded and -led movement fighting for the human right to housing for all. LATU organizes tenant associations, rent strikes, and eviction blockades through local chapters spread across the city of Los Angeles. **Rose Lenehan** and **Elizabeth Blaney**, who contributed art to this edited collection, are members of LATU and the Eastside local Union de Vencinos respectively.

Celia Magnone is a PhD student in criminology at the University of Illinois Chicago studying sex offence registration laws and the social, spatial exclusion of people on the registry.

Ari McCaskill is a graduate of the master's degree program in Africology and African American studies at Eastern Michigan University. The focus of his thesis was public housing activism and tenant-management.

Nina Medvedeva (she/her) has organized for housing justice, workers' rights, harm reduction, reproductive justice, and queer and trans rights over the last decade. She is a visiting assistant professor in women's and gender studies at Hamilton College in Clinton, New York.

Vladimir Mentus is a senior research associate at the Institute of Social Sciences in Belgrade, Serbia, and national coordinator of the European Social Survey. His research primarily focuses on economic sociology.

[people.power.media] broadcasts efforts and perspectives from marginalized communities where grassroots organizations are working to change housing and land issues. Founded originally in Toronto, PPM is currently based in San Francisco. **Jeantelle Laberinto** (she/her), **Priya Prabhakar** (she/her), and **Joseph Smooke** are members of [people.power.media].

Public Council is where **Greg Bonett**, **Faizah Malik**, **Katie McKeon**, and **Doug Smith** work in the Community Development Project and provide legal and policy support to community-led housing justice movements in Los Angeles using a movement lawyering model.

Remora House, co-founded by **Shannon Clark** and **Aaron Howe**, is an unhoused community support and defence group in Washington DC.

Rent Strike Bargain is a province-wide campaign in British Columbia that aims to build solidarity between tenants and organized labour across the unceded Musqueam, Squamish, and Tsleil-Waututh territories (Vancouver) and unceded Lekwungen territories (Victoria). **Anna Gabriela Doebeli** (she/her), **Ben Ger** (he/they), **Ryan Hong** (he/him), **Rebecca Kantwerg** (she/they), **Alex J. Kiczales** (he/him), **Alex McLean** (he/him), and **Pierce Nettling** (he/him) are members.

Saiyare Refaei (they/them/she/her) is a Chinese Iranian artist based on the traditional lands of the Puyallup and Coast Salish peoples, referred to as Tacoma, Washington. They are a member of JustSeeds and organize with La Resistencia for the freedom of immigrants detained in the detention centre in Tacoma.

Renters and Housing Union is a member-run union of renters and people in precarious housing in Naarm (Melbourne, Australia). **David Kelly**, **Prashanti Mayfield**, **Eirene Tsolidis Noyce**, **Zachary Doney**, **Jordan Adams**, and **Traça DeBarra** are members of the RAHU.

Right to Remain Research Collective is a group of SRO tenants, academics, organizers, students, and community allies collaborating in Vancouver's Downtown Eastside. **Aaron Bailey, Bryan Jacobs**, and **Dani Aiello** are members of R2R and a complete team profile of all our collective members who contribute to this organizing and intellectual work can be found on its website: righttoremain.ca.

Marena Skinner is a self-taught mixed media artist from Vancouver. She is known for her unique character style and subject matter about housing rights, sexual harassment, and mental health.

Samuel Stein writes and fights about New York City urban planning politics, with an emphasis on housing, real estate, labour and gentrification. He is the author of *Capital City: Gentrification and the Real Estate State*.

Ana Vilenica is a researcher, no border, tenants, and feminist organizer and activist from Pančevo, Serbia. She is a member of the *Radical Housing Journal* editorial collective, the Beyond Inhabitation Lab, and the Feminist Autonomous Center for Research.

ACKNOWLEDGEMENTS

The co-editors of this volume would first and foremost like to thank each of the contributors, both for your efforts in writing this book into existence and for the work we all share in struggling for more affordable, accessible, and racially and socially just housing in our communities and the world. Working in activist and social justice spaces with the knowledge that this work is always about keeping ourselves alive, fighting, and creating toward another world is an immense and necessary weight. All contributors are engaged in this important work, and we are grateful they lent their stories and knowledge to this book so that we all may read, reflect, learn, and continue creating a stronger housing justice movement together. Collecting and sharing the knowledge and experiences generated within movement spaces is an act of great trust that we do not take lightly. We are grateful for the support of the Urban Studies Foundation who supported this project as part of the organization's Pandemics and Cities grant program (USF-PCS-220102). We would also like to extend our gratitude to those within movements for housing justice who have yet to be thanked for their labour, commitment, and vision for a different world.

FOREWORD

Dispatches from the Threshold is a real-time document of organizing for housing justice in a time of multiple crises: an ongoing crisis of tenants' rights and housing affordability; a global pandemic; a climate catastrophe; a resurgent fascism; and more. Its contributors and those whose stories they tell have never had the luxury of organizing in anything but a moment of crisis. This is the reality of housing struggle in the twenty-first century.

We live in a time when the project of maximizing housing profitability is central to global financial accumulation, national development priorities, and local government finances. While housing struggles most often take the form of small battles between tenants and their landlords, or between residents of encampments and local police departments, they are always also imbricated in multiple levels of capital accumulation and public finance — in other words, in the mechanisms of the capitalist state. There is therefore no such thing as a simply small or local housing struggle. Though it may not always feel like it, the struggle for the most local thing imaginable — our own home — is one of many fronts in a global battle against the dominant economic, political, and social order.

The COVID-19 pandemic in some ways scrambled housing economics and politics. Suddenly, staying home was the central strategy for avoiding mass infection and death. For a great many people, that meant not going to work. Not going to work meant not earning the money to pay the rent, which in turn meant demanding that the rent be cancelled — by either the landlords or the state. Something had to give: either tenants would be thrown out of their homes, landlords would miss their mortgage payments, or banks would have to forgive their debts. Meanwhile, people with money and office jobs were suddenly able to sever the link between the geographic location of their home and their job, and many took off for greener pastures, setting off new dimensions of housing crisis in both the places they exited and the places they entered.

The various elements of COVID-specific housing crises were treated (but never resolved) in different ways in different places. What is remarkable is that despite this major global upheaval, not that much has seemed to change. Rents still outpace wages. Homelessness and displacement are still regular features of urban life. Evictions stopped, and then they started again. Some landlords exited the business, but new ones quickly replaced them.

This book positions itself at the "threshold" — an appropriately architectural metaphor for the subject of housing. This threshold could just as conceivably be a portal to the resurgent real estate state, capable of wiping away the advances of the past as it churns toward the corporate city of the future, as it could be one into a new era of housing justice, mass social housing, and universal rent control. The movements profiled in this book are actively adapting to the fast-changing landscape and will be the ones to carry us all over the threshold into a different future.

—**SAMUEL STEIN**, author of
Capital City: Gentrification and the Real Estate State

INTRODUCTION

THE STRUGGLE FOR HOUSING JUSTICE

DETROIT, MICHIGAN, UNITED STATES

WRITTEN BY
Rae Baker

In the process of assembling this volume over four years, much has transpired in the political and personal lives of the contributing editors and authors that has shaped our thinking about the work of housing justice movements in our own cities and in places where our activism, research, and politics have allowed us to develop relationships with people who, like us, are committed to the work of building tenant power. The Los Angeles Tenants Union (LATU) is one of just over a dozen organizations that are presented in this volume. To start us off on common ground, the co-editors of this volume are following the lead of LATU tenant organizers by adopting their definition of a tenant in our conceptualization of tenant power: LATU considers a tenant to be anyone who lacks control over their housing. Using this definition, tenants broadly include residents of encampments, squatters, tenants who do and do not hold leases, households with a mortgage or land contract, occupants of emergency hotel stay rooms, and many in between. Throughout this volume and in all our work beyond book writing, conceptualizing tenants in this way allows for the greatest abundance of connection and capacity in times of crisis and movements structured around scarcity and austerity. Building tenant power is and will continue to be an effort of significant magnitude in the crises of today and those yet to come. Conceptualizing tenants as anyone who lacks control over their housing most accurately and inclusively reflects the struggle against the compounding pressures of capital, racism, classism, gender inequality, ableism, settler colonialism, and policing — to name a few — that foreclose on people's access to housing. In the work of building tenant power, the collective power to challenge landlords, defend our neighbours from evictions, and radically transform housing from an asset into a public good, everyone is needed.

Amid the material and financial afterlife of the Great Recession (2007–09), during a global anti-racist uprising and reawakening, and the beginning of looming worldwide financial uncertainty driven by our latest global pandemic, this book was assembled to connect people engaged in the radical collective work of struggling toward housing justice. The following chapters offer up the stories of legal aid workers, tenant organizers, scholar activists, and encampment residents and advocates. Their words hold the potential to strengthen our tactics and deepen our collective (and diverse) visions for a more humane, equitable, and politically mobilized housing future. In our respective cities, Detroit and Los Angeles, the co-editors of this text have been engaged in housing activism through eviction and foreclosure defences, research, policy work, and tenant organizing for over a decade. As we assembled this volume, we each had landlord-tenant issues of our own, as did many of the contributing authors. Temporary protections against evictions, introduced during the most acute period of the COVID-19 pandemic, were eventually withdrawn, and some of the volume's contributors had to attend to the urgent work of eviction defences, encampment support, and, in some cases, attending the funerals of fellow tenants whose housing conditions proved deadly. Between these crises, contributors developed the stories and theories that make up this collection, shaping it into a living archive of experiences that demonstrate what it means to build tenant power.

Housing crises are one of many routinized catastrophes of capital, evidenced by the last decade and a half or so of the mortgage bubble of the Great Recession in the US, the mass wave of mortgage and tax foreclosures across parts of Europe and the US that followed, and the COVID-19 pandemic, in which renters' and mortgage holders' housing became suddenly imperiled, not by the virus itself but by landlord entitlement and the economic consequences of lost wages and workplace closures necessitated by public health protections. What is apparent to those of us in housing justice movements is that moments of mass crisis bring people together. From occupying and defending mortgage and tax foreclosed homes in the early 2010s, to rebelliously responding to the deaths of tenants in Grenfell Tower, to a mass influx of renters responding to the urgency of the pandemic in 2020: connecting with neighbours and strangers alike to fight for everyone's ability to have a place to call home is a tide that always rises to meet moments of crises with unrelenting persistence.

In 2020, with the housing crisis that ruptured out of the Great Recession just barely behind us, the first pandemic of the twenty-first century catalyzed a wave of tenant organizing across the globe. As COVID transmission spiked, so too did uncertainty and anxieties about how forced workplace closures, job losses, and shelter-in-place orders would impact people who were already experiencing economic precarity, disabilities, addiction, and the myriad structural effects of racism. Early pandemic uncertainties clarified that the potential of mass evictions seemed imminent for wage-dependent renters and people who were already financially struggling. The possibility of losing their homes politicized and radicalized tenants en masse.

In the early months of 2020, tenant organizing was reshaped by shelter-in-place restrictions and a dearth of public health precautions attempting to address the transmissibility of an illness we all knew little about. Housing activists and grassroots organizations who were seasoned in fighting evictions and their landlords in pre-pandemic times saw a rapid influx of enraged, scared, and newly energized tenants searching for and creating new outlets for collective organization in their apartments and across their neighbourhoods and cities. Another more chronic crisis was also bringing people into the streets.

In March 2020, just as the World Health Organization declared a pandemic, Breonna Taylor was shot and killed in her apartment by police officers who forcibly entered the wrong address. Just a few months later, George Floyd was murdered by a police officer in Minneapolis. Protests demanding an end to anti-Black police brutality and the defunding of the police spread across the globe and sustained for months following Taylor's and Floyd's murders, visibly commanding public spaces through rebellious resistance. At the time, analysis of these large demonstrations compared them to civil rights marches of the 1960s. However, Keeanga-Yamahtta Taylor urged that people rebelliously taking up public space in 2020 in response to police brutality more closely paralleled the 1992 protests in Los Angeles and beyond. Following the acquittal of the police officers charged for beating Rodney King, and reduced sentencing — from serving prison time for manslaughter to five years' parole — for a shop owner who murdered Latasha Harlins in his convenience store,[1] the public responded in an uproar. In both cases, the court sided with those who committed brutal acts of violence against Black people. Angelenos and people across the country marched on police stations and city halls, shut down roadways, and expressed their anger through congregating, property damage and arson. Just as George H.W. Bush invoked the Insurrection Act in 1992, Donald Trump and many state governors commanded the support of the National Guard to quell resistance against state-sanctioned police brutality in 2020. Both moments demonstrated the government's determination to defend property and the sanctity of policing from unrest that arises when police murder Black people without consequence. R.H. Lossin's essay "In Defense of Destroying Property" described property destruction of the 2020 uprisings as "reasoned, calculated acts" in the face of police brutality; not to be treated as an externality perpetrated by outside agitators but reckoned with as articulate expressions of refusal.[2] Whether responding to police brutality, defending our neighbours from evictions, stopping encampment sweeps, or resisting anti-Black racism, the structuring principle of these acts of defiance against the state-sanctioned violence of policing is always to keep one another alive.

Today in Canada, the United States, Australia, and across Europe, government funds intended to support financial recovery in what governments are calling a "post-pandemic" economy are using federal "post-pandemic" funds to inflate policing budgets and increase the pervasive spread of anti-Black surveillance technologies.[3] Those whose housing has been impacted by global crises, careless governmental preparation for emergencies, and the universal reality of how our housing needs change with age and ability, all live with the pain of foresight, that there must have been some other better way to have one's housing needs met. The rousing demand to defund the police that grew out of the anti-racist uprisings of 2020 posed a critical argument: that cities could reallocate municipal operating funds away from policing, which only reacts to — and perpetuates — violence rather than prevents it, and toward social resources like housing, food access, and public health services, which would proactively address the wellbeing and safety of residents.

The magnitude of social disinvestment came to a head in the context of the pandemic. As emergency shelter services panicked under the pressure of the 2020 pandemic response, homeless encampments expanded and became increasingly visible across Canada and the United States. Indigenous encampment residents and their allies importantly pointed out the pervasiveness of Indigenous populations experiencing homelessness and seeking out encampments as a place to find community and access to outreach and support services. The volume of Indigenous people experiencing COVID-19 and living at encampment sites was, as residents declared, directly proportional to the impact of settler colonial power over land and the violence that governing authorities have always depended on to enforce settler control. Homelessness, after all, is a construct based in settler colonial technologies of private property and land ownership.[4] Homelessness and encampments, both of which are most directly governed and presided over by laws and enforcement at the municipal level, are continuously met by authorities through evictions, criminalization, and "interlocking colonial and classist political economies."[5] Mounting public pressure to stop the sweeping of encampments in Canada and the US pushed back on NIMBY anxieties of encampments as sites of mass infection and blight by meeting settler authority with demands for Land Back! These declarations by Indigenous encampment residents and their communities enacted a politics of refusal against encampment evictions by asserting their right to self-determination on lands that were theirs to begin with.[6] These bold and valid declarations are imperative in informing and guiding how tenant power is politically conceptualized and carried out relationally among Indigenous Nations and settlers in our vastly disparate struggles for home.

One of the most important elements of organizing our communities, workplaces, and neighbourhoods is our capacity to locate and connect with one another. Connection is at least half of the struggle of being able to listen and learn from one another's experiences. With great intention, the everyday conditions of late-stage capitalism deeply alienate those who are most economically, legally, and racially excluded from civic and political life. Our individual and collective capacities to resist tactics of dehumanization, such as the criminalization of homelessness and poverty, profit-driven evictions and crises of housing greed, and the denial of necessary and lifesaving support from elected representatives during a pandemic are what has and will continue to enable compassionate dissenters to maintain a resolute grasp on the advancement of humanity, whatever our cause. *Dispatches from the Threshold* grew out of a desire to build connection and capacity across cities and communities where the struggle for rights to housing has been grappled with through a commitment to just, radical, and reparative outcomes and resistance to dehumanization.

Our intent in assembling this volume was to highlight the gains and mark the wins that housing and tenant activists were experiencing and witnessing in chronic and acute ways at the peak of the latest pandemic, for the purpose of learning from and tactically modifying in future moments of housing insecurity. We saw a need to reflect on the tensions and honestly assess the setbacks impacting the outpouring of housing activism around the globe, recognizing that movements for housing justice are geographically contingent and shaped by political and historic contexts of place. We saw a need to take stock of the strategies, contexts, and pressures under which tenants were struggling, winning, and having their homes taken from them. Most of all, we wanted to ensure that the knowledge and work made by movements simultaneously facing down the convergence of what Samuel Stein calls the "real estate state"[7] alongside broad public demands for the abolition of the police and state-sanctioned anti-Black racism, Land Back, and the COVID-19 pandemic was not lost. This volume, which we think of as a sort of snapshot or living archive, holds some of the stories of this time, so when the next crisis arrives, people engaged in the struggle for housing justice might have one more resource to turn toward to inform and guide our work to build tenant power.

In Manuel Castells' *The City and the Grassroots*, he assuredly claims that "urban structures will always be the expression of some institutionalized domination" and that,

> if urban research is to respond to the questions of our time — the urban crisis, the role of the state, the challenge of urban protest — we need to integrate our analysis of structures and processes, of crisis and challenge. Our purpose is to cautiously construct a new theory of urban change that can light a path to a new city.[8]

Having grown up in Franco's fascist Spain, Castells believed in the transformative power that theoretical and activist interventions could have on a society, specifically in transforming cities. The chapters of this book are written from a variety of perspectives and for a spectrum of audiences, many of whom often find themselves alongside one another. Activists, scholars, legal aid workers, and rabble rouser observations are included here because research is not confined to the work of academia, nor is theorizing the politics of civic life and political struggle. "Urban research" and theorizing the practice of politics that reflect anti-capitalist, socialist, anarchist, and undefined perspectives are shared in the chapters of this volume for the purpose of lighting, to echo Castells, and keeping the lights burning on the path of struggle for a new city. The experiences and knowledge shared in these chapters are deeply grounded in material, structural, and political change, at varied scales of impact and grown in different parts of the world, all committed to advancing the necessary work of actualizing a right to housing. Each moment of crisis presents an opportunity to take stock of what we have learned in the past and to adapt and find ways to deploy the strategies and resources available in the moment, be they legal, artistic, financial, or impactful forms of direct action. Though these chapters do not share a unified theory of social change, they share the perspective that the role of housing in cities holds a distinct and significant influence over the urban form and how people across classes, races, and abilities relate to property, safety, and belonging.

This volume's contributors offer perspectives from their tireless work as tenant organizers, legal aid workers, activists, court observers and counter mappers, housing agency workers, scholar-organizers, and renters. At their core, each chapter is a provocation for broader political change. One of the challenges the chapters attempt to meet is expressing what the housing questions of today are for those who are most susceptible to exploitative property relationships, vulnerable property tenure, and extralegal displacement from their housing, and those living in encampments or otherwise outdoors. Friedrich Engels' *The Housing Question*[9] addressed how the revolutionary goals of the organized working class could not be replaced by policy reforms at the onset of the Industrial Revolution, referencing that the increased population of workers in industrial centres were met with a lack of adequate and affordable housing that created a specifically proletariat housing crisis. Engels' question — how will workers overcome the exploitation that is ripe in a capitalist-controlled housing market characterized by high rents and low quality and quantity of homes — lives on in a near timeless and immortal state.

Collectively, the chapters of this volume think through the multifaceted dynamics of re-posing Engels' housing question in the twenty-first century, during a pandemic, in a time of growing abolitionist thinking, in a moment that prefigures a radical transformation that is being struggled for through a diversity of tactics across countless locations, even in our post-care and post-responsibility moment of ignoring the ongoing consequences of COVID-19 halfway through the 2020s. The conundrum at hand today, just as Engels presented it in 1886, is that policy reform is not the answer to the inherent inequalities produced by capital. Today, and over the last four years and one hundred and fifty years, this housing question has been compounded by two pandemics, increasingly militarized and brutal policing, ongoing resource wars and genocides, and a corresponding global anti-racist uprising. Poor and homeless people continue to be criminalized not only through local laws that restrict camping and sleeping outdoors, but by some countries' highest courts and governments (Denmark, Netherlands, Hungary, and the United States) making homelessness itself against the law. Responding to the housing question of today requires an understanding of its proximity to labour and wages, race and dispossession, to the politics of place and colonization, and the conceptualization of class positions. We may look toward the wealth disparities resulting from long-term global wage stagnation or the price gouging and rising rents that have been emblematic of the "strong" economic comeback of corporations in the post-2020 economy. The reality that wage stagnation, the cost of living crisis, and the likelihood of experiencing poverty particularly impact women, people with disabilities, trans people, and Black and brown communities means that responding to the housing question today requires thinking that incorporates experiences of class that are shaped beyond the capitalist mode of production alone, that include gender, race, ability, migration status, and the impacts of colonial traumas to name a few. Further, the housing question must be entirely reassessed in the context of the urbicide of Gaza, where entire cities are levelled as an act of Israel's violent occupation and people's homes become their forced graves and evidence of genocide.[10] How we think about housing today needs to extend beyond capital and labour alone and beyond the minimum of what it takes to keep one another alive. Tenant power is the horizon for radically transforming the housing conditions we struggle in today.

In issuing our *Dispatches*, we challenge the dominant market-oriented narrative about how supply alone will provide a grand fix to the housing issues of every variety. In most of the chapters in this volume, people are fighting to retain housing or living spaces they already have access to, as well as applying pressure to upend restrictions that govern how people may live and behave in those spaces. Challenging supply-side arguments, which are often most beneficial to housing developers rather than those who need access to safe and affordable housing, this volume centres a contentious range of arguments that demand more critical and radical actions than "build! build! build!" in the market-oriented sense. Just as Engels affirmed that policy was not the way out of the housing question of the Industrial Revolution, the authors of *Dispatches from the Threshold* are certain that we won't build our way out of any housing crises, because true transformation requires an immense shift in the balance of power on the side of people who lack control over their housing. For this shift in power to be realized, we need to build trust among fellow tenants, build class consciousness, and broadly practice greater commitment and follow through to anti-racist action and the actualization of land reparations and Indigenous reconciliation. In cases where reparative housing development is made possible through the rematriation of violently occupied lands, which is possible in our lifetimes, new housing questions will surely arise.

Housing insecurity is dangerous not only because of the inconsistent conditions people are forced to navigate while living between shelters, encampments, sofas, and vehicles but because people without adequate housing or access to shelter are murdered at the hands of police and violent civilians every day. People without consistent housing have shorter lifespans and trauma resulting from homelessness and time spent in shelters. The experience of being housing insecure or homeless is one of criminalization and at best exclusion from civic life through bylaws that restrict camping, sitting, and panhandling while city councils shell out tax abatements for condominium developments and sports facilities to bolster downtown economies. It is a gross understatement to say that those who need housing most experience the greatest hostility within housing and rental markets. Subjugation and dehumanization are near guaranteed byproducts of interacting with service agencies and non-profit organizations who are tasked through austere state disinvestment in assisting people with navigating the process of lily-padding from one assistance voucher or temporary transitional unit to the next while waiting on long registers for an "affordable" option, which are growing exceedingly less affordable.

The efforts of this most recent wave of tenants' movements have decisively re-politicized renting one's housing as the global rental market becomes more deeply financialized through the proliferation of real estate investment trusts, the continuous accumulation of properties by private equity firms, and rental units acting as assets for securitized bonds. Housing financialization — treating housing as a commodity and vehicle for the growth of wealth and investments — is in direct opposition to approaching access to housing as a right or a social good. One of the challenges in our collective ability to respond to the increasing financialization of housing will not necessarily be to match the pace of financialization and its operative institutions, but to consider the scale of financialization in relation to people power and direct action and to respond with appropriately scaled tactics and impact.

People who have been drawn into housing justice and tenant organizing work have often had encounters with the housing system, personally or as witnesses of immiseration, extraction, dispossession, and domination that enrol us into struggles for justice. A common theme throughout this volume is the question of how the tenant power that is built through organizing, campaigning, and supporting one another can be sustained in the face of seemingly endless crises of housing. *Dispatches* authors grapple with seeking to balance meeting the immediate material needs of tenants and creating systemic change, often without resolution, but with acceptance that our housing struggles are an avenue through which multi-issue organizing is possible and necessary and must be pursued. Though calls for structural level change are echoed throughout the pages of this volume, contributors demonstrate their priority and the clear need to place equal value and effort toward ensuring encampment residents have access to first aid materials, that we have the backs of our neighbours in court when they are at risk of eviction, and that tenants of a rural trailer park are not left behind in their struggle. The everyday needs that must be met to build tenant power is the necessary groundwork in making long range structural changes possible in the future. There is much work ahead.

Notes

1. Keeanga-Yamahtta Taylor, "How Do We Change America?" *The New Yorker,* June 8, 2020, https://www.newyorker.com/news/our-columnists/how-do-we-change-america.
2. R.H. Lossin, "In Defense of Destroying Property," *The Nation,* June 10, 2020, https://rhlossin.com/wp-content/uploads/2023/06/In-Defense-of-Destroying-Property-_-The-Nation.pdf.
3. "Rifles, Tasers and Jails: How Cities and States Spent Billions of COVID-19 Relief," *The Marshall Project,* September 7, 2022, https://www.themarshall-project.org/2022/09/07/how-federal-covid-relief-flows-to-the-criminal-justice-system; GOV.UK, Police to receive £60 million to support COVID-19 response, February 12, 2021, https://www.gov.uk/government/news/police-to-receive-60-million-to-support-COVID-19-response.
4. Rylan Kafara, "Dystopian Prohibitions and Utopian Possibilities in Edmonton, Canada, at the Onset of the COVID-19 Pandemic," in *Utopian and Dystopian Explorations of Pandemics and Ecological Breakdown* (Routledge, 2024).
5. Jessica Braimoh, Erin Dej, and Carrie Sanders, "'Somebody's Street': Eviction of Homeless Encampments as a Reflection of Interlocking Colonial and Class Relations," *Journal of Law and Social Policy* 36 (2023): 12.
6. Indigenous Peoples whose nations reside within settler colonial states have continued to struggle for self-determination, access and rights to lands against the persistent violence, and authorities of settler colonial governments. Land Back is not a prescriptive or unified set of demands held by all Indigenous Peoples. Each nation, clan, family, and person may have ways of thinking about how to create right relations between Indigenous Peoples, their land, and the presence of settlers and their institutions and economies. The Indigenous struggle to maintain relations to land under settler colonial control, and the fight for the repatriation of lands to Indigenous communities is not well categorized as part of an insurgence of Indigenous activity, as this struggle for land has been constant and is at the core of settler colonial claims to power.
7. Samuel Stein, *Capital City: Gentrification and the Real Estate State* (Verso Books, 2019).
8. Manuel Castells, *The City and the Grassroots: A Cross-Cultural Theory of Urban Social Movements,* No. 7 (University of California Press, 1983), xvi.
9. Friedrich Engels and Clemens Palme Dutt, *The Housing Question,* Vol. 23 (International Publishers, 1935).
10. Raffi Berg, "What Is South Africa's Genocide Case Against Isreal at the ICJ?" *British Broadcasting Corporation,* May 2024, 2024. https://www.bbc.com/news/world-middle-east-67922346.

TENANT-CENTRED PUBLIC HEALTH IN VANCOUVER'S DOWNTOWN EASTSIDE

VANCOUVER, BRITISH COLUMBIA, CANADA

WRITTEN BY
Aaron Bailey, Dani Aiello, Bryan Jacobs &
the Right to Remain Research Collective

The arrival of COVID-19 to Vancouver's Downtown Eastside (DTES) in the spring of 2020 generated intense anxiety for residents, community organizers, and public health officials. Many feared the worst for the low-income neighbourhood's nearly 16,000 residents, approximately 7,000 of whom reside in century-old single room occupancy hotels (SROs). These hotels, many of which are slumlord-owned, contain small-to-medium-sized rooms and communal washroom and kitchen facilities. The potential for a catastrophic pandemic scenario to play out in the DTES was anticipated by many community members who had already witnessed the systematic under-resourcing of the neighbourhood's physical, health, and social infrastructure over many decades. COVID-19 posed a new threat to the neighbourhood, and specific concerns arose around the potential for the virus to spread through the congregate housing setting of the hotels. This chapter tells the story of how organized SRO tenants have responded to repeated and concurrent public health crises in Vancouver's DTES, suggesting that tenant power is necessary for advancing community health and neighbourhood justice. The concentration of SROs, and the containment of low-income tenants within these poorly maintained buildings, is ultimately an outcome of the longer history of settler colonialism, racist twentieth-century planning policies, and ongoing cycles of displacement in the occupied territories of Musqueam, Squamish, and Tsleil-Waututh nations.

Beginning in the early 1900s, SROs proliferated throughout the DTES to cater to seasonal resource industry workers.[1] As a tool for dispossession of Indigenous people from the DTES, Vancouver's city planning policies segregated and ghettoized the area along racial lines, using the policies of public health and urban development to also target Chinese residents for surveillance and containment.[2] Later, during the Second World War, the Canadian government and local authorities forcibly dispossessed and interned a large community of Japanese Canadians. Eventually, downtown SROs became sites of home and community for low-income renters. SROs are still consistently the only remaining segment of the private housing stock renting for near the social assistance rental allowance in British Columbia.[3]

Decades of policy abandonment by federal, provincial, and municipal governments and the hollowing out of the Canadian welfare state soon intersected with gradual demographic turnover in SROs to create a unique experience of structural vulnerability for tenants of these hotels.[4] In the absence of federal investment in publicly built housing comparable to that in the United States and United Kingdom after WWII, the privately managed short-stay hotel or rooming house managed by private landlords, and increasingly charitable organizations, became a common form of low-income housing in Vancouver.[5] Until the late 1970s, responsibility for regulating safe and healthy housing in the city's privately owned SROs and other rental accommodation fell to the Vancouver Health Department.[6] In this time, SRO tenants were largely elderly and male, mostly former natural resource workers who settled in cheap, poorly maintained single units.[7] Changes to Vancouver's civic bureaucracy and the removal of SRO governance from public health's domain in the late 1970s cemented the city's laissez-faire approach to SRO landlords: costly bylaw and property-standards infractions were rarely addressed while conditions in SRO properties deteriorated at residents' expense.[8] As SRO stock fell into disrepair, a lack of clearly enumerated protections for SRO tenants under BC tenancy law, routine abuse and intimidation from unaccountable landlords, and a lack of responsiveness from City authorities to resident complaints largely blocked or discouraged legal recourse. The tolerated decline of private SRO housing conditions further obstructed state and tenant efforts to improve the stock because tenants who demanded bylaw enforcement faced homelessness at the risk of SROs being condemned.[9]

In the 1990s, as the Canadian government accelerated its divestment from publicly built housing, multiple levels of government began to acquire some SRO hotels, contracting management responsibilities to non-profit social service organizations. Since that time, multiple prohibition-related drug poisoning crises, stagnant social assistance rates, rising homelessness, insufficient investment in community-based mental health care, continued surveillance and separation of Indigenous families by the Canadian state, intergenerational trauma produced by settler colonialism, and increasing complexity of tenant support needs have continued to place immense pressure on tenant communities in privately owned and non-profit — sometimes referred to as "supportive" — housing.[10] Newer generations of SRO tenants are increasingly younger, disproportionately Indigenous, more gender diverse, more likely to access the unregulated drug supply, impacted by serious trauma, frequently live with challenging concurrent health concerns, including mental health diagnoses, and have previous experience of being unhoused.[11] It is in this context of historical and ongoing forms of extreme housing exploitation that our story of community public health unfolds — wherein residents and organizers activated deep relational networks of care and long-standing practices of mutual support for survival.

As housing precarity became more extreme with increasing rents and the shrinking of the affordable housing stock, by 2020 conditions had become dire in most of the approximately 4,000 privately owned SROs, and tenants were in increasingly exploited positions vis-à-vis their landlords in a climate of circumscribed legal rights.[12] As the COVID-19 crisis emerged, mutual aid networks led by SRO residents and organizers jumped in with efforts to keep residents safe, and an in situ research collective involving community-based academics and students from multiple Canadian universities called the Right to Remain research collective (R2R) stepped up to support the DTES SRO Collaborative Society (SRO-C), a non-profit organization that aims to advance SRO tenant–led social service and governance models. SRO-C and R2R had already worked together for years. For more than six years prior, R2R had organized weekly meetings for strategy and research activities, such as tenant interviews, archival visits, haiku poetry circles, town halls, outreach, tenant conventions, and other events to share the rich history of SROs and their tenants. With the onset of a pandemic, these intertwined tenant networks, peer-delivered programming, and participatory policy research activities proved to be essential components of the response to a new but familiar kind of health emergency in the privately owned SRO hotels. By detailing this pandemic response work in the hard-to-reach environment of the SRO hotel and highlighting the organizing model that relied on tenant expertise, care work, and labour to function, we make clear that DTES tenant networks are essential health infrastructure in our systemically unequal, austerity-driven city in times of crisis.

Long before the arrival of COVID-19, community-based public health solutions in the form of SRO tenant organizing and peer-to-peer[13] harm reduction were implemented in response to repeated policy-driven health crises in the DTES. In the 1970s and 1980s, the Downtown Eastside Residents Association (DERA) was formed in large part to improve legal protections for SRO hotel residents, and the association eventually became the eyes and ears of proactive SRO oversight, bylaw enforcement, and upgrading efforts to improve SRO conditions for tenants.[14]

The SRO-C had organized tenants against evictions and the many habitability problems in the hotels for five years before the COVID-19 pandemic hit, during a fentanyl-related drug poisoning crisis. Recognizing the SRO-C's deeper relationships into environments considered hard to reach by clinicians and public health professionals, Vancouver Coastal Health proposed a tenant-led program — the Tenant Overdose Response Organizers (TORO) — in response to rising numbers of overdose calls from SROs. Making use of existing relationships between residents of privately owned SROs, TORO coordinated naloxone and overdose reversal training workshops in their buildings while distributing harm reduction supplies.[15] Recognizing that housing and health are inherently linked, the SRO-C sought to expand the inter-building tenant-led social network developed under TORO. Local health authorities began to commit significant resources towards implementing this model through a form of tenant-led mutual aid.[16]

In mid-March 2020, before known COVID cases had reached the neighbourhood, staff, volunteers, and academic partners relied on existing community knowledge to complete a massive outreach campaign in nearly all the neighbourhood's approximately 104 private SROs. Lead tenants in SRO-C buildings were informed of the coming pandemic and were given new information about safer drug use and personal protective equipment (PPE) as soon as it became available. The sudden withdrawal of resources from the area associated with pandemic-related closures, especially honoraria paid for peers to support social service delivery, exacerbated pre-existing precarity. Many affordable cafes, the central community centre, reliable food programs, and harm reduction sites shut down without warning, leaving low-income residents especially with few options. Less traffic through the neighbourhood meant that economic opportunities for sex workers were severely limited, and drug markets became more volatile as global supply chains were disrupted. Overdose prevention sites reduced capacity and new "no-guest" policies in SROs increased the risks for tenants already vulnerable to isolation and fatal drug poisoning. Ultimately, state efforts to manage the social and economic effects of the pandemic did not account for the material conditions in the DTES and, in some cases created new, much more dire threats to residents.

In the first few weeks of the pandemic lockdown, the SRO-C quickly reallocated financial resources and connected with numerous other non-profit organizations[17] coordinating efforts in the DTES to set up a distribution hub where donations could be received, sorted, and repackaged to be sent back out for delivery to lead tenants in the SROs. The resulting collaborations led to a new program: the COVID Emergency Tenant Response initiative (CETR). SRO-C acquired and distributed personal protective equipment and cleaning and harm reduction supplies, food, and cell phones directly into buildings through the established tenant contacts in its network across the DTES and beyond. Door-to-door food distribution led by tenants and free access to cell phones had not previously been attempted on a large scale in the DTES, and yet these quickly became vital services. Extensive meal preparation and delivery programming were only made possible by collaborations with other community organizations who stepped in to adapt their grocery and hot meal programs. At the conclusion of the CETR initiative in 2021, the SRO-C continued many of these partnerships to make some food programming permanent, while R2R included digital justice and access to communications technology for DTES tenants a core focus of its work.

Responsibility for responding to the worsening toxicity of the illicit drug supply as a result of the pandemic, harm reduction service closures, and the sudden imposition of no-guest policies in many SROs that had not previously had them, fell largely to SRO-C's programs — especially TORO. Regular naloxone training and delivering harm reduction supplies made a difference. Tenant-driven TORO networks that had been established prior to the pandemic and identified leaders in new buildings became a lifeline to many residents who were regularly accessing the worsening drug supply. Lead CETR tenants in each hotel were carefully selected to coordinate the distribution of supplies in their building. People who possessed large peer networks, potential for leadership, and a visible interest in mutual aid work were identified and recruited as "super connector" tenants. Once a reliable contact was established in each SRO, supply distribution began. SRO-C staff called lead tenants and other residents of each building to check in with tenants, learn about overdoses and COVID-19 cases, determine supply needs, and request orders for each building. Meanwhile a team of organizers, volunteers, and staff received and sorted donations, fulfilled orders and coordinated teams of drivers to make no-contact deliveries. CETR programming continued to grow throughout the early months of the pandemic until delivery operations and tenant contacts equipped with free cell phones were established in over sixty buildings.

Throughout the SRO-C's development of the CETR initiative, R2R shifted its resources to support SRO-Cs operations, continue ongoing policy advocacy to improve SRO conditions, and provide support to R2R tenant co-researchers involved with the CETR project. R2R's lead investigators successfully navigated bureaucratic hurdles to secure the university project's status as essential, arguing that R2R's material and logistical support of the SRO-C's pandemic-related work could not be paused without serious negative consequences on the ground. Over several years, R2R had already developed a system of regular meetings and research co-production facilitated by regular online communication. Meetings themselves were deemed an essential health-related service and provided an opportunity to check in with tenant researchers. They became something to look forward to as a break from the monotony of self-isolation, improving morale and mental health, and providing a venue for tenants to reflect on their position as pandemic response leaders. Research activities facilitated these gatherings, where discussions shed invaluable light on SRO tenants' experiences of isolation, repeated loss related to drug poisoning, mental health and substance struggles, increased financial precarity, vaccine hesitancy within the community, the importance of communications technology, and involvement in mutual aid work. By materially supporting tenants to feel connected, continuing to contribute to policy advocacy efforts, and supporting organizers to remain on the ground with research funds, the collective was also able to support the CETR program and simultaneously learn more about the experience of the pandemic in this unique form of low-income housing.

Community coordinated mutual aid networks subsequently became a critical, albeit short-term, part of the success of Vancouver's pandemic response. The breadth and success of the CETR program relied on the existence of tenant networks tapped into by the SRO-C and the fundamentals of organizing: door knocking, conversation, learning about life in the buildings, and developing a democratic, collective response to the concerns of tenants in particular buildings. Local government and public health authorities did not have the pre-existing access, relationships, or trust of the community to meaningfully support DTES residents in the manner that SRO tenants and organizers did. Vancouver's Regional Health Authority acknowledged the unique risk environment of the SROs, considered a form of congregate housing, as it related to virus transmission, and sought out the SRO-C and other partners early on. These partnerships amounted to a form of temporary outsourcing and reliance on tenant groups to provide flexible, trust-based means of making the health authority known in the hotels. Our experience illustrates that resourced tenants were most able to meaningfully and safely provide the support needed to protect their neighbours' health from the beginning of the pandemic. However, it also suggests that these successes occurred under conditions of state retrenchment that required tenants to do so for their own protection, as they have always done,[18] supported by emergency funding that was eventually scaled back.

Public health's previous lack of attentiveness to SROs and collective action by tenants was the inevitable and systemic consequence of Canadian health promotion's neoliberal turn.[19] Outside of times of crisis and the observations of allied frontline workers, public health authorities are typically unwilling to recognize existing, and often politicized, tenant and community networks as health-promoting, though there are of course exceptions of supportive staff within some of the neighbourhood's public health services. But in the DTES, SRO tenant networks, in circumstances of austerity and epistemic drift, become essential public health infrastructure during public health emergencies. Tenant self-reliance, as effective and politically transformative as it may be in the DTES, often emerges in extreme conditions of exploitation, austerity, and state-led abandonment.

Public health's reliance on tenant networks to intervene in Vancouver's SROs is, ultimately, a related consequence of the withdrawal of the local state's public health apparatus from habitability enforcement in this part of the housing stock. State retrenchment in the form of neoliberal economic reforms between the 1970s and 1990s had severe consequences for both health care and housing. Today, the SRO-C continues to be supported by the provincially supported Regional Health Authority to carry out current programming that originated from CETR, namely tenant-led service-based initiatives. However, the conclusion of the emergency funding in 2021 meant that dozens of newly trained, highly skilled tenant organizers could not continue resourced mutual aid work beyond the crisis period. These tenants are called upon only when the most acute emergencies arise, neglecting the day-to-day health-promoting potential of their work within well-resourced tenant networks.

Tenant-led services in SROs, like those resourced by the SRO-C, and participatory academic partnerships, like R2R, provide a potential means of challenging mainstream social service provision and extractive research practice, respectively. Our partnership empowered and supported tenants to work together to solve collective issues and mobilize a rapid public health campaign based on mutual aid. That said, these successes occurred in response to state abandonment of the DTES, and pandemic-related resources have largely been withdrawn by the fiscally conservative state. By providing directly to tenants the resources they need to enhance how they already look out for each other, public health policymakers only stand to strengthen the bonds between neighbours and increase their willingness to contribute to the protection and growth of their community. Communities are already always having to save themselves, especially those that have been systematically ignored and abandoned, like SRO tenants. The SRO-C's existing tenant organizing networks across all its programs and R2R's research-as-organizing model together formed an essential aspect of public health infrastructure when required during the COVID-19 pandemic and stand to continue to operate as such.

The need for such tenant-centred, collective health intervention remains pressing. SRO tenant precarity has intensified as the pandemic has progressed. Illegal evictions, a new epidemic of SRO fires, and declining conditions in non-profit supportive housing present SRO tenants with new challenges. These are compounded by the ever-worsening unregulated drug supply and the overturning of small organizing victories in Vancouver, like restrictions on SRO rent increases to discourage eviction and preserve affordability. Tenant networks in the DTES will organize themselves to respond to these conditions, with or without state backing, in these contexts of dire need. The SRO-C, R2R, and other tenants' groups in the DTES continue to envision a future for proactive, well-resourced organizing towards community health that exists outside the constraints of overlapping crises.

Notes

1. Shlomo Hasson and David Ley, *Neighbourhood Organizations and the Welfare State* (University of Toronto Press, 1994).
2. K.J. Anderson, *Vancouver's Chinatown: Racial Discourse in Canada, 1875-1980* (McGill-Queen's Press, 1991).
3. Jeffrey, Masuda, Aaron Franks, Audrey Kobayashi, and Trevor Wideman, "After Dispossession: An Urban Rights Praxis of Remaining in Vancouver's Downtown Eastside," *Environment and Planning D: Society and Space* 38, 2, (2020).
4. Jeffrey Masuda and the Right to Remain Research Collective, "Abandoning the SRO: Public Health Withdrawal from Sanitary Enforcement in Vancouver's Downtown Eastside," *Journal of Urban History* 49, 4 (2023).
5. G. Suttor, Still Renovating: A History of Canadian Social Housing Policy, Vol. 6 (McGill-Queen's Press-MQUP, 2016); J. Wade, "Home or Homelessness? Marginal Housing in Vancouver, 1886–1950," *Urban History Review* 25, 2, (1997).
6. Masuda et al., "Abandoning the SRO."
7. Hasson and Ley, Neighbourhood Organizations; J. Sommers, "Men at the Margin: Masculinity and Space in Downtown Vancouver, 1950-1986," *Urban Geography* 19, 4 (1998).
8. Masuda et al., "Abandoning the SRO"; N. Blomley and the Right to Remain Collective, "Making Property Outlaws: Law and Relegation," *International Journal of Urban and Regional Research* 45, 6 (2021).
9. Masuda et al., "Abandoning the SRO."
10. J. Boyd, D. Cunningham, S. Anderson, and T. Kerr, "Supportive Housing and Surveillance," *International Journal of Drug Policy*, 34 (2016).
11. K. Shannon, T. Ishida, C. Lai, and M.W. Tyndall, "The Impact of Unregulated Single Room Occupancy Hotels on the Health Status of Illicit Drug Users in Vancouver," International Journal of Drug Policy 17, 2 (2006); S.P. Barbic, A.A. Jones, M. Woodward, M. Piercy, S. Mathias, F. Vila-Rodriguez, O. Leonova, G.N. Smith, T. Buchanan, A.T. Vertinksy, S. Gillingham, W.J. Panenka, A. Rauscher, A.M. Barr, R.M. Procyshyn, G.W. MacEwan, D.J. Lang, A.E. Thornton, M.K. Heran, A.M. Leon, M. Krausz, and W.G. Honer, "Clinical and functional characteristics of young adults living in single room occupancy housing: preliminary findings from a 10-year longitudinal study, *Canadian Journal of Public Health* 109 (2018).

12 Shannon et al., 2006, "The Impact of Unregulated Single Room Occupancy Hotels."
13 Toward the Heart, a key part of the BC Centre for Disease Control's harm reduction programming, cites Ti, Tzemis, and Buxton (2012) to define "peers" as "a person with equal standing in a community who share a common lived experience. Experiential workers use their lived experience with substance use in their professional work.... Experiential worker engagement can address equity of harm reduction services and interventions by fostering communication, building trust, increasing knowledge and reducing stigma and discrimination to reduce barriers and increase utilization of services," https://towardtheheart.com/peer-engagement; L. Ti, D. Tzemis, J.A. Buxton, "Peer Engagement in the Context of Policy and Program Development: A Review of the Literature," *Substance Abuse Treatment, Prevention, and Policy* 7, 47 (2012), http://www.substanceabusepolicy.com/content/7/1/47.
14 Masuda et al., "Abandoning the SRO."
15 Magnus Nowell and Jeffrey R. Masuda, "'You Need to Just Provide Health Services': Navigating the Politics of Harm Reduction in the Twin Housing and Overdose Crises in Vancouver, BC," *International of Drug Policy*, 82, (2020); G. Bardwell, T. Fleming, A.B. Collins, J. Boyd, and R. McNeil, "Addressing Intersecting Housing and Overdose Crises in Vancouver, Canada: Opportunities and Challenges from a Tenant-Led Overdose Response Intervention in Single Room Occupancy Hotels," *Journal of Urban Health* 96 (2019).
16 While the TORO program successfully empowers tenants to protect themselves and their neighbours from the ongoing violence of drug prohibition in Canada, the non-profit status, relationship with academic institutions, and state affiliations of the SRO-C allow for the collection of data on "high risk" SRO tenants by Vancouver Coastal Health, its circulation to policymakers, and the continued self-surveillance of this population. This exercise of biopower, mediated by a non-profit in a context of neoliberal state retrenchment, is much more cost efficient than the direct surveillance of SROs. The nature of tenant-led programming resourced by the local health authority is therefore complex and open to scrutiny that is beyond the scope of this chapter. We thank Eris Nyx for pushing us to think more critically about these power dynamics.
17 This includes groups such as DTES Response, WePress, Powell Street Festival, Watari, St. James Music Academy, and Everybody Is In, among many other community members and grassroots organizers.
18 Travis Lupick, *Fighting for Space: How a Group of Drug Users Transformed One City's Struggle with Addiction* (Arsenal Pulp Press, 2018); S. Boyd, D. MacPherson, and B. Osborn, *Raise Shit!* (Fernwood, 2009); S. Schulman, *Let the Record Show: A Political History of ACT UP New York, 1987–1993*, (Farrar, Straus and Giroux, 2021.; S. Hassan, Saving Our Own Lives: A Liberatory Practice of Harm Reduction (Haymarket Books, 2022); S.R. Friedman, D.C. Des Jarlais, J.L. Sotheran, J. Garber, H. Cohen, and D. Smith, "AIDS and Self-Organization Among Intravenous Drug Users," *International Journal of the Addictions* 22, 3, (1987).
19 Masuda et al., "Abandoning the SRO"; D. Raphael, "Grasping at Straws: A Recent History of Health Promotion in Canada," *Critical Public Health*, 18, 4 (2008).

COMMUNITY CONTROL OF PUBLIC HOUSING

NEWARK, NEW JERSEY, UNITED STATES

WRITTEN BY
Ari McCaskill & Peter Blackmer

Despite being long denigrated by policymakers and profiteers, public housing has been the bedrock of strong communities in cities across the United States. The COVID-19 pandemic raised fundamental questions about housing in our society and led many activists and some progressive planners to revisit public housing as a viable solution to precarity. It also presented an opportunity to refocus on the most important component of stable public housing — the people who call it home. In fighting for a renewed commitment to public housing, organizers must recognize that the past failures of public housing do not reflect the failures of its residents, that racial capitalism has been a driver of the decline of public housing, that strong organizations come from strong communities, and that understanding policy is vital for effective organizing. These important lessons become clear when we study the work of tenant organizers in Newark, New Jersey, during the Black Power Movement in the 1970s.

From 1970–74, tenants of Stella Windsor Wright Homes (also known as Stella Wright Homes) waged the longest rent strike in the history of US public housing and won tenant management of the housing project. In the wake of the 1967 Newark Rebellion and the election of Kenneth A. Gibson as the city's first Black mayor in 1970, working-class Black tenants blended grassroots militancy with political savvy as they successfully fought for community control of public housing in Newark.

Building upon social networks and leadership within the project, tenant organizers translated effective organizing into a model of tenant management that lasted for two decades. This chapter explores the campaign for tenant management at Stella Wright Homes, which unfolded amidst a similar era of vast housing precarity and great political possibility, to offer critical lessons about the importance and viability of tenant-led public housing in our current moment of desperate need.[1] With protections for renters evaporating post-pandemic, the histories of tenant organizing and collective management of public housing may offer valuable instructions and inspiration for mobilizing community resources and assets to ensure safe and affordable housing when the government abandons its citizens.

As African Americans came north during the Great Migrations, racist policies like redlining and restrictive covenants contributed to residential segregation in Jim Crow cities like Newark. The migration, containment, and eventual displacement of Black communities in Newark fuelled contentious struggles with local, state, and federal agencies. While federal programs enabled white citizens to buy homes in the suburbs during the Great Migrations, Newark's growing Black population was largely confined to the city's Central Ward. Housing segregation contributed to overcrowding and exploitation, and a housing shortage meant that working-class Black renters were forced to pay high rents to white absentee landlords for crumbling apartments.

This manufactured decay of the predominantly Black Central Ward made the area a target for federal "slum clearance" and "urban renewal" initiatives. Under the guise of eradicating "blight" and replacing old housing, these programs razed entire neighbourhoods with few provisions for relocating Black tenants or homeowners. As organizer Louise Epperson explained, "It wasn't urban renewal, it was Black folks removal."[2] These conditions spurred tenants of privately owned buildings to demand improved housing through rent strikes, while Black homeowners like Epperson built organizations to resist displacement wrought by urban renewal.

For working-class Black renters seeking safe and affordable housing amidst racist exploitation and displacement, public housing became a refuge. Most of Newark's projects, however, were concentrated in the Central Ward. The buildings were cheaply constructed, and the Newark Housing Authority (NHA) put little care into their upkeep and maintenance. In 1970, Stella Wright Homes became the epicentre of struggles to improve public housing in the city. Completed in 1959, the high-rise buildings housed 1,205 apartment units with nearly 5,000 tenants. Within just ten years, conditions had deteriorated to such an extent that tenants referred to their buildings as "hell-holes" or "concrete concentration camps."[3] Elevators failed, incinerators poured smoke and soot into hallways and apartments, rats and roaches were uncontrollable, and there was virtually no investment in public safety.[4] Contrary to age-old racist narratives about public housing, these conditions were caused by racist disinvestment, not careless tenants.

Mary Smith was among the first tenants to move into the nearby Scudder Homes project in 1959 and, like her neighbours in Stella Wright, soon began talking with tenants in other buildings to demand improvements. "I was a person who had never been involved in any kind of community action," she recalled. "Before I knew it, I was elected president of the tenants association."[5] Smith's experience was a familiar one for tenants whose anger over living conditions and strong relationships with neighbours vaulted them into the fray of tenant organizing.

Throughout the 1960s and 70s, tenants like Smith organized for more humane conditions, greater investment and accountability from local and federal housing authorities, and eventually tenant control of public housing. The budding tenant movement gained momentum on July 12, 1967, when a Black cab driver named John Smith was savagely beaten and arrested by Newark Police and taken to the Fourth Precinct, in the Central Ward. The precinct was in the vicinity of several public housing projects, where thousands of Black residents witnessed the brutality and responded in kind. The police beating of Smith was a tipping point after decades of struggles against systemic racism had been met with minor reforms and major police repression. Black Newarkers fought for their liberation in the streets for five days as the police and National Guard waged urban warfare to suppress the rebellion. Amidst the chaos, organizers issued a progressive set of demands, including that 50,000 new units of housing be built for relocation of residents displaced by urban renewal.[6]

The rebellion provided momentum and political leverage to ongoing struggles for housing justice and equitable development in the city. This was most evident in a campaign to prevent the construction of a state medical school on a 150-acre plot in the heart of the Central

Ward, which threatened to displace 20,000 residents. After the smoke cleared from the rebellion, however, the balance of the political scales had shifted. "The power structure was scared," organizer Junius Williams explained. "It was like we had that invisible nameless, faceless brother with a brick standing behind us."[7] Organizers used their leverage to reduce the acreage of the project to 58, secure 63 acres of vacant land for community-led housing development, and win guarantees of employment and community health programs from the medical school. Shaped by Black Power demands for community control of housing and urban development, this win influenced tenants to seek greater agency in public housing in Newark.

While urban rebellions have historically forced the nation to reckon with the causes and consequences of institutional racism, these fleeting moments of reckoning have seldom produced lasting systemic change. As public housing conditions continued to deteriorate after the rebellion, tenants organized to pressure the NHA and city government to make improvements. The rapid growth of tenant organizations in the late 1960s was aided by the social fabric that residents had cultivated over the years in their buildings. Many former tenants recall the familial bonds that were forged in the high-rise projects and the shared responsibilities among tenants for childcare, maintenance, and upkeep of their floors. Though often overlooked, these networks fostered the development of local leaders, laid the foundation for tenant organizations, and mobilized community assets and resources to ensure safe and affordable housing when the government proved unwilling to shoulder this responsibility for its most vulnerable citizens.[8]

While navigating the murky waters of the NHA, City Hall, and the federal department of Housing and Urban Development (HUD), public housing tenants often felt ignored and dismissed. When they complained about conditions, the NHA and City Hall cried poverty and offered weak promises of maintenance services. To add insult to injury, the NHA announced plans to raise rents in 1969. To top it off, when a sorely needed $7 million modernization grant from HUD to make improvements on Stella Wright came through that year, tenants were excluded from the decision-making process despite a legal mandate of tenant participation. Coming amidst heightened demands for Black self-determination following the rebellion, these actions proved to be a turning point for tenant organizing.

Inspired by the successful campaign for community control of development in the medical school fight, tenants fought for agency in how the funding would be spent. Organizers canvassed buildings and used newsletters for political education about the modernization grant, explaining the roles of federal agencies and local players in accessible language, while calling for tenant unity to determine funding priorities.[9] Frustrated by both the NHA and the ineffective Tenant League, organizers escalated their efforts. Toby Henry and Juanita Short called for a new election to supplant the League's existing leadership in March 1970 and were elected as president and vice president, respectively, of the newly formed Stella Wright Tenant Association (SWTA).[10]

The following month, Constance Washington, of the Poor and Dissatisfied Tenants Association (an affiliate of the militant National Tenants Organization), and Stella Wright tenant organizers Toby Henry and Rev. Thomas Comerford declared a city-wide rent strike in public housing to improve living conditions and demand greater representation in policymaking. Guided by dedicated tenant organizers, the SWTA quickly emerged as the leading force of the rent strikes. They also won the support of the Archdiocese of Newark, which backed Rev. Comerford's involvement and mobilized parishioners in solidarity. By November 1970, the strike spread from Stella Wright and Scudder Homes to include fourteen other projects throughout the city.

As the rent strike put pressure on the city, the NHA tried to end the strike through legal actions. By 1972, the NHA had lost nearly $2 million in rent from the strike and filed suits against the SWTA. Rather than turn over the rent being held in escrow to the NHA, which had failed to make necessary repairs, Henry and Comerford withdrew the funds and returned the money to the tenants. For this act, they were held in contempt of court and sentenced to forty-five days in jail. The trial drew the media spotlight, and celebrities like Bill Cosby, Bill Withers, and Erma Franklin showed up in court to lend support to the rent strikers. "The housing authority made a political decision to destroy the tenant leadership at Stella Wright," Greater Newark Urban Coalition president Gus Heningburg explained. "They figured if they could break Toby Henry, then they could break the strike. Well, it didn't work ... they made a martyr out of him."[11] Such acts of conviction in the face of repression helped to galvanize tenants while sharpening the contradictions between Black working-class tenants and the state.

The following year, the rent strikers cycled in and out of court, as the NHA brought eviction suits against 11,000 tenants (25 percent of Newark's public housing population), and settlement talks collapsed. When the first eviction cases came to trial in November, however, a judge refused to order any evictions and granted an 80 percent reduction of past and future rents, marking a win for the strikers. Furthermore, he recommended that if conditions could not be improved, Stella Wright should be torn down.[12]

With tenants withholding $6.5 million in rent by early 1974, the NHA was on the verge of bankruptcy and moved to shut down Stella Wright. Mounting frustrations and the daunting scope of repairs led some tenant leaders to support the plan initially, but the lack of affordable housing in Newark meant that if Stella Wright closed, more than 700 families would be left homeless. While some tenants were relocated to other projects, others stayed, insisting on running the project themselves. Although tenants obtained a court order postponing the project's closing, a long-term solution needed to be found.

After weeks of negotiations between tenants, the NHA, city officials, and HUD, an agreement was reached to end the longest public housing rent strike in the nation's history after four years. The terms of the agreement included a tenant seat on the NHA Board of Commissioners; an NHA pledge to continue operation of Stella Wright with maximum possible services; the dismissal of lawsuits against tenants; $1.3 million in HUD funding for the NHA to make improvements; a citizens task force to oversee the agreement; and one of the SWTA's central demands — tenant management of Stella Wright.[13]

As the NHA gradually turned over full control of operations, tenants became responsible for the allocation of funds, collection of rent, enforcement of regulations, and handling disputes between tenants. Tenant management existed in a small number of other cities, including Boston and St. Louis, which provided models for the newly created SWTA Management Corporation (SWTAMC). It was a daunting task, but one made more manageable by the organizational networks tenants had built through the rent strike. After a rocky start caused by delays in HUD funding, the SWTAMC quickly improved conditions. In a relatively short period, the SWTAMC cleaned, painted, installed security systems, trained staff, and implemented policies to ensure sustainability, despite lacking control over government funding.[14]

In many ways, the SWTAMC replicated the informal management systems that tenant organizations had previously built to maintain the project when the NHA proved unable or unwilling to do so. Each building had a director and each floor had a captain, which encouraged participation, agency, and collective action. As the SWTAMC explained in their tenant handbook, this organizational structure was intended to "offer tenant involvement in all aspects, i.e., socially, economically, educationally and politically of our community — knowing that our power and success lies along these lines."[15] The SWTAMC also leveraged HUD dollars to expand existing daycare and social service centres housed onsite, while partnering with community organizations to build the capacity necessary to meet the needs of people living in a city within a city.

The impacts of tenant management were felt by tenants and the NHA alike. In its first eighteen months, the SWTAMC filled 800 vacant units and more than doubled revenues collected from rents.[16] Journalists took note of clean hallways, freshly painted walls, new landscaping, and better security, which one building director attributed to the solidarity and energy born of the strike.[17] Reducing vacancies from 78 percent to a mere 2 percent was the standout achievement of the organization, and tenants felt more secure in their homes. Even HUD acknowledged the successes of tenant management in several reports in the late 1970s.[18]

At the same time, reports acknowledged the question of sustainability after HUD introduced Section 8 vouchers in 1974. This program provided federal subsidies to low-income tenants for rent in privately owned housing and consequently drained tenants and funding from public housing nationwide. This shift to free-market subsidies challenged the collectivism of the SWTAMC and tenant management more broadly. Even though residents had created an effective model for managing public housing, it was still reliant on federal funding and therefore vulnerable to the neoliberal agendas of the Nixon administration and its successors. Like Black Power–era experiments in electoral politics, this exercise in local self-determination demonstrated the power of collective action, while simultaneously revealing the need to build national power to create systemic change.

Nonetheless, the SWTAMC maintained tenant control until the early 1990s, when the city began demolishing its high-rise projects. The legacy of thirty years of organizing forged by poor and working-class Black tenants and the connectivity of a community was dismantled in favour of free-market solutions, and Stella Wright Homes was demolished in 2002. This privatization of low-income public housing diluted tenant power and marked the end of progressive era policy, thus making poor and working-class people more vulnerable to the Great Recession. The elimination of the federal safety net of public housing has allowed for a free fall of the most marginalized Americans in the years since and revealed the sweeping social consequences of housing precarity during the COVID-19 pandemic.

One of the primary lessons offered by the Stella Wright rent strike and resultant tenant management is that effective tenant organizations grow from the relationships and collectivity cultivated by tenants. In periods of social crisis and upheaval, like the rebellions of the 1960s and 2020, organizers can draw strength from social networks built by local people. Movements grow at the speed of relationships, and local leaders can quickly mobilize these existing networks for political power during such moments of possibility. This was seen most recently in the successful efforts of tenant organizers in the New York City Housing Authority to prevent the privatization of the nation's largest public housing authority. The people who live in low-income and public housing must have agency over their community. The history of the SWTAMC shows that tenant control of public housing can be mutually beneficial for tenants and municipalities alike but must be adequately funded to provide safe and dignified housing for the most vulnerable members of our communities.

As housing inequity has skyrocketed for poor and working-class renters since the Great Recession, activists, academics, planners, and policymakers have attempted to re-envision low-income housing. Experiments from portable tents affixed to repurposed shopping carts in Los Angeles's Skid Row to tiny homes in vacant lots are piecemeal responses to a systemic crisis. Absent from these stop-gap solutions has been the revisioning of public housing as a viable solution to contemporary housing inequity. Additionally, we still lack a holistic consideration of the lives, capabilities, and aspirations of public housing tenants.

The need for safe and quality affordable housing has grown in the decades since the creation of the Federal Housing Authority and the Newark Housing Authority. Housing insecurity could be drastically reduced if public housing projects like Stella Wright Homes remained operational and were adequately funded. Bloated military and law enforcement budgets in the United States clearly demonstrate that the housing crisis has not been created by a lack of resources, but by a violent society that values the profit and power of white elites over the needs of working-class communities of colour. The necessity of offering a public option has become an even greater moral imperative, yet has been subsumed by private developments that provide few low-income units. As Rev. Comerford explained, the Stella Wright rent strike represented "a struggle to moralize the priorities of our country. A struggle to prevent the abandonment of the cities. To protect the human rights of minority groups." This moral imperative remains today, but as in 1970, requires collective action, effective organizing, and protracted struggle to achieve.

Notes

1. For a more in-depth treatment of the Stella Wright Rent Strike, see Julia Rabig, *The Fixers: Devolution, Development, and Civil Society in Newark, 1960–1990* (University of Chicago Press, 2016); "Public Housing and the Stella Wright Rent Strike," Rise Up Newark, https://riseupnewark.com/chapter-4/housing-stella-wright-rent-strike/.
2. Louise Epperson interview with Blackside, Inc., 1994, Henry Hampton Collection, Washington University Libraries.
3. "Public Housing and the Stella Wright Rent Strike."
4. National Urban Coalition, "The Stella Wright Rent Strike and the Greater Newark Urban Coalition," Gus Heningburg Collection, Newark Public Library, https://riseupnewark.com/chapter-4/housing-stella-wright-rent-strike/.
5. Mary Smith interview with Blackside, Inc., 1995, Henry Hampton Collection, Washington University Libraries.
6. "Residents of Newark Statement of Demands," July 16, 1967, Newark Public Library, https://riseupnewark.com/chapters/chapter-3/part-2/actors/the-community/.
7. Junius Williams interview with Blackside, Inc., 1995, Henry Hampton Collection, Washington University Libraries.
8. Many former residents of Newark's public housing projects still hold reunions every summer where these stories can be heard. See Doug Doyle, "Former Residents of Scudder Homes Public Housing Project Tell Their 1967 Stories," *WBGO Journal* July 4, 2017, https://www.wbgo.org/show/wbgo-journal/2017-07-04/former-residents-of-scudder-homes-public-housing-project-tell-their-1967-stories.
9. "The Voice of Stella Wright Christian Community," October 28, 1969, Dennis Westbrook Collection, Rise Up Newark, https://riseupnewark.com/chapter-4/housing-stella-wright-rent-strike/.
10. Stella Wright Tenant Association, "Press Release," June 22, 1970, Dennis Westbrook Collection, Rise Up Newark, https://riseupnewark.com/chapter-4/housing-stella-wright-rent-strike/.

11 National Urban Coalition, "The Stella Wright Rent Strike."
12 Rabig, *The Fixers*, 161–63.
13 National Urban Coalition, "The Stella Wright Rent Strike."
14 Rabig, *The Fixers*, 165–66.
15 Stella Wright Tenant Association Management Corporation, "The New Stella Wright Handbook," 1975, Gus Heningburg Collection, Newark Public Library, https://riseupnewark.com/chapter-4/housing-stella-wright-rent-strike/.
16 Alan Gary Morley, "A Study of Tenant Management of Public Housing" (MCP thesis, University of Rhode Island, 1979).
17 Rabig, *The Fixers,* 166.
18 E. James Bradley, "The New Stella Wright Homes — Final TPP Report," Newark Redevelopment Authority, July 1978.

REHABILITATIVE CAPITALISM IN WINNIPEG'S RENTAL MARKET

WINNIPEG, MANITOBA, CANADA

WRITTEN BY
Stefan Hodges

In March 2019, at the height of a moral panic over methamphetamine use in Winnipeg, a twenty-unit apartment block on Jarvis Street in the city's North End transitioned into sober living housing for recovering addicts. In the following months, the private landlords who owned the building, Karin Harper and Patrick Penner, branded their new rehabilitative effort as the "Living Recovery Foundation" and began to transition a handful of the most run-down buildings in their portfolio towards a rehabilitative model. Some of the buildings required sobriety, while others were branded as "harm reduction" and allowed tenants to use drugs. In all buildings, however, access to the housing was contingent on a long list of house rules that aimed to regulate tenant behaviour in and out of the apartment.

Winnipeg's meth crisis and the COVID-19 pandemic punctuated a decade of relentless efforts to gentrify the city's downtown. The flagship of these efforts was the return of the Winnipeg Jets NHL hockey team in 2011, and the designation of a sports, hospitality, and entertainment district around the hockey arena that became a pleasure ground for suburban Jets fans. By 2018, True North Real Estate Development — a subsidiary of the Winnipeg Jets ownership — received $45 million from the city and province to build condos and luxury apartments next to the arena. Elsewhere, the city contributed $10.5 million between 2010 and 2013 to The Waterfront condo development on the northeastern corner of the downtown and offered tax rebates to new owners who would remain in the condos for five years.[1] Like earlier iterations of homesteading on the prairie, downtown development leaned heavily on support from what Neil Smith calls the "cavalry of city government" in an attempt to settle the "new urban frontier."[2]

The first signs of a meth crisis were evident as early as the fall of 2016. Police killed two people in ten days and attributed these killings to "wild behaviour" created by methamphetamine, implying that the drug posed a risk to the city at large.[3] This discourse simmered until late 2017, and by 2018, public opinion exploded over the crisis. That year, the *Winnipeg Free Press* published an average of 40.75 articles per month that mentioned methamphetamine — nearly ten times the rate of earlier years. Not a single article published by the local newspaper quoted an active user to describe the crisis. Instead, the mainstream media relied heavily on the testimonials of police and campaigning politicians, who blamed the crisis on "risky" subjects in inner-city communities. This rhetoric was easily adopted to shift the blame of poor social conditions onto people who use drugs.

A particularly relevant example is Armour, a property management company, which quickly became one of Winnipeg's largest landlords by buying up inexpensive buildings and rapidly raising rents while neglecting maintenance and repairs. Tenants organized media campaigns to decry renovictions and abusive management tactics,[4] and Armour attempted to shift blame onto meth users. Following a chain of tenant-organized attacks on social media and in the press, Armour's president, Mike Romani, tried to deflect criticism for fires in their buildings onto people who use drugs, suggesting that "every one of [the fires] would be drug-related."[5] Tenants countered Armour's rhetoric in their media campaigns by holding the focus on Armour's abusive management practices, including building-wide evictions, a refusal to maintain or repair units, and even a failure to install fire extinguishers.[6] Winnipeg's renters and Armour's investors began to pull away from the landlord as vacancy rates rose in their buildings. Harper and Penner, who had a large portfolio of eighteen apartment blocks managed by Armour, cut ties from the management company and formed the Living Recovery Foundation (LRF). From the outset, the rehabilitative rebrand was an attempt to fill units by attracting tenants back to their buildings.

The LRF took a different approach than Armour: instead of condemning meth use, they used the meth crisis to find profit in their run-down apartment buildings. Instead of barring or evicting people associated with meth use, the LRF proposed to house, control, and rehabilitate them. At the same time, the rhetoric of the meth crisis normalized policies of securitization that were convenient for the LRF. During the meth crisis, landlords lobbied to expedite evictions,[7] police justified lethal use of their weapons and applying more resources to fight meth use,[8] and public institutions like libraries, recreation centres, and liquor stores introduced new securitization policies to bar "risky" people from entering premises.[9]

There is a long history tracing back to Paris's seventeenth-century Hôpital Général of the state using housing as a tool of moral transformation.[10] Foucault described the Hôpital Général as an early biopolitical intervention — the government's management of people's bodies and lives — that would control its residents:

> The unemployed person was no longer driven away or punished; he was taken in charge, at the expense of the nation but at the cost of his individual liberty. Between him and society, an implicit system of obligation was established: he had the right to be fed, but he must accept the physical and moral constraint of confinement.[11]

Authors have continued to trace how public housing and its philanthropic precedents were designed to contain and reshape the lives of the lower classes. For example, late Victorian "model dwellings" were designed to separate households into nuclear families and to reinforce binary gender divisions between bedrooms.[12] Later, mid-century models of public housing were proposed to replace slum housing with the notion that modern architecture would uplift the working class.[13] Throughout the War on Drugs, American public housing came to resemble the prison, with added fences, metal detectors, curfews, and video surveillance.[14] And more recently, public housing in Canada implemented "supportive" programming, which has been described as a "regime of care" with "heightened surveillance of at-risk populations … merging enforcement and treatment in the places where they now live."[15] This is a rich and useful literature to analyze architectures of confinement in the state's housing system. However, when biopolitics is taken up by the private market, does rehabilitative housing operate differently than those state-led examples? More specifically, what happens when moral transformation and social control become subordinated to a search for profit?

This study of the LRF builds a theory of rehabilitative capitalism, where political economies are formed in disinvested spaces to produce value through the management of so-called "risky" subjects. Rehabilitative capitalism subjugates tenants to carceral conditions under the guise of benevolence. In the context since the onset of COVID-19, where "supportive housing" is growing as a solution to the homelessness crisis, it is crucial to disrupt strategies that find profit through confinement and to push instead for housing that is grounded in self-determination, community building, and poverty reduction.

Rehabilitative discourse allowed the LRF to position themselves as benevolent, despite their carceral nature. Their intervention treated drug use as a behavioural problem, and their aim was accordingly to transform behaviour. Borrowing from other examples of "carceral rehab,"[16] the landlords tried to instill a regimen of controlled routine and forced labour. Daily meetings, mandatory chores, and volunteer hours were intended to create a disciplined lifestyle that would ostensibly keep tenants sober. This made the housing look quite a lot like prison or rehab facility. If tenants stepped out of line, neglected to attend meetings, or relapsed, they were threatened with eviction. Despite these impositions flouting tenancy protections, the rehabilitative branding still coded Harper and Penner as "good" moral subjects. One local housing worker insisted that "they're folks that are good people, family people,"[17] lending them a moral value that aligns them, as Dorothy Roberts has theorized, with patriarchal and racial norms of a "good family" that have long been constructed in relation and opposition to the "deviant" poor and racialized household.[18] Moral value is a key component of rehabilitative capitalism because it structures a relationship where "good" subjects inherit positions of authority over "unfit" subjects to justify their intervention. Tenants knew very well that the LRF was "just another slum apartment,"[19] but state agencies and non-profit housing support workers treated the LRF as a partner and continued to funnel referrals to them.

Vacancy was not a problem specific to the apartment buildings owned by Harper and Penner. Before the pandemic, vacancy rates were already creeping above 5 percent in Winnipeg's central neighbourhoods, and these rates continued to rise to over 7 percent after the emergence of COVID-19. The LRF's rebrand worked to generate moral value, but it also produced scarcity to find demand in a high-vacancy market. While most landlords screened subjects whom they associated with the meth crisis, the LRF became one of the only housing options available for marginalized tenants. At first, the referrals helped to solve the vacancy problem, but since most tenants only received a basic housing allowance of $576 from Employment and Income Assistance, the rents were not very profitable. Once buildings filled, the landlords were able to "double tenancies" by encouraging tenants "to be roommates with each other whether they liked it or not," according to an LRF staff member.[20] The LRF's doubled tenancies, which were located in some of the most neglected buildings in Winnipeg, collected upwards of $1,152 per unit, making them far more profitable than other apartments in the same neighbourhoods.

Since the development of Victorian tenement housing, the architecture of the modern apartment has been designed to facilitate categorization, surveillance and controlled lines of communication.[21] This has made it easy to adapt rental housing to serve carceral purposes, otherwise found in other carceral institutions such as the prison[22] and the psychiatric institution.[23] The LRF's early referral network captured streams of tenants from drug addiction rehab, hospitals, and detention centres. The landlord's disciplinary rule system touted a program of spatial confinement that formed a logical continuity from carceral institutions into the community. On paper, tenants were expected to live under a curfew, had mandatory work hours, were not allowed guests, and followed a pass system reminiscent of Canada's Indian Act, which attempted to regulate and monitor the movement of Indigenous Peoples.

In response, tenants developed their own acts of refusal: they refused to follow rules, and many moved out as soon as they could find other options. These acts made it difficult for the landlords to enforce the rules of confinement, which relied foremost on the threat of eviction. Eventually the curfews and mandatory work hours were abandoned. Still, the LRF used surveillance to monitor and correct behaviour. They installed security cameras in the buildings, and staff entered units without notice to perform "wellness checks." Tenants described the wellness checks as contradictory and confusing interventions where the rhetoric of care was deployed to intimidate and repress tenants who questioned or opposed the landlord:

I'm trying to correlate this with the fact that they made it sound productive, when in reality these "wellness checks" were just to size up people or to make them feel like shit. ... The fact of the matter is that it was not what was agreed upon and that's angering.[24]

Winnipeg's moral panic over methamphetamine use waned in the initial months of the COVID-19 pandemic. Attention shifted towards a new crisis, and people associated with meth use were no longer seen as the biggest risk to urban capital. During the early months of COVID-19, the LRF shifted their focus away from drug addiction recovery. In early 2021, they rebranded again towards "housing first" and "family reunification." The so-called "harm reduction" buildings, which were the most neglected in the stock, were rebranded as "low-barrier housing" and the sober living buildings offered to house families that were reunifying with their children or that were flagged and monitored by Manitoba's foster care system (Child and Family Services [CFS]).

The new model was a logical outcome of the LRF's search for profit. As an accumulation strategy, rehabilitative capitalism relies on growing categories of damage to expand its intervention. The meth crisis was an important moment to justify a transition for the landlord, but the second transition towards housing first and family reunification allowed them to expand to a far wider referral network. In an email sent to a network of housing workers and government agencies in June 2021, Karin Harper wrote: "This city has a huge shortage of low barrier housing. It has been suggested to me by more than one agency that we are the only true Housing First in the city."[25] In addition to the demand for low-barrier housing, the landlord also tapped into a new referral network through the province's foster care system, where 90 percent of the 9,849 children in care are Indigenous. Their early model of rehabilitative capitalism certainly hinted at a continuity of colonial subject management, but this became even more clear in the shift towards family reunification.

Canada's National Housing Strategy follows a trajectory of neoliberal housing policy, which, on the one hand, has justified continued investment in public housing by targeting vulnerable populations,[26] and on the other hand, has funded initiatives that help people find housing and stabilize tenancies in the private market.[27] In 2021, the federal government launched the Rapid Housing Initiative, which aims to "address urgent housing needs of vulnerable Canadians, especially in the context of COVID-19, through the rapid construction of affordable housing." That same year, Manitoba created the Manitoba Housing Supports Initiative to fund the creation of programs to "increase access to affordable housing and to help reduce homelessness." Meanwhile, the federal Reaching Home initiative attempts to help people find and maintain tenancies in the private market by providing rent top-ups and arming social workers with funding to cover repairs and arrears.

Pandemic-era housing policy helped to frame the environment in which recovery landlords like the LRF operate. Though the programs named here at the very least provide necessary housing solutions in the short-term, it remains that the LRF is exploiting a growing political economy of housing for marginalized tenants where there is a recognized scarcity of housing options[28] and where a growing assembly of housing agencies are working to funnel people into whatever housing they can find, adding public funding to sweeten the deal. Non-profit housing providers were granted federal money to build housing for marginalized tenants, but at the same time, LRF copycats also appeared throughout the pandemic, turning existing apartments into carceral spaces. Recovery landlordism was developed during the meth crisis, but it expanded throughout the pandemic. In the words of a current LRF tenant, this made the apartment "like a jail, except even more dangerous."[29]

The LRF, and copycats Makoon Transition and Geoffrey's Garden (which were founded in an LRF building by staff who no longer work at the organization), have all reapplied the LRF's original model of disciplinary housing to their own brands of family reunification housing. Surveillance is a key feature of because CFS requires that families live under twenty-four-hour supervision while they are reunifying with children. Mandatory check-ins, wellness checks, and security cameras all serve the landlord by exerting disciplinary power over tenants, but they also allow the landlord to promote their carceral housing to the colonial state's foster care system.

Family reunification housing taps into a more robust and more profitable network of referrals than drug addiction housing. Harper explained that her direct line of communication with CFS allows her to speculate on how much rent she can receive for housing a family that is about to reunify:

> I've got somebody in the building, she's gone through everything she's supposed to go through, she's still doing programming outside of AFM [Addiction Foundation of Manitoba]. She gets three visits a week with her child, and again I'm accepting her single status and then one child ends up back in her care and then her rent will be according to that.[30]

Family reunification allows the landlords to increase rents to absorb additional resources that the family would otherwise receive to support their children. Under Manitoba's rent control, these are illegal rent increases, but welfare workers pay the rent directly to the landlords without asking questions, either unaware of rent protections or unwilling to jeopardize the housing of their clients. Similarly, Geoffrey's Garden openly admitted at a Residential Tenancies Commission hearing that they raised rents from $600 to $930 when parents received custody of their children, sometimes in studio apartments.

The LRF, Makoon Transition, and Geoffrey's Garden have all argued, incorrectly, that they do not fall under the Residential Tenancies Act. While they claim to support vulnerable populations, they also produce vulnerability by disregarding rent controls and other tenancy protections while subjecting tenants to policies of confinement. At the Geoffrey's Garden hearing, a tenant explained that she was evicted for not attending mandatory meetings. During the spread of COVID-19's highly contagious omicron variant, she had isolated in her apartment with her newborn to stay safe. The landlord determined that this was a breach of house rules and evicted her without notice at the end of December 2021.

Just as prisons, migrant detention centres, and long-term care facilities were sites of disproportionate infectious spread during the pandemic,[31] recovery landlordism also made tenants vulnerable to COVID-19 while stripping away basic rights. As landlords search for profit in political economies attached to homelessness management and the colonial state's foster care system, they capture value from the advanced marginality of their tenants. At the same time, housing that relies on confinement rather than care has proven to produce conditions of vulnerability to illness, violence, and poverty. The shift to family reunification housing during the pandemic meant that the harm produced in this carceral housing was highly gendered and colonial.

Recovery landlordism in Winnipeg's rental market has relied on colonial constructions of the benevolent settler subject to justify a paternalistic management of Indigenous Peoples. Sherene Razack explains that this relation is important for the performance of settler colonialism because "Indigenous suffering becomes something non-Indigenous peoples will ameliorate, and public discourse shifts from land claims to rescue."[32] The benevolent rhetoric of rehabilitation serves to deflect criticism away from illegitimate occupation and allows land-based economies to persist, but as Michelle Stewart and Corey Laberge recognize, it also functions to open new kinds of extractive economies:

> The twenty-first century settler colonial economy in Canada expands through narratives of welfare and care — where there is neither welfare nor care in these cases, but rather the extraction of surplus value found in disposable lives that render value through their management.[33]

This is where the logic of settler colonialism, which is ultimately about the appropriation of land, rubs up against the political economies of racial capitalism. Recovery landlordism is made possible by "the state-sanctioned, or extralegal production and exploitation of group-differentiated vulnerability to premature death."[34] Rehabilitative capitalism is a strategy of accumulation born of settler colonialism and racial capitalism that finds profit through the production and management of vulnerable or "risky" subjects. In Canada, post-pandemic recovery plans are homeward-bound and promoted in the name of care, but the LRF case reminds us to be mindful of the rhetoric of "care" and "cure." For settler colonial states, politics of care and cure have always been part and parcel of reaffirming and foreclosing the imagination of settler futures.[35]

The LRF also exposes the threat that recovery landlordism poses to tenant rights and wellbeing. Supportive housing and housing first programs are couched in benevolent rhetoric, but these interventions cannot be taken for granted. Housing advocates need to pay close attention to how supportive housing is structured. What supports are truly offered, and under what conditions? The defence of tenants' rights needs to be at the heart of this analysis.

In settler colonial cities like Winnipeg, recovery needs to be Indigenous-led, and non-Indigenous people like me should be attentive to how we participate. By building lines of communication with tenants, lending financial and organizing support to those who challenge policies of confinement, supporting move-outs, and sharing rights-based information widely, we can make small acts of solidarity to disrupt and undermine the expansion of carceral conditions in the rental market.

Notes

1. Bartley Kives, "City Council Approves $10-K Rebate for Exchange Condo Purchase," *Winnipeg Free Press* (blog), July 17, 2013, https://www.winnipegfreepress.com/breakingnews/2013/07/17/buy-new-condo-pick-up-10k.
2. Neil Smith, *The New Frontier: Gentrification and the Revanchist City* (Routledge, 1996).
3. Carol Sanders, "Chief Sees Meth Link in Shootings: Police Noticing More 'Wild Behaviour' on the Streets, Smyth Says," *Winnipeg Free Press* (blog), September 25, 2017. https://www.winnipegfreepress.com/breakingnews/2017/09/25/chief-sees-meth-link-in-shootings.
4. Isaac Wurmann, "Landlords cross Canada Are Pushing Tenants Out with Renovations," Vice (blog), November 2, 2018, https://www.vice.com/en/article/d3qajk/landlords-across-canada-are-pushing-tenants-out-with-renovations.
5. Marina Von Stackleberg, "Apartment Fires a Symptom of Winnipeg's Drug Use 'Epidemic,' Says Property Company," *CBC News,* January 16, 2019, https://www.cbc.ca/news/anito/anitoba/west-end-apartment-fires-1.4979553.
6. Austin Grabish, "Used Needles, Condoms and No Heat: Residents Say Problems in Winnipeg Block Make It 'a Nightmare,'" *CBC News,* January 18, 2019, https://www.cbc.ca/news/canada/manitoba/212-langside-building-issues-1.4984655; Cameron MacLean, "'Crumbling Down': Tenants Fear for Safety, Health in Winnipeg Company's Apartment Buildings," *CBC News,* March 27, 2019, https://www.cbc.ca/news/canada/manitoba/armour-property-management-complaints-1.5072887.
7. Larry Kusch, "Quick Evictions Touted in Fight against Meth," *Winnipeg Free Press,* October 12, 2018, https://www.winnipegfreepress.com/breakingnews/2018/10/12/quick-evictions-touted-in-fight-against-meth.
8. Ashley Prest, "Armed Man High on Meth Tasered Twice." *Winnipeg Free Press,* June 22, 2017, https://www.winnipegfreepress.com/local/2017/06/22/armed-man-high-on-meth-tasered-twice; Danielle Da Silva, "Police Community Engagement Program Concludes," *Winnipeg Free Press,* December 1, 2017, sec. Community Review, https://www.winnipegfreepress.com/our-communities/souwester/2017/12/01/police-community-engagement-program-concludes.
9. Sarah Cooper, Joe Curnow, Bronwyn Dobchuk-Land, Andrew Kohan, John K. Samson, and Brianne Selman, "Millennium for All Report on Securitization of the Millennium Public Library," 2019, Millennium for All.
10. Stefan Hodges, "Recovery Landlordism: Accumulation through Confinement in the Landscape of Winnipeg's Meth Crisis," master's thesis, Concordia University, 2021. https://spectrum.library.concordia.ca/id/eprint/989950/.
11. Michel Foucault, *Madness and Civilization: A History of Insanity in the Age of Reason* (Random House, 1988[1965]), 48.
12. Robin Evans, "Rookeries and Model Dwellings: English Housing Reform and the Moralities of Private Space," *Architectural Association Quarterly* 10, 1 (1978).
13. Ted Rutland, *Displacing Blackness: Planning, Power, and Race in Twentieth-Century Halifax* (University of Toronto Press, 2018).

14 Rashad Shabazz, *Spatializing Blackness: Architectures of Confinement and Black Masculinity in Chicago,* New Black Studies (University of Illinois Press, 2015).
15 Danya Fast and David Cunningham, "'We Don't Belong There': New Geographies of Homelessness, Addiction, and Social Control in Vancouver's Inner City," *City and Society* 30, 2 (2018), 245.
16 Teresa Gowan and Sarah Whetstone, "Making the Criminal Addict: Subjectivity and Social Control in a Strong-Arm Rehab," *Punishment & Society,* 14, 1 (2012), https://doi.org/10.1177/1462474511424684.
17 Hodges, "Recovery Landlordism" 2021, 57.
18 Dorothy Roberts, "Black Women and Their Families: Deviants or Resistors?" In *Changing Perspectives of the Family,* 77–95. (Des Moines: Drake University Law School, 1994).
19 Hodges, "Recovery Landlordism," 56.
20 Hodges, "Recovery Landlordism," 75.
21 Evans, "Rookeries and Model Dwellings"; Rutland, *Displacing Blackness.*
22 Shabazz, *Spatializing Blackness*; Hodges, "Recovery Landlordism," 57.
23 Greg Suttor, *Taking Stock of Supportive Housing for Mental Health and Addictions in Ontario* (Wellesley Institute, November 2016).
24 Tenant interview in Hodges, "Recovery Landlordism," 93.
25 Tenant interview in Hodges, "Recovery Landlordism," 75.
26 Greg Suttor, *Still Renovating: A History of Canadian Social Housing Policy* (McGill-Queen's University Press, 2016).
27 Jino Distasio, Jitender Sareen, and Corinne Isaak, "Winnipeg Site Final Report: At Home Chez Soi Project," (Mental Health Commission of Canada, 2014), https://mentalhealthcommission.ca/wp-content/uploads/2021/09/At2520Home2520Report2520Winnipeg2520ENG_0.pdf.
28 Morgan Modjeski, "'It's a Joke' Tenant Speaks Out on Winnipeg's Living Recovery Landlord," *CityNews,* January 11, 2023, https://www.youtube.com/watch?v=AuAPfdi9Y9w.
29 Hodges, "Recovery Landlordism,", 75.
30 Hodges, "Recovery Landlordism," 79.
31 Detention Watch Network, "How Ice Detention Contributed to the Spread of COVID-19 in the United States," Detention Watch Network, 2020, https://www.detentionwatchnetwork.org/sites/default/files/reports/DWN_Hotbeds%20of%20Infection_2020_FOR%20WEB.pdf; Megan Linton, "'Warehouses Like This Are Not the Answer': Exposing the Crisis of Long-Term Care in Manitoba," *Canadian Dimension,* November 18, 2020, https://canadiandimension.com/articles/view/warehouses-like-this-not-the-answer-exposing-crisis-long-term-care-manitoba.
32 Sherene Razack, *Dying from Improvement: Inquests and Inquiries into Indigenous Deaths in Custody* (University of Toronto Press 2015), 59.
33 Michelle Stewart, Corey LaBerge, "Care-to-Prison Pipeline: Indigenous Children in Twenty-First Century Settler Colonial Economies," In *Settler City Limits: Indigenous Resurgence and Colonial Violence in the Urban Prairie West,* edited by Heather Dorries, Robert Henry, David Hugill, Tyler McCreary, and Julie Tomiak (University of Manitoba Press, 2019), 209.
34 Ruth Wilson Gilmore, *Golden Gulag: Prisons, Surplus, Crisis, and Opposition in Globalizing California,* (University of California Press, 2007) 28.
35 Jasbir Puar, T*he Right to Maim: Debility, Capacity, Disability* (Duke University Press, 2017); Razack, *Dying from Improvement.*

LEVERAGING LAND AND HOUSING OCCUPATIONS

PHILADELPHIA, PENNSYLVANIA, UNITED STATES

WRITTEN BY
Amanda Ricketts & Claire Herbert

In early 2020, activists in Philadelphia began covertly moving precariously housed mothers and their children into homes left vacant by the local housing authority. Soon after, Center City tent encampment populations swelled to nearly 200, occupying prime urban space. Against the backdrop of Black Lives Matter protests and the Centers for Disease Control (CDC) guidance to desist from sweeps during the pandemic, activists and unhoused residents came together in a happenstance way, leveraging land occupations in Center City to aid families' ability to remain in vacant housing they took over, thereby resisting the violence of separation by child welfare agencies. Using interviews with organizers and media reports, as well as city and organizational documents, this chapter traces the way that housing and land occupations unfolded unexpectedly but mutually supported each other's objectives in Philadelphia. This cooperation was exemplified by encampment organizers and residents leveraging their visibility and power in the moment to support squatters. We describe how the unplanned, contentious nature of these occupations interacted with the manifold tactics of both activists and unhoused residents who came together to support these diverse causes. Weaving together the occupations' responses to and capitalization on the political moment of the pandemic and social unrest stemming from police violence, we find an ultimate solidification of homeless mothers' rights to house their children, uniting their families.

Organized takeovers of land and buildings as a strategy for gaining access to housing is commonplace across countries in the Global South and North. Scholars estimate that there are over a billion squatters globally.[1] In the United States, however, land and housing occupations have received little attention in academia.[2] Mainstream media tends to frame such direct action pejoratively, focusing on the illicit transgression of property rights and property owners as victims and deploying the term "squatters" in a disparaging way.

For societies founded on the principles of liberalism, private property is paramount as value, culture, and legal priority. One primary role of the government is to protect individual, exclusionary, contractual rights to property: taking over land and housing is a direct challenge to these values and legal rights. Taking a broader view historically and geographically, however, paints a more nuanced picture. Squatting — as the act of claiming right to land and housing on that land — has been foundational to the construction and expansion of the United States,[3] not unproblematically as settler colonial societies are founded on stealing land and turning it into property. Research reveals that squatting is simultaneously an economic survival strategy and a political refusal of the exploitative conditions that threaten vulnerable populations.[4] In the contemporary US, those without legal rights to property (be it use-rights as renters or control-rights as owners) are denied fundamental liberties. Lacking the legal right to be anywhere, people experiencing unsheltered homelessness have nowhere to legally carry out the practices essential to life. In this way, then, squatting is a radical assertion of belonging — of the right to exist as well as be included in the sphere of legally protected citizenship. This case of land and housing occupations in Philadelphia reveals the power of multiple forms of occupations to carve out space free from state violence in a society where property is often more protected and valued than the lives of vulnerable residents.

Philadelphia experienced significant population decline in the latter half of the twentieth century, largely due to historical forces impacting rust belt cities across the US.[5] Philadelphia's population peaked at just over two million in 1950, then lost around 500,000 residents by 2000, and has subsequently stabilized with around 1.6 million residents in 2020.[6] In that year, the dual concerns of family separation due to homelessness and of gentrification of formerly disinvested neighbourhoods intensified against the backdrop of the unfolding pandemic and Black Lives Matter protests against police violence. Sparked by revitalization efforts and incentives, gentrification has accelerated primarily in Center City and adjacent neighbourhoods, as well as surrounding anchor institutions like Drexel University and University of Pennsylvania in West Philadelphia and Temple University in North Philadelphia,[7] leading to an overall decline in low-cost housing in these neighbourhoods.[8] These revitalization trends interact with the city's highly racially segregated landscape in ways that exacerbate neighbourhood race and class inequalities, as more than 70 percent of its census tracts are either over 75 percent Black or over 75 percent white.[9] Despite the spread of gentrification, Philadelphia still has a high vacancy rate relative to other large US cities: the 2020 census counted 68,722 vacant housing units in Philadelphia.[10]

The Philadelphia Housing Authority (PHA), established under the federal Housing Act of 1937, is the fourth largest public housing authority in the United States and largest landlord in Philadelphia. It is also responsible for providing affordable housing for low-income residents.[11] The PHA manages an estimated 12,894 public housing units, and as of July 2020, the PHA had over 25,700 households on waiting lists.[12] Despite being a significant source of affordable housing in Philadelphia, residents and activists have accused the organization of accelerating gentrification through the sale of scattered sites of housing and land, contributing to the harmful displacement of communities of colour.[13] Residents complain of non-profit homeless service providers infringing on personal autonomy, of racially charged police violence, and of the violence of family separations. Regarding the latter, Philadelphia has the "highest child separation rate in the country — three times that of New York City and four times that of Chicago."[14] Resistance to these various forms of state violence coalesce in this case study.

A small local organization, Philadelphia Housing Action (PHAct), had worked to intervene in problematic housing authority practices years before the events of 2020. PHAct is a grassroots coalition of long-time housing and homeless activists, whose members "are grounded in years of agitation, work, and advocacy informed by collective experiences of homelessness, institutionalization, incarceration, family separation, foster care, public housing, interpersonal violence, immigration, substance use, mental health and all other forms of discrimination and oppression."[15] Central PHAct actors were galvanized by the PHA's private police force activity and role in gentrifying neighbourhoods (such as in North Philadelphia, where they flipped disjointed public housing sites and had plans to turn some sites into Temple University student housing). Near the end of 2019, PHAct and affiliated organizations, like the Workers Revolutionary Collective, had begun discussing the problem of housing in Philadelphia. By February 2020, PHAct had a broader scope, with increased community support, though the organization's core members never numbered more than five.[16] Viewing PHA as paradoxically violating its own mission and obligations, PHAct decided they should move families into vacant PHA housing.

Soon COVID-19 began impacting the wider community. Stay-at-home orders were put in place, and the CDC issued guidance prohibiting homeless encampment evictions. The pandemic made problems of homelessness more acute, as shelter capacity dropped and doubling up became riskier. On March 23, 2020, PHAct and its allies, including North Philadelphia Food Not Bombs, challenged the eviction of an encampment at the Pennsylvania Convention Center. PHAct members recall that the PHA's private police force was "basically paid by the convention center to do so."[17] Later the same day, PHAct occupied its first vacant PHA property, opening it to the homeless community. Vacant sites were chosen and subsequently selected for occupation through visual surveys and community knowledge networks. PHAct members acting as "surveyors" leveraged their privilege to go undetected by neighbours while entering PHA-owned housing. One PHAct member explained the process: "If a neighbour came out and asked what I was doing, I would tell them I [was] surveying vacant city owned property for emergency housing. And that was good enough for most people, especially at the very start of the pandemic."[18] Through April and May, PHAct identified and moved mothers with children into ten more empty PHA-owned houses. Many families agreed to participate not because of political alliances but because they wanted housing: everyone who was moved into a house was homeless.[19]

In May 2020, the George Floyd uprisings and subsequent critiques of state endorsed police violence further galvanized PHAct members and their allies. Members felt that collaboration between organizations was an essential tactic to maximize political cover. This broad collaboration enabled PHAct to organize local academics, frontline workers, and health care professionals to oppose evictions and CDC guideline violations. Allyship offered additional support and credibility in framing the organization's critiques of PHA's private police force and the intensity of violent state interventions: weeks of protests and marches locally were met with militarized policing that also included the eviction of homeless encampments from Center City areas by the National Guard. As a result, activists felt it was time to move forward with the comparatively less visible PHA housing occupations. However, there was not necessarily consensus on which tactics and outcomes to target; some organizations were wary that a focus on encampments would take away from housing objectives.[20]

PHAct's framework of abolitionist politics and its diversity of tactics was particularly important, as organizers realized "the revolution [would] not be funded." At the same time, the occupations were preventing the PHA from making money from the sale of these houses.[21] This entwining of government with the business of selling real estate further explains the persistent and violent enforcement of PHA's private police force throughout the summer. The PHA's role as a public agency operating as and with the interests of a "private property management company" betrays its public-serving operative.

On June 10, 2020, PHAct and homeless activists initiated a protest encampment, Camp James Talib-Dean (Camp JTD), under the collective cause of Housing Now. Housing Now is a slogan, a goal for the future, and an organizing objective for asserting the universal right to housing. The encampment occupied prime space in Center City, on Benjamin Franklin Parkway adjacent to several prominent museums and a Whole Foods store. Camp JTD quickly swelled to over 150 residents. It was additionally declared a no-cop zone, banning homeless outreach and defying police orders. Harm reduction was an important frame used to unite activists and motivate housing and land occupations as solutions, particularly concerning safe injection sites and controlled supplies of drugs. Harm reduction directed toward housing suggests that an important first step is allowing people space to live free from punitive state intervention. Citing the recent death of a resident, for whom the camp was named, an activist said the encampment was a "really good example of why people need a safe space.... More work needed to be done because the place [encampment] was not that safe, but the whole point was to create a space that was safer for people than the outside world."[22] Reducing harm by creating safer spaces for unhoused community members through both housing occupations and organized encampments, particularly mothers with families, is a central organizing tenet for PHAct members. Having no place to legally be subjects unhoused community members to additional risks and instability. Policies that illegalize community members leave people susceptible to further state coercion or violence. PHAct organized around solutions that met individuals where they were, creating spaces of security and belonging entirely separate from state surveillance.

Tactics both shifted and persisted over the next several months. On June 27, 2020, Camp Teddy, a smaller encampment — more strategically assembled through planned deliberation and prominently situated — occupied PHA-owned land in North Philadelphia. This encampment impeded breaking ground for a new $52 million mixed-use development, a project many nearby residents supported but that raised concerns about escalating gentrification pressures in a distressed neighbourhood. These two camps persisted for four months as residents continued their protest occupations, media showered attention on the encampments, and activists continued moving homeless families into PHA-owned homes.

In response, the PHA used their private police force to "eject squatters without a legal court process,"[23] bypassing the city police force, which does not typically evict squatters if they have established tenancy. Instead, the landlord is instructed to use the civil eviction process through the court, proceedings that could take between four and twelve months.

The unique politics of the coalition surrounding PHAct expanded and finally motivated the city to negotiate. Few non-profits were collaborators, or even allies in these occupations, because they were hesitant to risk their funding by directly opposing the PHA. Non-profit actors may have positioned themselves as rhetorical allies to the cause of housing justice, but PHAct members emphasized that these organizations had legal and philosophical limitations that were fundamentally misaligned with the political and strategic goals of PHAct. PHAct's housing occupations were particularly concerned with creating safe spaces outside of state structures that perpetuate housing injustice, particularly for homeless mothers and children. Abolition is the central politics orienting the activists' relations to the PHA and the demands of Camp JTD and Camp Teddy occupiers. At the same time as activists were identifying the limits of the non-profit industrial sector's support for PHAct's more extralegal and political strategizing, they found a bounty of ever-expanding support from affinity groups and individual activists. Activists noted that the prominence of PHAct's political mission resulted in an abundance of resources in the form of allies and educational materials, as everyone was "working really hard not to be racist, and [the input] wasn't necessarily useful for what we were doing, and there's many ways that it was very fraught, but nevertheless, there was a lot of energy."[24]

This immense energy garnered the attention of the city, and eventually a begrudging PHA, which set off negotiations over housing involving PHAct, the mayor, other high level city officials, and the CEO of the PHA. Camp residents, affinity groups, and individual activists united behind a common aim: to leverage these visible, spatially disruptive encampments to carve out access to more affordable housing, to ensure the stability of the homeless families squatting in PHA-owned housing, to hold PHA accountable to its mission of providing affordable housing, and to push back against forms of state violence.

Activists with PHAct achieved multiple successes. The particular historical moments of encroaching gentrification, evictions, policing violence, and Black Lives Matter protests, as well as the way the COVID-19 pandemic stressed formal housing solutions but provided some protection for informal housing solutions (like encampments) were integral to this outcome. On September 1, 2020, PHAct demanded that PHA transfer vacant city-owned properties to a land trust to be held as permanent low-income housing. The PHA announced on September 26 that the city had agreed to transfer fifty houses to a community land trust if all PHAct's encampments were dissolved. On October 1, the PHA promised "nine fully rehabbed houses, two empty lots, the transfer of any squats that have already been approved for disposition to the land trust, amnesty for all Philadelphia Housing Action squatters, an end to extrajudicial ejectments and evictions by PHA Police, jobs for encampment residents to rehab the houses, a one year moratorium on sales of PHA property and an independent study on the impact of PHA property sales, participation of PHA Police Department in City of Philadelphia reform initiatives, and to fully implement the Continuous Conservation Reserve Program (CCRP) with up to 300 vacant properties" for the dissolution of Camp Teddy.[25] On October 12, 2020, following multiple assemblies and canvassing at the encampment, PHAct signed an agreement to vacate Camp JTD on short notice in exchange for an additional fifty houses from PHA to hold in the land trust.

Despite previous criticisms of non-profit organizing, PHAct created a non-profit called the Philadelphia Community Land Trust to be a "container" for the newly acquired property, though it was conceptually "decoupled" from their political work. PHAct members internally approved of the land trust legal format for taking property off the speculative market but lamented that the format does not in and of itself challenge private property, noting that the necessity for a legal entity to own property reflects settler colonial relationships with the land.[26] Furthermore, members criticized land trusts for not serving the people, as community processes and decision-making were replaced with a corporate board structure. However, community land trusts are arguably the best legal vehicle in US common law for the creation of communal property, though the full desired extent of this form of relationship to the land has no clear articulations yet. This dispute shapes how PHAct continues to frame their work. The organizers note the contradictions inherent in creating a land trust, as the central organizational values of PHAct oppose the hegemonic structures of private property present in land trust policy. While housing struggles often pressure the state to uphold responsibilities such as the Fair Housing Act, tenant protections, and habitability standards, the case of PHAct and their allies shows the importance of carving space away from the violence of the state, which is often ever present in the lives of unhoused or precariously housed populations.[27] Squatting may be a radical assertion of belonging, and in this case PHAct also successfully claimed housing as belonging to the community.

Notes

1   Robert Neuwirth, *Shadow Cities: A Billion Squatters, A New Urban World* (Routledge, 2016).
2   For exceptions see: Amy Starecheski, *Ours to Lose: When Squatters Became Homeowners in New York City* (University of Chicago Press, 2006); Claire W. Herbert, *A Detroit Story: Urban Decline and the Rise of Property Informality* (University of California Press, 2021); John Atlas, *Seeds of Change: The Story of ACORN, America's Most Controversial Antipoverty Community Organizing Group* (Vanderbilt University Press, 2010).
3   Jason Jindrich, "Squatting in the US: What Historians Can Learn from Developing Countries," in *Public Goods versus Economic Interests: Global Perspectives on the History of Squatting*, edited by T. Aguilera and A. Smart (Routledge, 2006).
4   Asef Bayat, "Radical Religion and the Habitus of the Dispossessed: Does Islamic Militancy Have an Urban Ecology?" *International Journal of Urban and Regional Research* 31, 3 (2007); Nezar AlSayyad, "Urban Informality as a 'New' Way of Life," in Nezar AlSayyad and Ananya Roy, eds. *Urban Informality: Transnational*

Perspectives from the Middle East, Latin America, and South Asia (Lexington Books, 2003); Eduardo Moisés Peñalver and Sonia K. Katyal, *Property Outlaws: How Squatters, Pirates, and Protesters Improve the Law of Ownership* (Yale University Press, 2010)

5   Thomas J. Sugrue, *The Origins of the Urban Crisis: Race and Inequality in Postwar Detroit*, updated edition, Vol. 168 (Princeton University Press, 2014).
6   US Census 2020. Philadelphia Quickfacts.
7   Jackelyn Hwang and Lei Ding, "Unequal Displacement: Gentrification, Racial Stratification, and Residential Destinations in Philadelphia," *American Journal of Sociology* 126, (2020).
8   Seth Chizeck, "Gentrification and Changes in the Stock of Low-Cost Rental Housing in Philadelphia, 2000 to 2014." *Cascade Focus*, January 2017, http://www.philadelphiafed.org/-/media/community-development/publications/cascade-focus/gentrification-and-changes-in-the-stock-of-low-cost-rental-housing/cascade-focus_5.pdf?la=en.
9   Jackelyn Hwang, and Lei Ding."Unequal Displacement: Gentrification, Racial Stratification, and Residential Destinations in Philadelphia." *American Journal of Sociology* (2020),126(2):354-406.
10 US Census Bureau, "Philadelphia City Census" (2020), https://data.census.gov/.
11 Philadelphia Housing Authority, "About PHA," 2022, http://www.pha.phila.gov/aboutpha/about-pha.aspx.
12 Philadelphia Housing Authority, 2020 "Agency Overview," http://www.pha.phila.gov/media/189728/pha_fact_sheet_2020_july_10.pdf.
13 Interview with PHAct organizers, August 30, 2021.
14 Philadelphia City Council, Resolution No. 190798, "Special Committee on Child Separation in Philadelphia," sponsored by council members Oh and Bass, 2019.
15 Philadelphia Housing Action, "About," 2021, https://philadelphiahousingaction.info/about/.
16 Interview with PHAct organizers.
17 Interview with PHAct organizers.
18 Interview with PHAct organizers.
19 Samantha Melamed, "Once-Homeless Philly Families Are Squatting PHA Houses, The Agency Wants Them Out." *Philadelphia Inquirer*, August 5, 2020.
20 Interview with PHAct organizers.
21 Interview with PHAct organizers.
22 Interview with PHAct organizers.
23 Interview with PHAct organizers.
24 Interview with PHAct organizers.
25 Nichole Tillman, "PHA and Occupy PHA Reach a Deal to End Encampment," Press Release, Philadelphia Housing Authority, October 5, 2020; Wiley Cunningham and Jennifer Bennetch, "Philadelphia Housing Action Claims Victory after 6 Month Direct Action Campaign Forces City to Relinquish 50 Vacant Homes to Community Land Trust," Press Release, Philadelphia Housing Action, September 26, 2020.
26 Interview with PHAct organizers.
27 Deyanira Nevárez Martínez, "Homelessness in Southern California: Street-Level Encounters with the State and the Structural Violence of Performative Productivity," *Radical Housing Journal* 3, 2 (2020).

HOUSING AND HOME AS KEY SITES OF STRUGGLE

MINNEAPOLIS, MINNESOTA, UNITED STATES

WRITTEN BY
Nina Medvedeva

In 2020, anything seemed possible in Minneapolis. The Third Precinct Police Station was burned to the ground. People formed vast mutual aid networks. A new wave of support for houseless neighbours bloomed. At the seeming end of the world, people were ready to give revolution a chance. The response to the brutal police killing of George Floyd amidst the COVID-19 pandemic showed the power of communal action and care in resistance to widespread state abandonment of people's health and its twin, state-sanctioned racist police violence. One of the most remarkable efforts was the takeover and conversion of a Sheraton hotel into a mutual aid hub that provided food, rooms for the houseless, and harm reduction services. The day after the Third Precinct burned, the Sheraton hotel was evacuated due to safety issues. When organizers fighting against the displacement of unhoused neighbours learned about the evacuation, they quickly rushed in and negotiated with the hotel owner, Jay Patel, to let unhoused people stay there.[1] The newly dubbed Share-A-Ton Sanctuary Hotel was situated in Phillips — a working-class and racially diverse neighbourhood in the heart of Minneapolis. With a disproportionate number of houseless people being Black, Indigenous, and people of colour, volunteers saw the occupation as "a means of land repatriation ... addressing historic deep disparities."[2] Activists stepped up to support houseless people displaced by police from long-standing encampments. The hope behind the Share-A-Ton was to provide residents with a semi-permanent place to live during the pandemic while also supplying free meals, reliable access to assistance and social workers, and a sense of stability in a tumultuous time. As Charmaine Chua writes in her analysis of the hotel, the goal was to create a "resident-centered environment ... grounded in principles of harm reduction, autonomy, mutual aid, anti-racism, and abolition."[3]

After a little over a week, things fell apart at the Share-A-Ton when the hotel owner called the police to evict residents and deactivated keycards, making it impossible for residents to access their rooms.[4] Evicted hotel residents moved to encampments set up in public parks across the city, most prominently in Peavy Park and Powderhorn Park. The Minneapolis Park Board attempted to evict these camps several times, but physical confrontations with the police, call-in campaigns, and lobbying from encampment residents, activists, and neighbourhood groups forced the board to declare a temporary stay on evictions. During that time, there were hundreds of people living at the encampments. These sites provided residents with a space to meet and discuss their needs, bathroom and washing facilities, open-air kitchens, access to health care and social services, and even amenities like a library.

COVID-19 strained an already underfunded shelter system to the point where the system could not accommodate more people. Congregate settings acted as major sites of COVID-19 transmission while depriving residents of respect and autonomy. When no individual housing options were available, moving houseless populations out of centralized spaces like shelters and into decentralized spaces like encampments became a CDC best practice — one ignored by the city as it sought to evict residents. One encampment resident told the *Star Tribune*: "Most of us have had bad experiences with shelters. They get you under their thumb, they treat you like children.... I literally would rather take a chance on hypothermia than go back to the shelter. That's how a lot of us feel."[5] Temporary shelter housing couldn't be guaranteed from one day to the next, and encampment residents also worried that taking the city's offer for indoor shelter space would provide the city with cover to clear the encampments. There's little surprise that houseless residents choose places like the Share-A-Ton and encampments over traditional shelters.

Encampment residents and their comrades stood up to continuous waves of opposition from city legislators wanting to remove the encampments, while homeowners, police, and Park Board members argued that the encampments infringed on the rights of property owners to enjoy the parks. Encampment residents refused the city's "housing solutions" that provided residents with temporary access to a shelter bed or hotel room and instead fought for robust communal permanent housing alternatives — ones that kept people together in community and gave them a sense of autonomy over their living space. Encampment residents stood firmly for the right to occupy space, build a good life free from incarceration and police violence, and receive care. These goals presented clear resistance against notions of private property, neoliberal imaginaries of space, and the designation of public land for exclusive use by housed residents. By working to create spaces attuned to the needs of houseless people, encampment residents and their comrades created and politically embodied central components of housing justice: the conflict over people's lives, their ability to decide how to live, and the prioritization of those needs against and above private property relations.

After a long summer of struggle in 2020, police cleared many encampments. Some were evicted because the Park Board decided the camps were an illegal use of the park or because they deemed residents' use of space heaters and campfires as dangerous. Others were evicted due to homeowner complaints about drug use, gun violence, sexual violence, and sex work. In response, encampment residents either took the city's limited shelter and housing offerings, started new encampments, or moved elsewhere. The city project of housing the houseless was limited to begin with and gradually lost funding as politicians normalized mass death and infection from COVID-19.

The ongoing Minneapolis encampment movement carries an important lesson for all activists engaged in the work of housing justice: the right to shelter and housing is a social project that can be used as a political weapon against the unhoused. I want to use the movement as a provocation for rethinking how the concept of "housing" operates within housing justice struggles. The concept of "housing," if left unexamined, limits our ability to respond to attacks on the poor and unhoused. Housing is not just a building one occupies. It is produced by a complex interrelation of domestic labour, government regulations, market forces, tenant advocacy, and the system of property that makes ownership possible. Expansive notions of housing justice take "full account of the structural processes of housing precarity as well as the continuous and complex contestations through which rights to housing are conceptualised, claimed and consolidated."[6] Housing justice requires community control, non-market social housing, reparations to racialized communities, and high-quality living environments for all involved.[7]

As the temporary COVID-19 support for renters and the ongoing eviction crisis have shown, the state offered limited concessions while maintaining a system of property that created a common precarious existence for nearly everyone. These concessions obscured the core issues in housing justice struggles: a fundamental transformation of social relations into one in which tenants have power over how they live. The government's temporary policy responses to the heightened housing precarity early in the pandemic were short-lived as business, landlord, and conservative interests pushed the federal government to end social assistance programs by 2021 and shift to a "new normal" even as COVID-19 reached unprecedented levels. As the government relaxed its COVID protocols, its policies took on a revanchist edge. When eviction moratoriums expired, the limited programs that persisted, like the COVID-19 Emergency Rental Assistance Program, could be refused by landlords if they chose to evict due to non-payment of rent.[8] This created a ticking time bomb for a rise in houselessness and subsequent disease spread. People were forced to return to work to pay rent arrears or face eviction. Data on these impacts remains limited, but there was a sizable shift in power back to property owners and business interests following the gradual end of eviction moratoriums implemented by cities and states across the country. Grassroots housing justice groups were left to pick up the pieces as government funding and support programs ended.

The difficulty with these social welfare measures as forms of housing justice is that they are bound to a particular arrangement of property and family. While the disruption of housing by a global pandemic may feel rare or unprecedented, our most recent global public health crisis is one event in a longer history of disease restructuring the home. The government has long paired housing policy with disease control. One need only look at the brutal quarantining of Chinese immigrants in San Francisco during the 1920s flu epidemic, historical and contemporary "slum" clearance, and the racist zoning laws meant to protect the white bourgeois family from so-called racial contagion.[9] Housing disruption, governance, and disease management go hand-in-hand. More central than the housing unit itself are the underlying social relations that make it possible: the social relations of property and home constituted by historically, geographically, and culturally specific forms of capitalist production, domestic labour, and household consumption. Emergency relief policies and their withdrawal show how state-mediated access to housing through these social relations can be a means to discipline and punish communities of colour, workers, unhoused people, disabled people, and anyone else the state deigns deviant to the white supremacist project of capitalist accumulation.

The house has long been a shifting political unit. The single-family home, the apartment, and the hotel/motel room arose through a series of deliberate urban policy decisions. Cities in the late 1800s were populated with apartment hotels, boarding houses, and rooming houses. Multi-family unit tenements with shared kitchens and washing rooms were a common form of working-class dwelling. These forms of working-class living were seized or made illegal during the standardization of zoning laws in the US. Between 1930 and 1950, government as well as local and national banking and real estate interests incentivized white single-family home ownership through racially biased lending and outright segregation, all while destroying urban life under the guise of slum clearance. In response, housing justice movements pushed the federal government to desegregate the housing and mortgage markets as well as to create public housing — a public goods project that was largely abandoned by a combination of state and industry forces in the 1970s in favour of subsidizing private-sector tenants and real estate developers who made some of their units rent-controlled. Since the 1980s, a wave of financial deregulation, racist and classist predatory lending, and weak government protections for affordable housing created today's unequal housing landscape.

These historical trends in regulation, development, and financialization delimit the kinds of housing that are possible in the US. Today, the home serves as a dense and contested ideological site of subject formation, political inculcation, and rest. Ananya Roy argues that

> the home ... is a problematic object not because it will be lost in the future, through foreclosure or eviction, and not because it cannot be legally claimed through emplacement and occupation, but because it was always insecurely possessed by dispossessed subjects, those rendered outside the grid of white normativity.[10]

The racialized and class politics of home should be apparent in this short history: homes conducive to working-class life were targeted for destruction by racist housing policies that left working-class people of colour in the lurch while incentivizing white middle-class family life.

Property relations — the laws and social practices that define people's ability to own and make use of buildings, businesses, and pieces of land — are central here because they delimit the home as a site. For the home to be a legitimate object in the eyes of the state, it must conform to state-sanctioned conceptions of ownership, land use, taxation, and countless other bureaucratic, judicial, and financial norms.[11] These property relations have racialized and gendered dimensions. Cheryl Harris describes whiteness as a status property that guarantees a person's access to health, wellbeing, and basic rights such as property ownership, the right to vote, and the right to state protection.[12] K-Sue Park argues that race is central to the founding of property relationships as we know them in the US. In the colonial era, Indigenous Peoples' and people of colour's relations to land and housing were destroyed by force, and the state did not recognize land as a commodity unless it was settled by white people.[13] These initial forms of property in the colonial US were concretized through racialized and colonial dispossession and institutionally cemented during Reconstruction, Jim Crow, and now the post-Civil Rights eras. The dispossession and continued exclusion and predatory inclusion of racialized peoples through land theft, redlining, and secondary mortgage markets have come to constitute contemporary property relations.

The home is always ungraspable for those outside of white normativity. People of colour, particularly Black and Ingenious Peoples, remain forcefully excluded from the property regime, whether through projects of land seizure, eviction, or police violence.[14] This is especially true for houseless residents who were forced out of a hotel by a vindictive property owner, and later, forced from encampments in public parks through a combination of legislative, police, and property-owner interests. When houseless people try to build a sense of home, however temporary, it is under attack for failing to align with white supremacist property relations.

The originary rot at the heart of the US property relation shows how the home must be rethought as a political object. This is not to say that the efforts by activists to keep people housed are misguided. It is to draw our attention to the ideas of home, housing, and property that shape our housing justice activism — to push for analysis that helps us theorize another way forward.

One way to advance housing justice is through what I call "autonomous cooperative living." This ideal, when paired with an anti-property praxis, creates a framework through which to understand the potential and future directions of housing justice struggles. The concept of autonomy owes its origins to anarchist housing movements. Autonomy is the right to make decisions, starting with people most impacted, and then act on those decisions, rather than relying on the state to act. Autonomy is a communal value that respects individual desires while aiming to do best by the collective whole. It is deeply entwined with abolitionist politics of transformative justice and mutual support.

At encampment sites in Minneapolis, the value of autonomy has been practised in the prioritizing of community need over and above local government and law enforcement's desire to maintain public parks as a manicured space of leisure for housed residents. Encampment residents and volunteers as well as housed neighbours worked together, came into conflict, and worked through the contradictions of their opinions and political positions about housing and communal living. Likewise, encampment volunteers and residents worked to respect resident autonomy at all stages. Encampment volunteers helped residents cook food, launder clothing, travel to appointments, resolve inter-camp conflicts between residents and volunteers, and access resources they needed, and they supported resident needs during eviction processes.

The value of autonomy goes together with the value of cooperation. Cooperation here has a wide range of meaning that must be decided upon by the collective members, but I want to highlight the cooperative principles of voluntary and open membership, democratic member control, autonomy and independence, and concern for community.[15] Dean Spade's definition of mutual aid as "collective coordination to meet each other's needs" underscores the interdependence of collectivity, mutual support, and participation as cooperative principles.[16] Cooperation not only creates the conditions for survival but also expands into broader social movements. At Minneapolis encampment sites, cooperation was practised through the conflict management and resource provision mentioned above. It was also practised during community defence. In the zine "So You Want to Stop an Encampment Eviction… 4 Lessons from MPLS Camp Defense 2021–2022," encampment defenders laid out four principles for successfully deterring encampment evictions: 1) Get there first with the most; 2) Deterrence is critical; 3) It's time the class war had two sides; and 4) No engagement with eviction collaborators.[17] The main lessons of these four principles were to anticipate encampment evictions and show up early, support encampment residents regularly in person to deter bad practices among city and police intervention, and directly confront encampment evictions when they happen through direct action. This cooperative approach puts the needs of encampment residents above the state and property owners who claimed the exclusive right to public space. These principles make encampment life possible by fighting against, and gradually learning how to anticipate and counter, the actions of agents of systemic dispossession and prioritizing the needs of encampment residents.

Finally, the value of "living" instead of housing highlights the political project at the centre of housing justice: a collective control over life and social reproduction. What is at stake in housing is less the property itself and more the kind of life that is housed and reproduced. Social reproduction is a Marxist theoretical lens used to theorize how identity categories, institutions, social patterns, and logics are maintained and replicated in society. Social reproductive labour, sometimes called care labour, reproduces certain modes of life that are then put to work in the economic system. Typically, care labour and socially reproductive labour are theorized with the figure of the white housewife and the work she does in reproducing the nuclear bourgeois family through childrearing, cooking, cleaning, education, household management, emotional support, and other work. However, more innovative uses of social reproduction feminism grounded in Black feminism, Third World feminism, and queer of colour critique push us to think about alternative forms of sociality that persist despite dominant (white and middle-class) forms of social reproduction.[18] It is in these alternative ways of life that we can find the values and shape of a different world. In 2023, the autonomous and collaborative power of encampments, as well as the skills of those who took part in encampment struggles in 2020 and 2021, were harnessed through an Indigenous-led fight against the demolition of the Roof Depot, an abandoned warehouse in Minneapolis's Phillips neighbourhood. Activists claimed that demolishing the depot would unearth arsenic from a long-shuttered pesticide factory near the site and spread this toxin into the surrounding neighbourhood.[19] Community members established Camp Nenookaasi near the Roof Depot to protest the demolition.[20] In their initial demands, the activists not only called to hand over the Roof Depot site to the community but also to "enact a moratorium on encampment evictions and invest in pilot programs to provide shelter and services to the houseless community."[21] The encampment residents underscored the interrelation between struggles for housing, land, autonomy, cooperation, life, police abolition, and environmental justice. The encampment has since transformed into a healing camp grounded in Indigenous practices and inclusive of all unhoused residents.[22] It has been forcefully evicted multiple times by the city, but residents and supporters have helped it relocate and re-establish. Nenookaasi remains active in 2024 as a paradigmatic example of autonomous cooperative living.

The project of houseless and encampment support, anti-property politics, and eviction defence all serve as examples of a kind of life that does and could exist if contemporary property relations are overturned — one that people are putting their bodies on the line to defend.[23] The prevalence of autonomous cooperative living at the Share-A-Ton and the subsequent encampments is an important provocation for those engaged in housing justice work to remember and learn from. Building people's capacities to act autonomously and live together without fear of state violence is at the heart of housing justice projects. In fighting for these possibilities, we may just create a world worth living in.

Notes

1 Julia Lurie, "They Built a Utopian Sanctuary in a Minneapolis Hotel. Then They Got Evicted," *Mother Jones*, June 12, 2020, https://www.motherjones.com/criminal-justice/2020/06/minneapolis-sheraton-george-floyd-protests/.
2 Lurie, "They Built a Utopian Sanctuary."
3 Charmaine Chua, "Abolition Is a Constant Struggle: Five Lessons from Minneapolis," *Theory & Event*, 23, 4 Supplement (October 2020).
4 Lure, "They Built a Utopian Sanctuary."
5 Susan Du and Nicole Norfleet, "City's Attempt to Clear Minneapolis Homeless Camp Leads to Scuffles between Police, Camp Defenders," *Minneapolis Star Tribune*, March 18, 2021, https://www.startribune.com/city-s-attempt-to-clear-minneapolis-homeless-camp-leads-to-scuffles-between-police-camp-defenders/600035818/.
6 Valesca Lima, "Urban Austerity and Activism: Direct Action against Neoliberal Housing Policies," *Housing Studies 36*, 2 (February 7, 2021), https://doi.org/10.1080/02673037.2019.1697800.

7   Housing Justice Platform, "Housing Justice National Platform for a Homes Guarantee," 2020, https://www.housingjusticeplatform.org/.
8   Home Line, "Eviction Moratorium Phaseout Information," June 1, 2022, https://homelinemn.org/phaseout/.
9   Nayan Shah, *Contagious Divides: Epidemics and Race in San Francisco's Chinatown* (University of California Press, 2001).
10 Ananya Roy, "Dis/Possessive Collectivism: Property and Personhood at City's End," *Geoforum* 80 (March 2017), https://doi.org/10.1016/j.geoforum.2016.12.012.
11 Brenna Bhandar and Alberto Toscano, "Race, Real Estate and Real Abstraction," *Radical Philosophy*, 194 (2015), https://www.radicalphilosophy.com/article/race-real-estate-and-real-abstraction.
12 Cheryl I. Harris, "Whiteness as Property," *Harvard Law Review* 106, 8 (1993). https://doi.org/10.2307/1341787.
13 K-Sue Park, "Race and Property Law," *Georgetown Law Faculty Publications and Other Works*, January 1, 2021, https://scholarship.law.georgetown.edu/facpub/2405.
14 Aileen Moreton-Robinson, *The White Possessive: Property, Power, and Indigenous Sovereignty,* 1st edition (University of Minnesota Press, 2015).
15 International Co-operative Alliance, "Cooperative Identity, Values & Principles," 2014, https://ica.coop/en/whats-co-op/co-operative-identity-values-principles.
16 Dean Spade, *Mutual Aid: Building Solidarity During This Crisis* (Verso, 2020).
17 Near North Supporters, "4 Lessons from Minneapolis Camp Defense 2021–2022," Near North Camp Defense, May 1, 2022, https://northdef.wordpress.com/2022/05/12/4-lessons-from-minneapolis-camp-defense-2021-2022/.
18 Jan M. Padios, "Labour," In *Keywords for Gender and Sexuality Studies,* (New York University Press, 2021). https://keywords.nyupress.org/gender-and-sexuality-studies/essay/labour/.
19 Environmental Protection Agency, "EPA Finalizes Partial Deletion of Superfund Site from National List," October 2019, https://semspub.epa.gov/work/05/951026.pdf.
20 Nicole Perez. "Native People Will Not Be Silenced," *Minneapolis Star Tribune*, February 27, 2023, https://www.startribune.com/native-people-will-not-be-silenced/600254866
21 Defend the Depot, "Neighbourhood Residents Occupy Roof Depot Site, Demand the City Call off Demolition Plans," https://www.defendthedepot.com/updates.
22 Camp Nenookaasi [@campnenookaasi], Image of how to support the camp, Instagram, published by Camp Nenookaasi, September 25, 2023, https://www.instagram.com/p/CxojbE8xG0z/?hl=en.
23 Anonymous, "Militant Defense Helps Delay and Prevent Encampment Evictions in Minneapolis," *It's Going Down*, January 24, 2022, https://itsgoingdown.org/militant-defence-helps-delay-and-prevent-encampment-evictions-in-minneapolis/.

BUILDING TENANT POWER OUT OF CRISES

ATLANTA, GEORGIA, UNITED STATES

WRITTEN BY
Natalie McLaughlin, Dani Aiello, Karimah Dillard-Mickey & the Housing Justice League

The stories of how we struggle to build power out of crises are widespread in past and present housing movements. So often, the line between service provision and organizing to build a base of active and engaged leaders within the movement is one we straddle uncomfortably as organizers. As we work tirelessly to craft methods of political education and meaningful pathways to organizing, we notice the programmatic creep of the tools and projects we build and the serious challenges of converting the shared class position of those most impacted among us into a basis for power. This reflection piece on the Housing Justice League's Tenant Power Hotline aims to share one site of this universal struggle. Situated at the intersection of the pandemic and the 2020 uprisings, the hotline became a central feature of housing justice organizing as political and class consciousness in Atlanta and across the United States transformed at the beginning of the decade.

The Housing Justice League (HJL) is a small, grassroots non-profit based in Atlanta and rooted in Peoplestown, a historically Black community south of downtown. Having been subject to decades of disinvestment and displacement cycles, Peoplestown and nearby neighbourhoods are a key site of Black social life and community building in Atlanta. Founded in 2017, HJL has its roots in the Peoplestown Listening Project, created by community members to push back against displacement, and in Occupy Our Homes Atlanta,[1] which grew out of the 2011 Occupy movement.[2]

Relationships were built across these groups to ultimately form HJL, whose ethos has informed its present-day core focus on bottom-up organizing: a theory of change rooted in the importance of building the power and leadership of people with low or no income through their relationships and unity in fighting for better housing circumstances.

In 2018 the board, staff, and membership of HJL passed bylaws that established working groups as a way to distribute leadership and grassroots organizing work among members, staff and board members. It was in this context that a small group of organizers went on to create the Eviction Defense Working Group (EDWG). Its purpose was to build tools and increase political education around tenants' rights in an effort to stem the eviction crisis in Atlanta. Nearly 47,000 annual eviction filings passed through the Fulton County Magistrate Court during this time,[3] and to build knowledge of tenants' rights about housing court, the Eviction Defense Manual[4] was born.

Intended as a tool for harm reduction and outreach, the manual was envisioned by HJL as a conduit for the relationship-building, knowledge transfer, and ultimately mutual aid necessary for deeper tenant base-building with those most affected by evictions. Our hope was that being able to offer something tangible would open up much-needed conversations with neighbours on doorsteps and at kitchen tables — the lifeblood of base-building. The arrival of the COVID-19 pandemic, however, upended more intimate approaches to organizing and instead led us to a whole new method of mutual aid via digital networks through our Tenant Power Hotline. At the same time, this digital shift significantly highlighted long-standing racial and class tensions within our own work. Since its beginning, the demographic make-up of the EDWG has been more white and wealthier than the directly impacted neighbours HJL seeks to organize with. While this is not a new dynamic, major shifts in our approach constrained by the pandemic made this much more glaring than before. In this chapter, we share the story of how organizers in the EDWG worked to transform crisis into power through the development of digital and material resources to fight eviction and how this process came with hard lessons about race, class, and power. While the organizing work itself is collective, as always, this story is told from the perspective of only a few individuals close to the work.

In the first few months of 2020, the EDWG carefully strategized community outreach and the distribution of the Eviction Defense Manual.

Following some of our earliest canvassing efforts in February 2020, rumblings of COVID-19 were already present. In Atlanta, many grassroots initiatives sprung up early on to defend marginalized communities that would be most deeply impacted. Many supporters, especially progressive people with stable jobs now working from home, were looking for ways to "plug in," often for the first time. Just a few months later, in May and June 2020, in the midst of the murders of George Floyd, Ahmaud Arbery, Breonna Taylor, and Rayshard Brooks, Atlanta protesters unleashed the largest wave of civil unrest the city had seen since the 2008 financial crisis. Many HJL members were organizing with HJL by day and protesting racial injustice at night. There was an unrelenting energy of resistance and militancy in the streets, bringing even more progressives into the work of the hotline as they sought to respond to the protesters' demands for racial justice in tangible ways.

This was the context in which HJL began the largest volunteer initiative in its history. The first iteration of the hotline was operating in a matter of weeks. HJL board leadership put out a call for hotline volunteers to the membership and publicly on social media, and dozens of people signed up, many being completely new to housing justice organizing. During the first few months of the pandemic, we held hotline volunteer training for over thirty newcomers on a weekly basis. Soon we had enough volunteers to operate seven days a week for nine hours a day, with many shifts covered in both English and Spanish.

Along with the flood of volunteers came a flood of hotline callers. At a time of unprecedented employment instability, the hotline rang off the hook with callers from all over Georgia already facing significant rent debt and eviction notices. Indeed, COVID-19 quickly revealed how dysfunctional the housing market is, with millions of people only a paycheque away from losing their homes. In these early stages, we were already hearing from people who had quickly become homeless or were pushed into housing of last resort — extended-stay hotels. The large number of eviction filings in Metro Atlanta had already been pushing many vulnerable renters into substandard housing prior to the pandemic. Tenants in the extended-stay hotels found themselves with fewer tenant protections and increased housing precarity as these hotels were not included in the federal ban on evictions introduced in April 2020. Taking a volunteer hotline shift during this time meant spending hours on the phone with people who were experiencing incredible stress from dealing with serious housing emergencies. Unsurprisingly, most people calling the hotline, especially in the early months of the pandemic, were desperately seeking financial assistance, which HJL was unable to provide.

In these early stages, it was unclear how the hotline would serve callers or the mission of HJL to organize with tenants to build a movement for tenant power. The description in our original hotline volunteer protocol[5] and recruitment materials outlined that our intention with the initiative was to build a "statewide reporting system," so that tenants could 1) call to report illegal or dangerous landlord behaviour; 2) receive updates on policy changes and information about community resources; and 3) receive advice and support to organize in their apartment buildings and wider communities. While we clearly stated that the hotline was both a source of information and a pathway to learning about organizing, our base-building goals were often overshadowed by the practical and urgent matters of rent-relief resources, paperwork, and referrals for legal support. Even while we referred many callers to direct-service organizations, we knew that these organizations would be unable to meet most requests for rent relief or legal aid. The pandemic exacerbated many pre-existing dynamics of racialized expropriation in Atlanta's lowest income and historically Black neighbourhoods — cycles of eviction and homelessness, people being pushed into dangerous living conditions, and families forgoing basic necessities in order to pay rent.

From its outset, the hotline had an underlying intention similar to the Eviction Defense Manual: to build relationships and ultimately work toward class consciousness and organizing capacities of tenants in precariously housed majority Black communities. To tie the hotline to HJL's broader goals of tenant organizing, volunteers were trained to attempt to "build a bridge to organizing" with hotline callers. Through a series of training and one-on-one sessions that included role playing and written protocols, HJL organizers helped new volunteers understand what tenant organizing is and how to go about broaching organizing conversations over the phone. Despite these in-depth mentorship and support efforts, organizing digitally proved to be extremely difficult. Many hotline callers expressed interest in organizing, but prioritizing COVID-19 mitigation at the time meant we could not provide in-person support. Without the crucial face-to-face conversations happening at kitchen tables and doorsteps, most tenants were quick to fall out of touch. Further, many people calling the hotline were in acute crisis, and initiating an organizing discussion at times felt inappropriate or simply too abstract in a way that did not map onto people's immediate needs.

HJL organizers were faced with some big questions regarding strategy at this point. On the one hand, in all our time in this work, it had never felt like a more strategic moment to organize. Tenants across the country and beyond were suddenly without rent, angry that there was no help from the government, and much more willing to act. On the other hand, many tenants were in violation of their rental leases due to nonpayment. This wasn't anything new, and we were faced with the same familiar and now more emergent problem: what leverage did tenants really have without any rent to withhold in a state where it is simply against the law to withhold rent? While we were encouraging tenants to come together to make collective demands of their landlords to cancel rent and cease evictions, we were also learning that public pressure has limitations when it fails to impact a landlord's bottom line.

Further, while the goal of the hotline was to support tenants to organize, many HJL volunteers answering calls had little understanding of organizing — this was largely due to HJL's inability to offer meaningful political education and mentorship following the sudden influx of volunteers and technological barriers. Without hands-on experience and with the limitations inherent to digital relationship-building, we continued to feel like our hotline was filling more of a direct-service role than one of organizing tenants. Years later, and through ongoing reflection, we have come to realize our hotline efforts were more about mobilizing to respond to a worsening housing crisis than serving the deeper goals of organizing we had aimed for. While mobilizing is an important way in which broad numbers of people can act, organizing is the deeper work of leadership development, skill building, and development of political consciousness. Ultimately, while any mobilizing tactics can serve deeper organizing, in many ways the emergency of the pandemic resulted in mobilizing tactics being goals in and of themselves.

Building the relationships needed to centre and support Black leadership in majority-Black low-income communities with limited time and resources was a persistent challenge within HJL and the wider movements beyond it. There has also been a tendency in our work towards something we call "reactive organizing," where organizers find themselves responding to crises and trying to convert those experiences into class consciousness. These are too often ad hoc responses which take us away from our longer-term group visions. When we reflect on our efforts, we recognize the limited reach of our work, the short-term effects of our "wins," and, most importantly, the inconsistent presence in our meeting spaces of those most impacted by racial and housing inequality. While our group is multiracial, we had more white folks engaging in organizing work with us than not, and increasingly so during the pandemic. With the arrival of over a hundred volunteers looking for ways to engage, we noted that most of these volunteers were white, and few had experience with organizing. Meanwhile, many longer-term Black members of HJL were Elders encountering sudden barriers to meaningful participation in the work as we shifted to virtual communication platforms like Zoom and Slack. This significantly exacerbated a pre-existing tension between HJL's mission of organizing with and for the most-impacted Black community members and the presence in our meeting spaces of many middle-class students, academics, attorneys, and non-profit workers.

Those resourced by whiteness and class often have more time, resources, or specialized legal or research know-how through access to higher education. Further, while their skill set in honing tools, data, and technology for movement work is a much-needed element of housing justice organizing, these interests can end up shaping the strategic direction of the work at the expense of other priorities and ways of knowing and responding. Within HJL, Black residents, and Black women in particular, had a long history of contributing to the work through their lived experience, place-based institutional knowledge, and social capital. These crucial relational matrices were upended by the forced pivot away from in-person engagement to a reliance on technology. For these reasons and others, online meeting spaces even today reveal significant differences across race and class, even down to how language is used and how experiences are shared.

Some of these racial and class tensions played out in the organizing HJL supported at the extended-stay hotel Efficiency Lodge. A rising housing option of last resort across the Southeast, extended-stay hotels ostensibly provide flexibility like weekly rent cycles, no credit checks, and low or no security deposits, but this can come at the expense of flagrant violations of tenants' rights and protections. In recent years, extended-stay markets have made record profits as more and more tenants found themselves pushed into increasingly severe contexts of housing precarity due to rent debt and evictions exacerbated by COVID-19. In October 2020, HJL hotline volunteers received multiple calls from tenants of Efficiency Lodge, owned by former Georgia governor Roy Barnes. Tenants, many of whom had been living at Efficiency Lodge for years, reported being threatened with eviction for nonpayment of rent. The hotel hired private security to carry out these evictions — in some cases at gunpoint — rather than going through the eviction-court process. Not only were hotel tenants being refused the basic rights of housing court, but hotel managers and owners were denying that a landlord-tenant relationship even existed, which in fact it did under Georgia law, given that tenants had been staying at Efficiency Lodge for more than thirty days.

Over the weeks and months that followed, HJL organizers supported a small group of Efficiency Lodge tenants with landlord research, getting connected to legal aid, planning rallies and phone zaps, and spreading awareness with social media campaigns. Throughout this time, HJL organizers noted that tenants were met with many challenges to meaningful organizing, from hostile security to dangerous habitability issues, extremely high tenant turnover, and minimal time and resources. Extended-stay hotels are emblematic of the ways in which some property owners tap into markets of precarity by renting to super-exploited, often racialized people whose credit and eviction records exclude them from accessing safe housing and the minimal protections that other tenants are afforded — in this case a lease and right to legal eviction proceedings. While the pandemic heightened the number of renters pushed into these types of housing arrangements, HJL's experience with Efficiency Lodge illuminated the size of the extended-stay population that had existed long before the pandemic hit.

As HJL organizers and tenants faced down newly exacerbated problems of precarity, the long-standing dynamics of race and class in our organizing crept in, where white logics played too significant a role when ostensibly working with and for majority-Black and most-impacted communities. The three main organizers from HJL setting up tenant meetings were young, white and from upper-middle-class backgrounds. Due to the urgency of the situation, there was a big disconnect for the organizers, who wanted to encourage bigger-picture analysis and public-pressure campaigns, and the tenants, who had a pressing need to address immediate housing urgency in their lives. This dynamic revealed a problematic white logic to jump on a hot issue without the critical infrastructure built up over years or decades to support such a campaign in a way that both addresses immediate needs and protects tenants from retaliation or additional harms and builds political consciousness and power at the same time. These experiences are ultimately what have pushed us to reflect more carefully on the differences between mobilizing and organizing and, specifically, on the problem of reactive organizing and the ways in which already-existing race and class differences among us map onto all these tensions.

These dynamics around technology, access, whiteness, and class have been a regular area of discussion within the EDWG and among HJL leadership. A key conclusion we reached was that HJL needed to be much more intentional in creating space and meaningful leadership opportunities for tenants most impacted — Black women in particular. In response to this, the Tenant Working Group was created by HJL director Alison Johnson in 2021 to support such work. Since its creation, the Tenant Working Group has been working on the longer-term goals of deeper base-building, while also ensuring collaboration with the EDWG and other working groups within HJL. Our hope is that creating such Black women–led spaces within our organization will help us better address the challenges of whiteness and class in trying to foster Black-led social movement organizations. Despite all this intentional work, we still struggle in this area. We have lost some of our Black Elders, who have passed on; some have shifted their focus to other issues — another key leader is facing eviction and unable to put as much time into organizing. The reality is that sustaining the deeper relational and care work required to support those most impacted to be in leadership is a long-term commitment with many challenges and limitations.

Stepping back to consider the wider perspective, the Tenant Power Hotline has fostered countless hours of connectivity and network-building between tenants and organizers across Metro Atlanta and beyond. It fielded well over four thousand calls across two years. This opening for deeper connectivity with tenants has revealed to us a great deal about previously more invisible aspects of housing precarity in the South, particularly the plight of extended-stay hotel tenants and subsequent legal battles that brought their struggle to public attention. This work has generated many important opportunities for political and rights-based education with far wider reach than we had previously thought possible, even as the limitations and exclusiveness inherent to digital platforms revealed themselves within our own organizing relationships. The pandemic clearly exposed the state's complete failure to support tenants in a time of crisis. In spite of the limitations we now reflect upon, the manual, the hotline, and the countless volunteers and tenants themselves stepped in to build what has become important scaffolding — a capillary network of mutual aid and outreach that showed us new possibilities for building a wider base of power among those least resourced by property in Atlanta and the wider US south.

Members of the Housing Justice League contributed to the writing of this article in 2022. As the organization evolves and members join and transition out of this work, we want to thank and acknowledge our fellow members from 2022 for the thought and analysis contributed to this chapter.

Notes

1 Sarah Jaffe, "Whose Homes?" *Dissent Magazine*, August 24, 2016, dissentmagazine.org/online_articles/sarah-jaffe-necessary-trouble-occupy-homes-atlanta/.

2 Occupy Our Homes Atlanta built relationships with long-term residents of Peoplestown during the Peoplestown Listening Project, conducted by and with residents to identify community concerns and set the groundwork for issue-based organizing. Community leaders emerged and began receiving administrative support to build the Housing Justice League's infrastructure from Peoplestown Revitalization Corporation, American Friends Services Committee, and the Rick McDevitt Youth Center. These organizations continue to shape the growth and general operations of HJL today.

3 Elora Raymond, Richard Duckworth, Ben Miller, Michael Lucas, and Shiraj Pokharel, *Corporate Landlords, Institutional Investors, and Displacement: Eviction Rates in Single-Family Rentals,* Community & Economic Development Discussion Paper no. 4–16, Federal Reserve Bank of Atlanta, December 2016; C. Joyner, J. Ernsthausen, and W. Mariano, "Eviction Tactics Squeeze Renters," *Atlanta Journal-Constitution,* July 24, 2018.

4 Housing Justice League, *Eviction Defense Manual,* housingjusticeleague.org/evictiondefense.

5 Housing Justice League, "Tenant Power Hotline Volunteer Protocol," docs.google.com/document/d/e/2PACX-1vSTq9bVV8zBhG7-A5yvbrY4S35QMA3LFcPJZteW3RJSWaUSjaqIRNVFL-12QbSGr1wkO4JRADKc96Lp/pub.

CONTRADICTIONS IN INFRA-COMMONING NETWORKS IN SERBIA

BELGRADE, SERBIA

WRITTEN BY
Ana Vilenica & Vladimir Mentus

In April 2020, activists from the anti-eviction organization Joint Action Roof Over Head (aka the Roof) distributed food and hygiene products to twenty-two families in the Kamendin social housing neighbourhood as part of their pandemic response initiative No One Hungry, No One Without a Roof. Kamendin is a neighbourhood where 80 percent of all social housing constructed by the City of Belgrade is located.[1] Hundreds of people in this area face the threat of eviction due to accumulated debts stemming from their inability to pay bills. In some of the reports, members of the anti-eviction group described the food distribution program initiated in Kamendin as "challenging"[2] because of the sheer lack of social infrastructure throughout the neighbourhood. In an effort to address the breakdown of infrastructure during the pandemic, the Roof initiated a parallel distribution stream of food and everyday necessities as an explicit project of urban commoning[3] that operated alongside their anti-eviction practices.

Urban commoning is conceptualized in contrast to enclosures of public resources. The practice includes making temporary and permanent infrastructure of care work, political work, and direct action that emphasizes the effect of these modes of labour as the "infrastructure of housing struggle."[4] Though it has great emancipatory potential, some argue that urban commoning, also called infra-commoning, also produces contradictions.[5] In this chapter, we discuss the contradictions of infra-commoning processes during the COVID-19 pandemic in Serbia that emerged due to complex dynamics between the anti-eviction movement and new pandemic-induced solidarity practices and relations. We look at these contradictions as potentially generative sites for mutual analyses and work.

Moving beyond binaries and deterministic views on the commons, we embrace a dialectical approach built on the assumption that infra-commoning action is linked to its structural context and in turn, is complex and sometimes chaotic. We examine how people come together in the process of infra-commoning and what kind of collectivities emerge, what kind of economies emerge, and what kind of politics are produced. We base the analysis on observations during our engagement in the anti-eviction organization the Roof. We finish with a reflection on how the housing crisis was deepened by the COVID-19 pandemic and how organized resistance and infra-commoning networks persist today.

Profit-motivated evictions were not an everyday urban practice of the socialist experiment in Yugoslavia. Evictions, more generally, intensified during the wars across the country in the 1990s as a tool of turbo-fascist[6] expulsion across Yugoslav republics in a process of redistributing property and establishing new national borders. After the war, massive evictions re-emerged as a tool of racist urbanization practices of reordering Serbian territory with European infrastructure projects and profit-motivated redevelopment projects. Contemporary eviction infrastructure has been set up under pressures from the European Union (EU) as a part of the integration process into the EU. In order to continue the negotiation process, Serbia was forced to reform the country's legal system, and the regime of public-private bailiffs was introduced to relieve the courts of excessive caseloads. The public-private bailiffs form a new part of the eviction infrastructure. While ostensibly public, they are, in essence, private companies that mobilize both state police and private security forces to evict people from their homes. With this eviction infrastructure in place, a new epidemic of evictions started in 2017. People are targeted with eviction in Serbia for multiple reasons, the most prominent of which are settling debts by selling evicted people's homes, mortgage installment delays, property restitution to pre-WWII owners, and eviction of residents living in informally settled or squatted housing.[7]

As a reaction to the regime of public-private bailiffs under the EU-reformed Serbian legal system, a new anti-eviction movement was founded by left-political organizations, urban and sociopolitical movements, and associations dealing with urban and social issues. This movement uses direct action to prevent eviction at the doorstep of people's homes as well as legal support and solidarity related to particular situations, such as collecting money for rent and support in paying bills and buying basic necessities such as food and hygiene products. This is a very popular movement in Serbia, and at its peak, several years ago, it was able to mobilize hundreds of people to protest and undertake anti-eviction actions. This movement can be described as an infra-commoning movement and should not be confused with mutual aid; infra-commoning is a practice of creating temporary solidarity infrastructures to defend homes and lives in times of crisis. The narrative of the crisis allowed for leftist charity actions to be confused with practices of mutual aid. While the concept of mutual aid was present in this movement's imaginary, it has rarely been practised in a way that engages people in need to take part in solidarity actions in a structural way. Infra-commoning mostly involves activists who undertake political and direct actions and do care work in a top-down way, while people in need stay on the receiving end.

Thanks to this movement, bailiffs became one of the most despised professions in the country, but state repression of the movement has also been constant. This culminated in revisions of the law on bailiffs that further criminalized anti-eviction solidarity work by introducing higher fines against protesters. In the last seven years, the movement created an unstable but effective anti-eviction commoning infrastructure comprising people and resources that have helped many defend their homes in a communal way.

People in Serbia rely on multiple forms of informal economy to sustain their everyday lives, such as informal financial support, goods exchange, shared childcare and elder support. These practices repair and bridge places and lives where formal infrastructures have been dismantled through building new informal institutions, connections and networks that preserve life. When basic formal (institutionalized) socially reproductive resources — like public health initiatives and emergency shelter services — are scarce, informal social networks are the most reliable determinants of quality of life and survival. These networks are an effect of the repeated and incomplete post- or anti-socialist institutional evolution in Serbia, as well as persistent racialization and social and economic hierarchies in urban world-making in Eastern Europe. Inadequate state measures during the COVID-19 pandemic crisis in Serbia further degraded the already broken social infrastructure. In a situation of generalized precarity, new forms of commoning emerge through acts of caring that underline interdependence and reciprocity as fundamental components of the social world.

With the first lockdown to contain the COVID-19 pandemic in Serbia, it became clear that the state was unwilling to take precautions to prevent a social catastrophe on the ground. Many people dependent on informal work and public resources were left without basic means of subsistence during the lockdown, while evictions by public-private bailiffs continued. The state issued a recommendation to the bailiffs to pause evictions, but there were no legal consequences for those who continued. At the same time, with heavily policed streets, both formal and informal social reproduction infrastructures were temporarily brought to a halt during the lockdown, and inadequate state measures further degraded Serbia's already broken social infrastructure. As a response to these issues, anti-eviction activists intensified mobilization and solidarity work to protect homes and lives by creating temporary networks of care in the gaps produced by the emerging public health situation.

The Roof's anti-eviction activism in 2020 and 2021 focused on mobilizing public support to redistribute resources by donating money to those in dire need. The money was collected via open calls on social media. The peak in fundraising was reached following a call for donations at the onset of the pandemic, where the minor funds distributed by the government to all adult residents were reallocated by solidary citizens to the Roof. Funds were later used to buy and distribute consumer goods for those facing housing insecurity and who have been evicted from their homes, to provide legal assistance for them, as well as for paying fines for activists due to their participation in anti-eviction actions. At first, the resources were redistributed to those that the movement already had contact with due to eviction threats as well as those in similar need who requested support. With multiple lockdowns, the anti-eviction movement identified houseless people as the most affected and started a working group that allied with those residing on the streets of Belgrade. Inspired by the actions of the anti-eviction movement, new groups, such as Solidarity Kitchen in Belgrade, Kitchen of Solidarity in Novi Sad, and Solidarity Meal in Subotica, were formed under the slogan "Solidarity, Not Charity."

The economic position of Serbia's lower classes in the last thirty years has become extreme, with the escalation of disparity lasting longer than in other European countries. The average income in Serbia is among the lowest in Europe, and economic inequality and inter-class barriers are among the highest, especially since the onset of the COVID-19 economic era.

The social divides between people in need and mostly middle-class activists and the people from both the middle and working classes who donated money to anti-eviction initiatives were to some extent blurred during the pandemic, as were territorial borders between areas inhabited by the poor and those inhabited by the rest. The care network that emerged produced a temporary infrastructure that allowed encounters between groups of people that would usually not meet in their everyday lives. This also created tensions within the movement, especially between the old and allegedly politicized members and new members with their own new ideas of organizing.

Activists, as initiators of anti-eviction and food distribution networks, made decisions in assemblies on how to redistribute resources and who would receive them. Those who donated money and other necessities, such as clothing and hygiene products, remained outside the decision-making process. The poor and heavily racialized people remained in the role of aid recipients. This often led to situations where activists were misidentified as NGO workers during the distribution of aid, including instances when their cars were raided by dissatisfied people who were not on the list to receive aid during delivery days. Part of this dissatisfaction was directed toward state restrictions that dictated that households in need would be limited to only one share of aid delivery.

In order to understand the structural place of this care network, it is important to contextualize it in the broader informal economy of day-to-day life in Serbia. "People as infrastructure" was a generalized condition after the wars in the 1990s. Those who rewire and maintain social infrastructure most are often the racialized urban poor. The lockdowns, as the main logic of pandemic management, temporarily disabled some of the existing infrastructure networks, forcing the racialized urban poor to search for alternative solutions to finding income. In this unequal network, people were able to access the resources necessary for survival while continuing to fight for their homes. When activists in the distribution network decided to close down operations due to limited people capacity, many recipients demanded that distribution continue, though activists were determined to dedicate their time to stopping evictions rather than distributing resources.

Financial resources, originating from citizens' donations, continued to be used to pay court costs for activists and were directed toward outstanding fees for tenants who resisted evictions. Part of the funds were used to help with rent or court fees for evicted families and households and to fund the Solidarity Kitchen. Funds were utilized to procure supplies such as clothes or wood stoves that were given directly to unhoused people. As the pandemic wore on, various domestic and foreign foundations offered to extend material and financial resources to support people experiencing economic hardship and housing insecurity, but the question of whether to accept their donations posed significant discord within the collective. Collective members were suspicious about foundations and corporations donating explicitly to gain publicity or forms of taxation benefits. In the few cases when funds were accepted from such entities, activists were intermediaries between donors and end users, procuring and distributing necessities and sometimes liaising with other organizations and collectives.

The politics practised through infra-commoning encounters create a kind of radical housing politics — radical in the sense that housing was a gateway to engage with and politicize issues of social reproduction while expanding informal social infrastructures.[8] In the eyes of anti-eviction activists, the action was helpful in further politicizing issues of housing and food precarity, but many activists were skeptical about their long-term engagement with such a practice, sometimes not sharing the perspective that food distribution and anti-eviction work both contribute to forms of commoning that make networks of social reproduction more mutual, stronger, and focused on collective wellbeing. When energy was completely directed back toward anti-eviction organizing, which ended food distribution efforts, the decision created a political sphere that felt hostile to the coexistence of diverse forms of socioeconomic and political organizing. Activists were concerned that among us, there was too limited a perspective held about the potential for further radicalization of distribution networks. The closure of the distribution network left activists seeking alternative outlets for their energy and labour. Some members joined a reformed leftist political party whose main proclaimed goal is to actualize the right to housing. Others joined related care infrastructure collectives, while some members remained engaged in the Roof's anti-eviction struggles and legal assistance, and organized various direct actions aimed at drawing public attention and pressure against public-private bailiffs and others responsible for evictions.

With the Russian invasion of Ukraine, the housing hyper-precarity of the pandemic era has only increased with the arrival of people displaced by war and war politics. Additionally, energy crises have dramatically increased the cost of living, with ongoing inflation adversely affecting housing loans. In this period, precarious conditions of renters have come into public focus for the first time since the end of the socialist experiment. The rental sector in Serbia is almost entirely informal and poorly regulated, with no protection for tenants. Serbia is a post-socialist super-homeownership country, with the 2021 census reporting that the population of renters ranges between 18 and 19 percent of the total population. The arrival of well-off Russian citizens fleeing forced conscription and awaiting work visas has created a micro-housing crisis alongside an epidemic of evictions against the local people. To take advantage of the new situation in the rental market, landlords evict their tenants with little notice to rent their property to tenants who are perceived as being more financially stable. There remains no legal protection for evicted renters during the pandemic era and no state support for them.

The anti-eviction movement never took a stance against anti-migrant eviction violence happening in informal settlements of people from the Global South on the borders of the EU travelling on the Balkan route, and it didn't engage with the newly emerged situation after the arrival of migrants from Russia. Migrant solidarity infrastructures remain separate from the renters' struggles and anti-eviction organizing in Serbia in the aftermath of COVID-19. In November 2022, a political campaign called "Don't Let Belgrade Drown" emerged from a protest movement against the Belgrade Waterfront mega project, a corrupt and non-transparent project driving gentrification and privatization of public land in central Belgrade by foreign private companies.[9] Shortly thereafter, Don't Let Belgrade Drown was elected to enter the National Assembly of Serbia and proposed a new law intended to introduce rent-control measures.

The measure outlined how rent control would be calculated based the average salary of citizens, as well as additional measures to achieve legal security for both tenants and landlords. In the media, these measures were characterized as communist,[10] which indicates how the ideology of anti-communism continues to discredit any form of social justice and measures for equity in Eastern Europe.

The contradictions of the anti-eviction movement in Belgrade have had the effect of demobilization and "de-movementization" due to disagreements among activists about who donations may be accepted from, as well as a tendency to gravitate toward more public facing anti-eviction work rather than the care network labour that often took place in the more private sphere typical of socially reproductive labour. In 2024, an era of public health, politics, and social practice in which care and responsibility have waned significantly since the arrival of COVID-19, the Roof continues to organize actions against eviction and contribute to legal fights for the right to housing, though with much less public presence. In October 2023, the Roof handed in a request to the Ministry of Justice to abolish public-private bailiffs and to return the enforcement proceedings to the court's control. In the struggle for the right to home, infra-commoning with all its contradictions remains a necessary home-making practice in conditions of extreme precarity that challenges apparatuses of the state, capital and police in order to support life.

Notes

1   Ana Vilenica," Contradictions and Antagonisms in (Anti-)Social(ist) Housing in Serbia," *ACME: An International Journal for Critical Geographies* 18, 6 (2019), https://doi.org/10.14288/acme.v18i6.1731.
2   Marina Sitrin and Colectiva Sembran, *Pandemic Solidarity: Mutual Aid during the Covid Crisis* (Pluto Press, 2020).
3   Ana Vilenica, Vladimir Mentus, and Irena Ristić, "Struggles for Care Infrastructures in Serbia: The Pandemic, Dispossessed Care, and Housing," *Historical Social Research*, 46, 4 (2021), https://doi.org/10.12759/HSR.46.2021.4.189-208.
4   Žarana Papić, "Evropa posle 1989 - etnički ratovi, fašizacija društvenog života i politika tela u Srbiji," *Sociologija* 43, 3 (2001).
5   Papić, "Evropa posle 1989."
6   Ana Vilenica, Aleksa Petković., "Zašto nas iseljavaju. In Ovo može svakom da se desi: Iskustva borbe protiv prinudnih iseljenja", *Združena akcija Krov nad glavom*, (Beograd: Prelom, 2020) 9-13.

7 Michele Lancione, "Radical Housing: On the Politics of Dwelling as Difference," *International Journal of Housing Policy* 20, 2 (2020).
8 Zeković, Slavka, Ana Perić, and Miroljub Hadžić, "The Financialization of 'the Urban' in the Post-Socialist Serbia: Evidence from the Belgrade Waterfront Megaproject," *Journal of Urban Affairs*, September 7, 2023.
9 Bogdan Petrovic, "Communist Measures: Dangerous Illusions of State Determination of Apartment Rents," *Vreme*, November 25, 2022, https://vreme.com/vesti/komunisticke-mere-opasne-iluzije-drzavnog-odredjivanja-zakupnina-stanova/

DETROIT RENTER CITY

DETROIT, MICHIGAN, UNITED STATES

WRITTEN BY
Rae Baker

Amid the dirty dishes and leftovers on the dining room table sat blight violation notice #19062104DAH, issued by a housing inspector of the City of Detroit's Buildings, Safety Engineering, and Environmental Department (BSEED), that read "failure of owner to comply with an emergency or imminent danger order." Three of the five of us seated around the table that night had been active for many years in various housing activist groups in Detroit, and lately the hits were feeling closer to home — including the house we were sitting in that night in the fall of 2019. There was standing sewage in the basement below us settled around an inoperable furnace that emitted frequent gas leaks. The ceilings and floors in several rooms were giving way to gravity, and holes surrounding window and door frames allowed gusts of wind to enter the house. Although anti-displacement and housing activism were alive and well in Detroit, ranging from the non-profit and deeply saviour-oriented white liberal advocacy end of the spectrum to more militant and direct-action organizations fighting anti-Black gentrification, what was lacking was a specific focus on the needs of tenants: the results of more than a decade of fighting mortgage foreclosures followed by a wave of property tax foreclosures that dispossessed Black homeowners at record-breaking rates. That night, with the city inspector's notice on my kitchen table with friends gathered, we decided to form a group that would rabble rouse, organize, and educate tenants across Detroit, and in doing so address a void within housing activism as well as a need to collectively struggle against the forces of deteriorating rental conditions and simultaneously rising rental prices that were pushing more Black Detroiters out of the city. And so, Detroit Renter City was formed in October 2019 and would become a city-wide tenant advocacy group of anti-racist feminist housing activists.

Detroit Renter City (DRC) actively operated between October 2019 and August 2021, and the organization's work connected resistance against the displacement of Black Detroiters with abolitionist politics and approached housing as a public good. The small team of organizers involved throughout DRC's existence utilized our past organizing experiences, research and policy skills, and a trusted working relationship with the movement for Black lives to develop and deploy education materials, conduct city-wide canvassing and other forms of direct tenant outreach, including political education, challenging the local court to adopt anti-eviction policies drafted by DRC members and collaborating with fellow activist organizations to increase the capacity and impact of direct actions to stop evictions and keep Detroiters housed.

Detroit is a majority Black city that was once heralded as having the highest rate of Black homeownership in the United States. Following the late 2000s subprime mortgage crisis and the Great Recession and the radical responsiveness of the global Occupy movement of 2011, housing activism in Detroit grew while becoming laser focused on defending homeowners from evictions resulting from mass foreclosures on defaulted predatory subprime mortgages. In the latter half of the 2010s, the mortgage foreclosure crisis was followed by a multiyear tax foreclosure crisis across Wayne County. Between 2011 and 2018, Wayne County foreclosed on one in every four homes in Detroit over unpaid property taxes; only later was it discovered that the Office of the Assessor had been systematically over assessing home values since the crashing onset of the Great Recession and the city's 2013 Chapter 9 bankruptcy filing.[1] During that time period, the sale of tax foreclosed homes in the Wayne County tax auction generated a surplus revenue of over $420 million for the county.[2] After a decade of focused resistance and defence against mortgage and tax foreclosures, issues impacting tenants and the struggles of renters, rather than owner-occupants, were almost entirely absent from organizing spaces in Detroit. That changed in March 2020 when the World Health Organization declared COVID-19 a pandemic. Not uncommonly, Detroit housing activism was oriented around defensive rather than preventative strategies. The challenge at the beginning of the pandemic was for housing activists to pivot from our familiar focus of defending owner-occupants' legal title toward the rapidly rising number of renters, who as of 2024, comprise upwards of 60 percent of Detroit's population, according to a February 2024 investigative report by Detroit-based journalism non-profit Outlier Media.[3]

The City of Detroit has had a rental property ordinance on the books since 1984. The ordinance outlines structural, maintenance, and habitability standards to ensure safe living conditions and reasonable tenant-landlord relations. Unfortunately, the ordinance has largely been left unenforced by the city's BSEED inspectors and entirely ignored by city officials, which allowed landlords to neglect the stock of rental housing throughout the city and created conditions of deep disrepair. In 2017, Mayor Mike Duggan announced that he was determined to bring all rental properties into ordinance compliance, which would require landlords to register each of their rental properties, have their rental units pass an annual inspection of habitability, and pass a lead safety and remediation clearance in order to obtain a certificate of compliance. These are the basic requirements listed in the ordinance that, if complied with, enable a landlord to legally collect rents from tenants who occupy residential units. Since 2020, compliance with the ordinance increased from approximately 5 percent of rental units across the city to a little more than 8 percent in 2024.[4] Duggan said compliance would be accomplished on a rolling schedule, with rentals in some zip codes needing to comply by 2019, others in 2020, and some in 2021. Updates made to the ordinance in 2017 state that only once a certificate of compliance has been obtained and the rental property has been registered can a landlord legally collect rent. This means that tenants living in rental units in Detroit that lack a certificate of compliance cannot be required to pay rent — a critical strategy point we learned in DRC's early days through research and policy analysis.

Late in 2019, DRC members attended a series of meetings hosted by the Detroit Property Maintenance Division intended to inform city staff about issues faced by renters. At each of the meetings, property managers and tenants were present in the audience. Tenants spoke openly about not being aware of the rental ordinance or of having very limited understanding of the purpose it served, which was likely a consequence of the ordinance largely being unenforced. Similarly, as DRC members conducted outreach to tenants outside of city-run meetings, we noticed it was common for renters not to be aware of the ordinance and to have limited knowledge about their rights as renters in general. When COVID-19 arrived in Michigan in March, already-extended deadlines for rental ordinance compliance continued to be delayed as the pandemic and multiple COVID illnesses and a COVID fatality resulted in a shrinking employee base within BSEED, which decreased the number of inspectors available to assess properties. The potential to use a lack of a certificate of compliance as a tactic to prevent evictions became clearer as people lost wages during the shelter-in-place closure of businesses in the spring of 2020 and stopped being able to afford rent.

Members of Detroit Renter City spent the early winter months of 2019 and 2020 researching statewide landlord tenant laws, familiarizing ourselves with habitability requirements of residential rental properties outlined by BSEED, and honing the art of policy translation to create tenant resource materials for Detroiters and tenants living in Wayne County. Within days of the pandemic being declared, Detroit Renter City took note of nationwide demands by tenants to federal and state governments that rental payments be suspended and that rent be cancelled to enable tenants to shelter in place without being at risk of losing their housing. Through our online platforms, including our website, Facebook, and Instagram, we wrote and circulated the Secure Homes: Rent Suspension for MI Tenants petition, which collected 1374 signatures and was delivered to Governor Gretchen Whitmer (D) and all state senators in Lansing, Michigan's state capital — to no avail and without any direct response.

In the meantime, forty miles away, former members of the Ann Arbor Tenants Union became aware of the Secure Homes petition and reached out to Detroit Renter City, extending an invitation to be part of a pandemic response coalition. The coalition, No Rent MI (NRM), formed in April 2020 as a statewide umbrella for Michigan tenants' organizations to work together to prevent evictions using abolitionist and anti-racist frameworks for thinking about housing justice. NRM wanted to prevent tenant interactions with police, advocate for the removal of police from all landlord-tenant interactions across the state, and ensure Black and brown tenants were not disproportionally impacted by evictions during the COVID-19 pandemic. Detroit Renter City joined NRM, alongside members of the Grand Rapids Area Tenants Union, Ann Arbor Tenants Union, Kalamazoo Union of Tenants, Lansing Tenants Union, Yoopers'

(Upper Peninsula) Tenants Union, and Villages Property Tenants Union (Detroit) in statewide organizing campaigns ranging from petitions and phone zaps to coordinated car caravans demanding a statewide pandemic rent freeze and then extensions of the State of Michigan COVID-19 eviction moratorium. NRM member groups discussed strategies and concerns about our local contexts, shared our knowledge, written materials and political education leaflets, and organized strategies across the group which had the intentional effect of preventing evictions locally through statewide collaboration. In addition to two statewide days of action to outright cancel rent, NRM held several online teach-in broadcasts live over Facebook offering information about defence strategies against illegal evictions — which landlords were carrying out despite the statewide eviction moratorium — the power dynamics of organizing rent strikes, and how to organize a tenants association. One of the teach-in events was watched by over 5000 viewers.

During the NRM meeting in the final week of May 2020, members discussed the murder of George Floyd in Minneapolis, which had taken place the day before, on May 25. A few activist organizations in Detroit organized a rally that would meet at Detroit Police Department (DPD) headquarters on May 29 in solidarity with demonstrations happening across the country to honour Breonna Taylor and George Floyd. The coordinated demonstrations would demand an end to anti-Black police brutality and act in solidarity with people whose lives were taken through acts of police violence. Days before the rally, Detroit's Chief of Police, James Craig, made a statement openly condemning the degree of violence wielded by Minneapolis police officers.

The rally was DRC's first in-person canvassing event since the pandemic began, at which we distributed a letter throughout the crowd and directly to DPD officers addressed to Chief Craig. The letter urged DPD officers to stop issuing pandemic loitering violation notices to Detroiters who were unable to shelter in place due to lack of housing and to refrain from aiding landlords with eviction activities. In Detroit, evictions are ordered by the 36th District Court and are to be carried out by court-appointed bailiffs, not police; however, landlords and bailiffs often call on police to attend evictions even when no backup is warranted. DPD officers and landlords often work together to remove tenants through intimidation tactics resulting in illegal non-court-ordered evictions. Given that Breonna Taylor was murdered by police in her rental apartment on a no-knock warrant when police entered the wrong address in Louisville, Kentucky, in March 2020, DRC's outreach focused sharply on mobilizing fellow tenants to demand that police stop taking part in evictions, both legal and via landlord collusion. Decreasing interactions between renters and police in general, but specifically in relation to the civil matter of landlord-tenant issues, was clearly a matter of life and death, particularly in a majority Black city.

Following this initial rally against anti-Black police brutality, hundreds of people continued to gather daily in Detroit for just over a hundred consecutive days, coordinated by an organization called Detroit Will Breathe (DWB), which formed in response to the international Breonna Taylor and George Floyd uprisings. Several long-term housing activists were deeply involved with DWB and in coordinating daily marches, which facilitated a close partnership and an onramp for co-conspiring between DWB and DRC organizers. This multi-issue organizing of racial justice and resistance against police brutality converging with tenant struggle was not a political or academic experiment for actualizing the theorization or praxis of conjunctures. This dissemination plan was hatched and carried out by organizers, both newly arrived and deeply seasoned within movement work, whose lives taught them what they needed to know about keeping their neighbours and one another alive. During these daily marches against police brutality, DRC and DWB organizers distributed thousands of "know your rights" leaflets. Since the marches were intentionally held in different neighbourhoods throughout the city, tenants across Detroit were receiving important eviction prevention materials, including strategy and tactical education, at their doorsteps, in both English and Spanish, throughout the summer and fall of 2020. Through direct outreach to a few more progressive members of city council, two council members carried out mass distribution of DRC's tenant political education materials to constituents across their districts that digitally reached the inboxes of residents in two of the city's seven council districts.

DRC organizers coordinated several door-to-door canvassing events on weekends in neighbourhoods with especially high rates of looming evictions, despite the standing state and federal eviction moratoriums that were in place at the time. Through daily canvassing with DWB and neighbourhood canvassing pop-up events and targeted distribution, this partnership and dozens of volunteers distributed more than

120,000 pieces of literature between May and October 2020. In addition to distributing paper copies of materials to tenants, DRC developed a reputation for social media graphics containing critical information for eviction prevention, and our website offered printable downloads of fliers and landlord-tenant rights materials. These online digital materials acted as a resource for tenants who were not being reached by canvassing initiatives. Statewide member organizations of NRM were able to repurpose many of DRC's tenant resources and were invited to rebrand the flyers with their own local tenant association graphics. We also conducted direct tenant outreach in multi-unit apartment buildings when tenants contacted us with concerns, always donning facemasks and meeting with tenants in building common spaces, parking lots, and on stoops.

In July 2020, we learned about an apartment located in Southwest Detroit where tenants were being threatened with eviction by their landlord despite the eviction moratoriums. The building, called The Barbara, was located on West Grand Boulevard. The Barbara is a fifty-unit building located in Southwest, Detroit's majority Latin American neighbourhood. In 2020, only nine units remained occupied in The Barbara. Reports in the local news and complaints issued to BSEED indicated that tenants of The Barbara had been experiencing gross negligence and uninhabitable maintenance conditions since 2015, and many of the former tenants self-selected to leave the building. Like many rental buildings in Detroit, The Barbara had changed ownership multiple times over the previous decade. The current owner was gutting and renovating the property in order to justify higher rents, which meant near complete tenant turnover in a previously majority immigrant and low-income apartment building. As of July 2020, the owner lacked registration and a certificate of compliance, which meant rents were not being legally collected.

By July 2020, when members of DRC visited The Barbara to conduct outreach to the nine remaining inhabited units, the building's common spaces and vacant units were active construction sites. The current landlord was ignoring structural hazards and habitability concerns, such as pests, plumbing and heating issues, and failing walls in units still occupied by long-term tenants, many of whom were low-waged, multigenerational and immigrant households. Electrical cables hung loosely in corridors, the elevator had been inoperable for almost a year, and there were holes in the concrete flooring large enough to fit a leg through and see into neighbouring units or for water from broken pipes to flow freely between them. An industrial dumpster loomed in the parking lot, and the property manager was threatening the remaining tenants that their belongings would be thrown out if their units weren't vacated before the end of the month, despite the eviction moratoriums. Coordinating with tenants of The Barbara, we issued a complaint to the district's city council member and the representative state senator, reporting the threat of illegal evictions as well as the structural and safety concerns about the condition of the building. The complaint demanded that the eviction moratorium and rental ordinance be upheld citywide and that elected representatives act when their constituents were at risk of losing their housing, particularly during a pandemic and in relation to evictions that lacked a court order. We also contacted BSEED and requested that a building inspector visit The Barbara. This visit resulted in the halting of all evictions, and the landlord was fined $7000 for negligent conditions.

The Barbara is one of more than 850 host sites of a public-private community surveillance program in Detroit called Project Green Light (PGL), of which forty sites were located at residential apartment buildings in 2020. PGL mounts closed circuit television cameras to host buildings and streams their digitized video footage to the Detroit Police Department's Real Time Crime Center (RTCC), where facial recognition software is applied to the video footage. The RTCC was modelled after federal Department of Homeland Security post-9/11 fusion centres, which investigate suspected matters of homeland terrorism through broad multi-agency data analysis.[5] The Detroit RTCC reviews all surveillance data and shares data, analysis and reporting with the Michigan State Police, the Wayne County Police, and US Customs and Border Protection, because of Detroit's proximity to the Canadian border — a true digital panopticon in the largest majority Black city in the nation. PGL host locations undergo a site inspection by a city staff member to determine suitability for surveillance equipment and pay a minimum of $6500 to the DPD for program start-up fees, plus annual cloud data storage fees. Through some stroke of luck or negligence, The Barbara passed the required inspection to become a PGL host site but not the inspection that would certify the building as safe enough to legally house tenants and charge rent. Though the apartment was operating illegally, The Barbara was streaming video surveillance footage to the RTCC twenty-four hours a day, seven days a week. Clocking this disconnect — the priority of the landlord to collude with the police despite his own extralegal rental operation, certainly not a coincidence in a majority Black city — DRC created a public information campaign called "Spotlight on Green Light." The campaign highlighted how of the city's forty PGL host apartments buildings, only one was in full compliance with the city rental ordinance. The campaign received wide attention, and we were invited to join a citywide abolitionist and anti-surveillance coalition called Green Light Black Futures (2019–21) that worked to end the police surveillance of Black communities. The living conditions, threats of extralegal eviction, and presence of constant police surveillance at The Barbara acted as an important inroad to expand our own approach to talking to tenants about policing, not only as an occasional potential threat but as a constant presence in their housing experience.

Learning from the tenants and conditions at The Barbara made us think deeply about policy tools and habitability issues we could leverage against landlords to prevent evictions beyond the temporary eviction moratoriums. If landlords in Detroit were legally obligated to comply with the structural and safety standards outlined by the building department and to register their rental properties in order for rents to be legally collected, the small number of landlords who were actually in compliance seemed like a point of leverage worth exploring. Prior to the pandemic being declared, Detroit's 36th District Court already had a thousand backlogged eviction cases, causing the chief judge to extend Detroit's citywide eviction moratorium by an additional month, until the end of August 2020, to allow time to process the deluge of existing cases. The extension bought time for tenant organizers, and at the beginning of August members of DRC authored a policy resolution that outlined a requirement for landlords to submit a certificate of compliance and proof of registration with all eviction filings in order for the filings to be considered complete by the court. The proposed draft resolution was emailed by a prominent housing rights attorney directly to the chief judge. Within a week, the judge adopted the resolution. However, less than two weeks later, Michigan's Supreme Court Administrative Office advised the 36th District Court to revoke the resolution, citing concerns that it may result in landlords bringing an equal protections suit before the court, because the enforcement schedule of Detroit's rental ordinance did not yet require compliance in all zip codes and would not until 2021.[6] Not wanting to abandon a potentially deeply impactful policy change, DRC forwarded the resolution to the office of the mayor and each member of city council with the hope they would implement the resolution by amending the rental ordinance, which would have supported the court in maintaining the resolution. However, members of city council refused to amend the ordinance. Following months of waiting, we received communication from one member of council expressing concerns that housing inspections would lead to landlords having to make costly home repairs, which would in turn drive up rents and decrease the city's stock of "naturally affordable housing."

In 2024, the city's new Safety Ain't Surveillance coalition, of which I am a member, pressed for a policy resolution with two members of city council that would restrict landlords from hosting Project Green Light if they are not in compliance with the rental ordinance. This anti-surveillance coalition has a broadened focus that includes all forms of police surveillance technology used by DPD, including automated licence plate readers and gunshot detection, as well as Project Green Light, In addition to this policy work, members of the coalition hosted five action and education workshops in 2024–25.

We learned important lessons from our organizing efforts prior to the onset of the pandemic and during its early years. Fighting for rights that tenants in Detroit already had enshrined in law directed our energy and efforts almost entirely toward political education and know-your-rights approaches to organizing, even when these rights were not being upheld or enforced. Though members of DRC were well aware and critical of historical and contemporary racialized relationships and access to property in the city, and larger national and global regimes of Black and brown displacement ranging from neighbourhood gentrification to international resource wars, we believed that the law just needed to be enforced to prevent ongoing racialized dispossession in Detroit. While it is true that we spent significant time mulling over legalese and creating tenant education materials, we were also regularly on the inside of eviction dumpsters pulling cherished belongings out after the careless wreckage left by bailiffs and packing up apartments with donated boxes when attempts at eviction defence had failed. We marched almost daily for a hundred days and constantly updated activists, who orchestrated daily outreach to residents in the early months of the pandemic about upcoming changes to eviction moratorium protections and where tenants could access legal support.

All kinds of work that is required to stop evictions and build tenant power was underway among members of DRC throughout the nearly two years that we organized together. If the self-reflection about our focus on policy and the law being a misstep appears like an over-correction or too self-critical, it is shared here because it is what we need to learn from the most and do differently in the future.

This is not to say that DRC was an ineffective organization during our years of operation. Our know-your-rights tenant education materials that were distributed across the city and the partnerships we entered with fellow grassroots housing, abolitionist, and anti-gentrification groups contributed to igniting a much stronger tenant movement that continues to evolve in Detroit today. Self-reflection and retrospection are hard and necessary teachers within social movement spaces. As much as we have learned from this work, we also need to acknowledge the important accomplishments that came from multi-issue organizing and collaborating with fellow activists and neighbours in Detroit and across the state. Our organizing connected tenants to legal aid resources, increased tenant knowledge of the difference between legal and extralegal landlord-initiated evictions, and converged with abolitionist calls to defund the police with tenant rights and anti-eviction politics. Members of DRC and the many organizations and volunteers we worked with accomplished what felt like a miracle in tenant organizing during a time of righteous anti-racist uprising amid a public health crisis that required us to think about keeping ourselves and one another safe in ways we never had before. The collective tenant outreach initiative carried out by DRC, DWB and countless volunteers was the largest tenant rights and political education campaign to prevent tenants from eviction conducted in the state of Michigan in response to the COVID-19 pandemic. This initiative surpassed all face-to-face and door-to-door efforts by municipal governments, which had access to federal COVID-19 Emergency Rental Assistance funds. Our collective effort is indicative of a shared political commitment to disrupt ongoing Black dispossession and our ability to adapt to the conditions of the political moment, when it counts most. It is energizing and inspiring to remember that work of this scale, fortitude, and impact is possible, and that we did it together.

In addition to focusing on organizing people to fight for the enforcement of rights tenants already have, an intervention worth exploring in cities where property inspections determine compliance with habitability standards is to organize for an expansion of who holds decision-making power in the process of determining compliance. Currently in Detroit, municipal property inspectors decide whether a rental unit is suitable for habitation based on a list of structural, functional, and livability criteria. Conversations about compliance take place between landlords and inspectors and sometimes agents of the 36th District Court. Tenants' intimate knowledge of living in their rental units is excluded from informing an inspection process that directly impacts their personal safety and emotional and mental wellbeing. Fighting for an inspection process that requires equal tenant and inspector input would provide tenants with some authority while enabling inspections to become an additional point of disruption and insertion of tenant power in the struggle for safe living conditions. Such a process would also create a climate that would encourage collective knowledge sharing and communication among renters and a strengthening of their political power.

Movements for housing justice and tenant power need the skills of people who focus on data and legalese just as much as they also require deep and continuous organizing and direct action that stretches far beyond looking to courts and elected officials to determine and enforce tenant rights. Though part of the work of tenant organizing is to understand and tap into the legal rights available to us, and to know our rights, tenant organizing is also a matter of collectively developing a class position and analysis that aligns with the intention to undermine the exploitative landlord-tenant relationship and to deepen and broaden this position through fighting for conditions that disrupt ongoing racialized dispossession, unaffordability, habitability issues, and challenges of tenure and the right to remain. To maintain perspective, another part of our work of building tenant power is to acknowledge the scale of this struggle beyond our own neighbourhoods and cities (when possible).

Gratitude is extended to all those who made the efforts, operations, and organizing of Detroit Renter City possible: Josh Akers, Julian Del Campo, Alexa Eisenberg, Eric Hanss, Danko Krouse, Petra McAninch, Brian Silverstein, all the canvassing volunteers, Detroit Will Breathe, and everyone who donated their time, door knocking skills, and funds to make the enormous outreach effort we accomplished together possible.

Notes

1. Timothy R. Hodge, "Decreasing Delinquency through Assessment Reductions: Evidence from Detroit," *Journal of Urban Affairs* 43, 5 (2021).
2. Joel Kurth, Mike Wilkinson, and Laura Herberg, "Sorry We Foreclosed on Your Home. But Thanks for Fixing Our budget," June 6, 2017, *Bridge Magazine*, https://www.bridgemi.com/urban-affairs/sorry-we-foreclosed-your-home-thanks-fixing-our-budget.
3. Sarah Alvarez, "In Detroit's Housing Market, Rentals May Be Outpacing Owner-Occupied Properties," *Outlier Media*, February 21, 2024, https://outliermedia.org/detroit-rental-market-properties-increase-data/#:~:text=Donate%20now%20to%20keep%20accountability,over%20a%20relatively%20short%20time.
4. Mondry, Aaron. "Why most Detroit rentals aren't up to code-and how the city could fix that," *Outlier Media*, June 25, 2024. https://outliermedia.org/rental-registry-detroit-ordinance-landlords-inspections/
5. Torin Monahan, "The Future of Security? Surveillance Operations at Homeland Security Fusion Centers," *Social Justice* 37, 2/3 (2010).
6. At the time that the resolution was adopted by the 36th District Court in Detroit, the property rental ordinance did not yet apply to all rental properties in the city. The resolution would have therefore created different standards for evicting tenants depending on the zip code and location in which the landlord operated their buildings and was seeking eviction. The resolution could have created an issue of unequal protection for landlords and risked the court and the county being sued in an equal protection case brought by impacted landlords. To learn more about the 14th amendment and equal protection under the law, see John P. Frank and Robert F. Munro, "Original Understanding of Equal Protection of the Laws, The," *Columbia Law Review* 50 (1950).

AGAINST LANDLORD TECHNOLOGY IN SAN FRANCISCO

SAN FRANCISCO, CALIFORNIA, UNITED STATES

WRITTEN BY
Erin McElroy, Matthew Martignoni, Jeantelle Laberinto, Joseph Smooke & Priya Prabhakar

This chapter explores the expansion and impacts of technology used by landlords, or what we describe as "landlord technology," in San Francisco. We also explore tenant struggles against landlord technological systems and the corporate landlords who deploy them, with a focus on surveillance platforms implemented in and around tenant housing, as well as digitally enhanced modes of real estate speculation and ownership. We illustrate how the deployment of landlord technology instigates gentrification, drawing upon our collective research as members of [people.power.media] (PPM) and the Anti-Eviction Mapping Project (AEMP). PPM is based in San Francisco, where it produces research and media on housing and land use issues for policy change. The AEMP is a data visualization, digital media, and counter-mapping collective that produces maps, stories, analysis, tools, murals, zines, and more to support housing organizing in the San Francisco Bay Area, New York City, and Los Angeles. Both groups are also members of the San Francisco Anti-Displacement Coalition, a network of housing justice–based organizations across the city. Both groups are also part of Landlord Tech Watch, a coalition that focuses on producing public-facing research to support tenant organizing against landlord technologies.[1]

In this chapter, we focus on the gentrifying impacts of landlord technology, or what those in the real estate industry often refer to as property technology, or "proptech." Housing scholars meanwhile refer to the digital mediation of landlordism as "platform real estate."[2] These terms refer to a range of technologies, including surveillance-based building access systems; "digital doormen," or camera and audio-based intercom systems often compatible with phone apps; virtual property management platforms through which tenants pay rent and file maintenance requests; tenant screening algorithms used to vet potential tenants and deny housing to tenants with criminal records, eviction histories, or poor credit; and price-fixing algorithmic systems used to determine rents for corporate landlords; as well as short-term rental (STR) platforms, such as Airbnb, and intermediary lease occupancy (ILO) platforms, known to transform long-term affordable housing into lucrative short-term vacation and corporate rentals. We refer to this array of platforms, devices, and algorithms not as proptech, but rather as landlord technology, or landlord tech, in order to better signal that the arbiters and beneficiaries of these systems are landlords, often at the expense of tenants.[3]

The landlord tech industry is often framed as an outcome of the 2008 subprime crisis, when large-scale Wall Street investment companies, such as Blackstone and Invitation Homes, purchased foreclosed single-family homes en masse and needed new systems to automate property management.[4] This saw the proliferation of virtual property management platforms, which often integrate with tenant screening systems to vet potential tenants. This era also saw the boom of app-based "smart" building entry systems and short-term vacation rentals. While critical scholarship has mapped the rise of such technology throughout the 2010s and 2020s globally,[5] many landlord technologies in fact predate this time. Tenant screening, for instance, was first launched in the 1970s in California before expanding to the rest of the United States and then experiencing a major boom following 9/11, with heighted and often racist security measures implemented.[6] Yet tenant screening was actively practised even prior to formal 1970s institutionalization. Throughout the first half of the twentieth century, it was common for landlords to collect data about prospective tenants' racial, gender, and sexual identities, and at times, to use this data to deny housing. Housing segregation, racial covenants and deed restrictions, and other discriminatory housing practices were profuse throughout the US — often enabled through analogue demographic data collection.[7] Civil rights housing measures, such as the 1968 Fair Housing Act, made overt housing discrimination more difficult, so abstracting tenant information through datafication vis-à-vis the tenant screening industry blossomed in its wake.[8]

Other landlord technologies, such as the implementation of closed circuit television (CCTV) cameras, also have analogue antecedents prior to the 2008 subprime crisis. CCTV was first developed by Nazi Germany and then began to be used by police in the United Kingdom in the 1960s and in the United States in the 1980s. In 1997, thirteen US cities implemented their own public surveillance programs making use of CCTV cameras. In 2005, San Francisco's mayor Gavin Newsom launched a similar program in the historically Black neighbourhood of Western Addition, installing thirty-three cameras for "community safety."[9] By 2007, up to 178 cameras had been deployed across the city in public housing developments, such as Sunnydale, Bernal Dwellings, Alemany and Plaza East, all managed by the San Francisco Housing Authority and funded by the federal government.[10] As scholars Simone Browne, Brian Jordan Jefferson, and many others have noted, CCTV and digital surveillance in public spaces, including public housing, often amplifies racial surveillance and carcerality, and in the US draws upon a much older history of anti-Black racism.[11]

Because of community pressure to restrict real-time data collection and storage by the police in San Francisco — which was understood to result in disproportionate criminalization[12] — the city's CCTV cameras were not updated for over a decade. In response to bad quality footage, police began collaborating with the private sector to access data. Landlords' cameras, some of which collect data about tenants, as well as cameras in public housing, can all transmit data to San Francisco Police Department (SFPD) — an agency notorious for enacting racial bias.[13] The city adopted the Surveillance Technology Ordinance in 2019 to restrict municipal agencies from acquiring or using surveillance technology, but the SFPD soon violated it to target Black Lives Matter activists.[14] Then in 2022, a law was passed permitting police to access privately owned surveillance cameras and surveillance networks in their investigations.[15]

Like tenant screening, landlord technologies bear long and uneven histories that only become exacerbated through digitization. Often, new landlord technologies get rolled out in times of crisis — 9/11, the subprime crisis, or the COVID-19 pandemic[16] — when they are introduced under the auspices of solving societal problems, but they end up reproducing existing biases, as Virginia Eubanks puts it, by "automating inequality."[17]

One of landlord technology's most worrisome implications today is its acceleration of gentrification. Landlord tech gives property owners data they can leverage to evict and fine tenants, with some landlord tech companies even advertising this explicitly.[18] Landlord tech in this sense contributes to the automation of gentrification: tenants are dispossessed from their homes after cameras capture a particular violation, at which point landlords increase their rents and attract a wealthier subset of tenants.[19] High-end "digital doorman" intercom systems meanwhile get implemented in luxury and market-rate housing specifically as a perk, aimed at attracting wealthy residents less likely to worry about increased surveillance.[20] This too contributes to gentrification by incentivizing wealthier and often whiter tenants to move to "digitally securitized" locations.

Short-term rental (STR) platforms, another form of landlord technology, are similarly responsible for deepening gentrification. Airbnb, which was formed in San Francisco in 2008, soon after triggered the proliferation of STRs locally and globally, along with ballooning rents as long-term housing was converted into vacation rentals.[21] San Francisco tenants are now struggling against ILOs, which similarly seek to replace long-term residential units with digitally mediated shorter-term, lucrative corporate, or "membership" housing.[22]

Advances in technologies and their marketing, for instance artificial intelligence and algorithmic processing, also induce gentrification. Today tenants are often worried about facial recognition capabilities in building access systems, as well as the role of algorithms in tenant screening software, given the many racial and gender biases that such tools have been seen to reproduce.[23] Tenants are rightfully concerned these tools will lead to landlords and law enforcement overmatching people of colour, which could then skew eviction and incarceration rates. Price-setting rental algorithms, also increasingly used by corporate landlords across the US, often to normalize untenably high rents, similarly contribute to gentrification and have actively been opposed by tenants in San Francisco.[24] These examples get at how landlord technologies automate gentrification and create additional work, stress, and precarity for tenants. This is not to overemphasize, spectacularize, or fetishize the role of technology when it comes to housing, given that many digital practices employed in the housing sector today are rather mundane.[25] But these techniques are mobilized by landlords to abet their accumulation of capital and concentration of land and property ownership; the shifting housing landscape of downtown San Francisco is evidence of this intensification of landlord control.

While there is nothing new about landlords surveilling tenants and calling upon the state to punish those who defy what they perceive to be the sanctity of their private property, corporate owners rely on standardized management systems and building controls to protect their investments. Landlords' business models, especially when it comes to private equity landlords, is to cut expenses and raise revenues for short-term gains.[26] This often means entering and exiting particular property relations quickly and selling units for much more than they were purchased at, as well as charging steep rents while failing to provide basic property management services, such as appliance repairs and regular garbage collection from dumpsters. Depending on shifting market conditions and demand, a landlord may be able to make more money by renting a unit to a business that manages non-residential uses such as STRs or ILOs. Surveillance and building control systems enable corporate owners to transition between residential and non-residential uses depending on which might amass more revenue.

Veritas, the largest private landlord in San Francisco, exemplifies the trend of mobilizing technology to control building use. As Yat-Pang Au, Veritas's CEO, revealed at the September 2021 Marcus and Millichap real estate conference, the company uses its apartment buildings as testing grounds for new surveillance technologies. When it finds products and companies that are particularly promising, Veritas invests directly in them. Veritas's investments are significant because they proliferate and normalize the use of landlord technologies for smaller landlords.

In the first years of the 2020s, tenants said that Veritas and other San Francisco-based corporate landlords, such as Mosser, Trinity, and Ballast Investments, threatened eviction and harassment as people struggled with the inability to pay rent due to pandemic wage loss, even as Veritas and Mosser received $3.6 million in Paycheck Protection Program loans intended to support small businesses and retain workers during the pandemic.[27] Veritas created its own application forms to collect information about tenants in advance of the California state application for rent relief. These surveys assembled more information about tenants than was required by state regulation, suggesting that they were screening out tenants who would otherwise have been eligible.

Veritas has long used cloud-based systems such as RentLytics and RealPage to administer rent collection and maintenance — an increasingly common landlord and property management trend. This type of software tracks construction projects and rent increases, maximizing rental income. Several cities and tenant groups throughout the US have brought litigation against RealPage, calling their practices "price fixing," and the San Francisco Board of Supervisors is considering legislation to deem RealPage's business practice illegal. RealPage, based in Texas, claims to serve 10 percent of the San Francisco rental market with "revenue management" products, which have been shown to overcharge rents.[28]

In addition to using price-setting algorithms, throughout the pandemic, Veritas additionally began demanding that tenants use an online-only rental payment system, which had previously been optional. It now largely uses Yardi (a landlord tech company that emerged in California in the 1980s and that today coordinates with RealPage and several other tools) for property management across the US. Another Veritas tenant reported now having to use another platform, Bilt, to pay rent, which they are wary of, given that in the past Veritas stole money from them through autopay software. The use of virtual property management systems overcomplicates the rent payment process and has been accompanied by hidden fines alongside increased screening demands. A Veritas tenant reported that they were told they could not transfer to another vacant unit in their same building unless they showed consistent income of 2.5 times the rent, a tax return showing that they make four times the rent, and a bank account with more than $37,000 balance for more than a year or a co-signer. These requirements far exceed "normal" expectations.

Meanwhile, other Veritas tenants have reported multiple instances of the landlord installing camera-based "digital doormen" made by a New York City landlord tech company, Carson, in which Veritas is an investor.[29] This shift to surveillance technologies essentially creates a "one size fits all" landlord technology suite that can be integrated into other services, such as virtual property management and utility monitoring. While used voluntarily before, the technology became mandated by Veritas during the pandemic, with tenants not being able to opt out. In a survey administered by the AEMP between 2020 and 2024, hundreds of tenants across the US complained about increased labour, stress, and at times inaccessibility that digital doormen, building access technology, and virtual property management platforms impose.[30] These complaints range from difficulty in entering their own home if without a cell phone or if in an area with poor wi-fi, to fines and penalties imposed for refusing to use an invasive technology in their home. Other tenants worry about increased policing in their building due to new cameras.

Trinity Properties — another large San Francisco-based corporate landlord and serial evictor — increased its use of landlord tech throughout the pandemic. At one property, Trinity employs several guards to monitor live video feeds of the building's many cameras, advertising them as "24-hour Front Desk Associates" and a "24-hour Courtesy Patrol" on its website. In our research, we were able to identify six smaller cameras at the main entrance alone and several in the lobby; however, the size of the building suggests that the surveillance network is more extensive.

One of the surveillance companies that Trinity uses is Axis Communications, which provides cameras in a wide range of spaces, from residential and retail buildings to public transport, to education institutions and prisons. Regarding the latter, Axis claims that their "tough and resilient devices … provide live views and enable mitigation of security risks and increase safety for inmates and staff."[31] This language around inmate safety eerily mirrors that around tenant protection, highlighting the extension of the prison-industrial complex into residential space.[32] That Trinity labels their cameras as amenities to protect residents from intrusive outsiders highlights how they aim to use landlord technology to surveil and determine who gets to enter, who gets locked up, and who gets locked out.

Mosser Companies, another corporate landlord, has instituted similar amenitization practices by advertising properties with controlled access and other "security" measures to ensure tenant safety. According to housing organizers, when tenants in one building requested camera data from these alleged safety-enhancing amenities, the property managers denied the existence of any footage. Tenants further noted that there is often surveillance tech like Amazon Ring doorbell cameras at entryways to individual units, which tenants are unlikely to install themselves. Ring partners with over 2,000 police departments across the US, supplying over 20,000 police data requests in 2020 alone.[33] Meanwhile, other corporate landlords, like Lennar, explicitly advertise Ring systems as amenities on their websites.

While seemingly separate from carceral examples of surveillance, many "high tech" and "smart" features are sold as a package deal in the form of a "post"-pandemic lifestyle. Importantly, "community" spaces from where one can "work from home" are often surveilled. The landlord thus surveils tenants in both the residential common areas and in workspaces provided to tenants. While there are plenty of troublesome privacy violations associated with this scopic network alone, often enough, these cameras also monitor adjacent streets, empowering corporate landlords as extensions of law enforcement. This is particularly troubling given ongoing misidentification, over-identification, and corollary punishment of people of colour, whether related to Ring cameras or other neighbourhood surveillance technologies, such as automated licence plate readers.[34] Indeed, there have been ample examples of passersby being misrecognized or falsely recognized by surveillance technologies, often along familiar anti-Black colour lines.[35] At the same time, implementing security measures such as Ring cameras often attracts wealthier residents unafraid of heightened surveillance, while targeting less privileged and unhoused neighbours. Either way, landlord tech bolsters property owners' ability to profit, often at the expense of poor and working-class tenants and community members.

The landlord tech landscape is barely regulated, and municipal officials generally have little understanding of what technologies landlords in their cities are using. Although Airbnb hosts are required to register with San Francisco (thanks to rigorous tenant organizing) and while there has been an ongoing push to better monitor and regulate STRs and ILOs more broadly, there is no recorded dataset of the various landlord technologies deployed by private landlords. Nor are tenants informed of potential harms caused by such technologies. This underscores the urgency of tenant-led data production, advocacy, and broader tenant organizing against landlord tech. Accordingly, as members of PPM and the AEMP, we have produced public scholarship and popular educational materials about landlord tech that categorizes landlord tech platforms and explains why they are harmful. Meanwhile, the Landlord Tech Watch network hosts a crowdsourced survey useful in tracking locations and harms associated with landlord technologies across the US.[36] We have also built networks with other organizers in New York City, such as the Ocean Hill-Brownsville Alliance, who successfully organized against their landlord from installing a facial recognition technology system at the entrance of the building.[37] But this public scholarship is only as powerful as organizing itself.

As the examples in this chapter show, the expansion of landlord technology has increasingly shaped the landscape of tenant and community experiences, as well as the ongoing work of organizing for housing justice. Prior to the pandemic, tenants already faced the pressures of steep rents, harassment, and threats of eviction under corporate landlords. The proliferation of landlord technology amid the COVID-19 pandemic only exacerbated tenant harms, making it even more critical for tenants to organize to build power and effect policy change.

In San Francisco, where 65 percent of housing units are renter-occupied, housing justice organizers understand how critical it is for tenants, especially those with corporate landlords, to both know and advocate for their rights. The Veritas Tenants Association (VTA), made up of members living in more than a hundred Veritas properties throughout San Francisco, Oakland, Alameda, and Los Angeles, serves as an exemplary model of tenant organizing in response to corporate landlordism. Veritas received nearly $6 million cumulatively in federal loans on top of state aid while tenants suffered from loss of income.[38] The VTA, supported by the Housing Rights Committee of San Francisco (HRCSF), urged Veritas to allocate those funds towards back rent collectively owed by Veritas tenants, amounting to an estimated $5.7 million, though unsurprisingly, Veritas did no such thing. In response, in September 2021, the VTA in San Francisco began an unprecedented debt strike lasting five months. According to organizers, tenants had numerous conversations about the stakes and risks and followed up with each other on a regular basis to keep morale and participation steady. They eventually won groundbreaking concessions from Veritas, including cancellation of all remaining rent debt for tenants and a waiver of annual rent increases for 2022.[39]

Concurrent with VTA's debt strike, HRCSF led the effort for the city of San Francisco to pass an ordinance legally empowering tenants to form tenant associations and requiring landlords to negotiate with the associations. The ordinance also stipulates that if landlords fail to follow the ordinance, their tenants may petition for rent reductions with San Francisco's Rent Board.[40] The SF Board of Supervisors unanimously passed the ordinance, which went into effect in April 2022. Though just one example, VTA's successful debt strike underscores the power of tenant organizing and lays the groundwork for further such work.

The convergence of real estate platforms and tech — which accelerated during the pandemic — has made corporate landlordism even more harmful to tenants. Yet digital mediation is not unique in real estate, especially given the growth of data-driven and algorithmic policing that dictates who and where people are surveilled.[41] Abolitionists today are fighting to abolish private property and the carceral state, which together reinforce racial capitalism and the prison industrial complex — a system that also encompasses the securitization of private property by landlords.[42]

Because of the shared tactics of data-driven policing and landlord tech, the struggle against surveillance must be taken on by both housing activists and police abolitionists. In 2019, San Francisco passed an ordinance banning the SFPD from using facial recognition systems. During the 2020 protests following George Floyd's murder, the SFPD violated the ordinance by using a business district's surveillance camera network to monitor the protests, resulting in three activists of colour suing the department.[43] These organizers importantly link struggles of police abolition, housing justice, anti-gentrification, and anti-surveillance, providing a framework for coalition-building. At the same time, there have been significant advances in organizing against RealPage price-setting software, which the SF Board of Supervisors began the process of regulating against in July 2024. If it all goes through, this would be the first ban on algorithmic price-setting software in the US.

As members of PPP and the AEMP, we draw upon collective research to study new technologies of landlordism and their housing impacts. From tenant screening to contactless property management through high-definition cameras, from platform-enabled housing for residential and commercial use to "smart" data-grabbing amenitization and algorithmic price-fixing systems, landlord technologies capitalize upon our homes and data to automate dispossession, housing precarity, and at times, carcerality. As these exploitative and dispossessive practices continue, we hope that collective research can fuel the ongoing work of producing housing justice knowledge to resist technologies of gentrification.

Notes

1. Anti-Eviction Mapping Project, [people.power.media], Ocean Hill Brownsville Tenants Alliance, AI Now Institute, and Anti-Eviction Lab, "Landlord Tech Watch," 2020, https://antievictionmappingproject.github.io/landlordtech/.
2. Mara Sanyal, "Digital Informalisation: Rental Housing, Platforms, and the Management of Risk," *Housing Studies*, 37, 6 (2022); Dallas Rogers, Sophia Maalsen, Peta Wolifson, and Desiree Fields, "Proptech and the Private Rental Sector: New Forms of Extraction at the Intersection of Rental Properties and Platform Rentierisation," *Urban Studies,* July 27, 2024, https://doi.org/10.1177/00420980241262916.
3. Erin McElroy and Manon Vergerio, "Automating Gentrification: Landlord Technologies and Housing Justice Organising in New York City Homes," *Environment and Planning D: Society and Space*, 40, 4 (2022).
4. Alexander Ferrer, "Beyond Wall Street Landlords: How Private Equity in the Rental Market Makes Housing Unaffordable, Unstable, and Unhealthy," *Los Angeles: Strategic Action for a Just Economy*, https://www.saje.net/wp-content/uploads/2021/03/Final_A-Just-Recovery-Series_Beyond_Wall_Street.pdf.
5. Desiree Fields, "Automated Landlord: Digital Technologies and Post-Crisis Financial Accumulation," *Environment and Planning A: Economy and Space*, 54, 1 (2022); Julien Migozzi, "The Good, the Bad and the Tenant: Rental Platforms Renewing Racial Capitalism in the Post-Apartheid Housing Market," *Environment and Planning D: Society and Space,* September 17, 2023, https://doi.org/10.1177/02637758231195962; Rogers, Maalsen, Wolifson, and Fields, "Proptech and the Private Rental Sector."
6. Erin McElroy, "Dis/Possessory Data Politics: From Tenant Screening to Anti-Eviction Organizing," *International Journal of Urban and Regional Research* 47, 1 (2023); Rebecca Oyama, "Do Not (Re)Enter: The Rise of Criminal Background Tenant Screening as a Violation of the Fair Housing Act," *Michigan Journal of Race and Law* 15, 1 (January 1, 2009).
7. Keeanga-Yamahtta Taylor, *Race for Profit: How Banks and the Real Estate Industry Undermined Black Homeownership* (University of North Caroline Press, 2019).
8. Wonyoung So, "Which Information Matters? Measuring Landlord Assessment of Tenant Screening Reports," *Housing Policy Debate* 33, 6 (November 2, 2023).
9. Erin McElroy, Noah Cohen, Shiyu Catherine Xu, Andrew Liquigan, Gracie Harris, Maggie McCarroll, Lulia Liu Pan, Matthew Martignoni, Alyssa Ramirez, and Paula Garcia-Salazar, "San Francisco Landlord Tech Report," University of Washington: Anti-Eviction Lab, 2023, https://www.antievictionlab.org/sf-report.
10. Heather Knight, "SF Public Housing Cameras No Help in Homicide Arrests," *SFGATE*, August 14, 2007, https://www.sfgate.com/news/article/S-F-public-housing-cameras-no-help-in-homicide-2510907.php.
11. Simone Browne, *Dark Matters: On the Surveillance of Blackness* (Duke University Press, 2015); Brian Jefferson, D*igitize and Punish: Racial Criminalization in the Digital Age* (University of Minnesota Press, 2020).
12. McElroy, Cohen, Xu et al., "San Francisco Landlord Tech Report."
13. Anti-Eviction Mapping Project, "Killings by Police, San Francisco, 1985–2020," June 8, 2020; https://antievictionmap.com/blog/2020/6/8/killings-by-police-san-francisco-1985-2020; *Electronic Frontier Foundation*,

"Activists Sue San Francisco for Wide-Ranging Surveillance of Black-Led Protests Against Police Violence," October 7, 2020, https://www.eff.org/press/releases/activists-sue-san-francisco-wide-ranging-surveillance-black-led-protests-against.
14 Electronic Frontier Foundation, "Activists Sue San Francisco."
15 Jessica Lyons, "San Francisco Cops Can Use Private Cameras for Surveillance," The Register, Sept. 21, 2022, https://www.theregister.com/2022/09/21/san_francisco_private_cameras/.
16 Erin McElroy, Meredith Whittaker, and Nicole Weber, "Prison Tech Comes Home," *Public Books*, August 18, 2021, https://www.publicbooks.org/prison-tech-comes-home/; Erin McElroy and Wonyoung So, "Landlord Tech in Covid19 Times," *Metropolitics*, March 30, 2021, https://metropolitics.org/Landlord-Tech-in-COVID-19-Times.html.
17 Virginia Eubanks, *Automating Inequality: How High-Tech Tools Profile, Police, and Punish the Poor* (St. Martin's Publishing, 2018); Naomi Klein, "Screen New Deal: Under Cover of Mass Death, Andrew Cuomo Calls in the Billionaires to Build a High-Tech Dystopia," *The Intercept*, May 8, 2020, https://theintercept.com/2020/05/08/andrew-cuomo-eric-schmidt-coronavirus-tech-shock-doctrine/.
18 Ari Teman, "5 Ways to Maximize Evictions (NYC Multifamily)," Linked In, November 9, 2018, https://www.linkedin.com/pulse/5-ways-maximize-evictions-nyc-multifamily-ari-teman.
19 McElroy and Vergerio, "Automating Gentrification."
20 ButterflyMX, "From Amenity to Necessity," *Video Intercom System for Apartment Buildings* (blog), https://butterflymx.com/resources/ebooks/from-amenity-to-necessity/.
21 Anne-Cécile Mermet, "Can Gentrification Theory Learn from Airbnb? Airbnbfication and the Asset Economy in Reykjavík," *Environment and Planning A: Economy and Space* 54, 6 (2022); David Wachsmuth and Alexander Weisler, "Airbnb and the Rent Gap: Gentrification through the Sharing Economy," *Environment and Planning A: Economy and Space* 50, 6 (2018).
22 Joseph Smooke and Dyan Ruiz, "Exclusive Exposé: The Wild West of Landlord Technology," [People.Power.Media.], September 29, 2020. https://www.people-powermedia.org/solutions/exclusive-expose-wild-west-landlord-technology.
23 J. Khadijah Abdurahman, Tranae' Moran, and Fabian Rogers, "Organizing as Joy: An Ocean-Hill Brownsville Story, with Tranae Moran and Fabian Rogers," *Logic Magazine,* December 25, 2021, https://logicmag.io/beacons/organizing-as-joy-an-ocean-hill-brownsville-story-with-tranae-moran-and/; Laura Kirchner and Matthew Goldstein, "Access Denied: Faulty Automated Background Checks Freeze Out Renters," *The Markup,* May 28, 2020, https://themarkup.org/locked-out/2020/05/28/access-denied-faulty-automated-background-checks-freeze-out-renters.
24 Stephen Council, "Hoping to Cut San Francisco Rents, Supervisors Approve Software-Pricing Ban," SFGATE, July 31, 2024, https://www.sfgate.com/tech/article/sf-realpage-software-ban-aaron-peskin-19610723.php.
25 Agnieszka Leszczynski, "Digital Methods III: The Digital Mundane," *Progress in Human Geography* 44, 6 (December 1, 2020).
26 Heather Vogell, "When Private Equity Becomes Your Landlord," *ProPublica,* February 7, 2022, https://www.propublica.org/article/when-private-equity-becomes-your-landlord.

27 Aidin Vaziri, "SF Landlord Veritas to Repay, Not Return, Big Loan after Pelosi Demand," *San Francisco Chronicle*, May 18, 2020, https://www.sfchronicle.com/business/article/SF-landlord-Veritas-responds-to-Pelosi-s-demand-15276352.php.
28 Council, "Hoping to Cut San Francisco Rents."
29 McElroy and Vergerio, "Automating Gentrification."
30 Anti-Eviction Mapping Project, [people.power.media], Ocean Hill Brownsville Tenants Alliance, AI Now Institute, and Anti-Eviction Lab; Erin McElroy, "The Work of Landlord Technology: The Fictions of Frictionless Property Management," *Environment and Planning D: Society and Space* 42, 4 (May 8, 2024), https://doi.org/10.1177/02637758241232758.
31 Axis Communications, "Prisons and Correctional Facilities," 2022, https://www.axis.com/solutions/prisons-and-correctional-facilities.
32 McElroy and So, "Landlord Tech in Covid 19 Times."
33 McElroy, Whittaker, and Weber, "Prison Tech Comes Home."
34 Jason Kelley and Matthew Guariglia, "Things to Know Before Your Neighbourhood Installs an Automated License Plate Reader," Electronic Frontier Foundation, September 14, 2020, https://www.eff.org/deeplinks/2020/09/flock-license-plate-reader-homeowners-association-safe-problems.
35 Jason Kelley, "Amazon's Ring Enables the Over-Policing Efforts of Some of America's Deadliest Law Enforcement Agencies," Electronic Frontier Foundation, July 2, 2020. https://www.eff.org/deeplinks/2020/07/amazons-ring-enables-over-policing-efforts-some-americas-deadliest-law-enforcement.
36 Anti-Eviction Mapping Project, [people.power.media], Ocean Hill Brownsville Tenants Alliance, AI Now Institute, and Anti-Eviction Lab.
37 McElroy and Vergerio, "Automating Gentrification."
38 Bay City News, "SF's Largest Landlord Launches Program to Cover Back Rent for Tenants Denied State Funds." *NBC Bay Area*, December 18, 2021, https://www.nbcbayarea.com/news/local/san-francisco/sfs-largest-landlord-launches-program-to-cover-back-rent-for-tenants-denied-state-funds/2759277/.
39 Joe Kukura, "Veritas Tenants End Rent Strike after Winning Significant Concessions on Back Debt," *SFist*, January 29, 2022, https://sfist.com/2022/01/28/veritas-tenants-end-rent-strike-after-winning-significant-concessions-on-back-debt.
40 Sarah Klearman, "The SF Board of Supervisors Just Passed Unprecedented Protections for Tenants' Unions," *San Francisco Business Times*, February 16, 2022, https://www.bizjournals.com/sanfrancisco/news/2022/02/16/peskin-tenant-organizations-rights.html.
41 Stop LAPD Spying Coalition, "Automating Banishment," https://automatingbanishment.org/.
42 Ruth Wilson Gilmore, *Abolition Geography: Essays Towards Liberation* (Verso, 2022); Rinaldo Walcott, *On Property* (Biblioasis, 2021).
43 Electronic Frontier Foundation, "Activists Sue San Francisco."

TENANT-ORGANIZED EVICTION COURT WATCH

PORTLAND, OREGON, UNITED STATES

WRITTEN BY
Colleen Carroll (Don't Evict PDX)

GRAPHICS BY
Saiyare Refaei

Tenancy is, by definition, a precarious position. As tenants, we do not have full control over our housing. In fact, we have very little control. We are temporary holders of access to housing, access which can be withdrawn quickly and violently through the eviction process. In many countries, including the United States, legally removing tenants from a rented residential property requires multiple steps, which is why I refer to evictions as a process instead of an event.[1] Perhaps when you read the word "eviction" you imagine a sheriff or a marshall escorting a family out of a unit, disposing of their belongings on the sidewalk, and changing the locks on the doors behind them. This scene, formally known as a lockout, is the last step in a long eviction process, but it is not the only way tenants are displaced or evicted.

I began court-watching in eviction courts in the summer of 2020. I had only moved to the Portland, Oregon, area a few months prior and was renting a new apartment that I could barely afford. Then I got laid off. For tenants, losing a job can mean losing your home in a matter of weeks, because evicting a tenant for missing a single rent payment is often lawful. In August 2020, many nations had placed temporary restrictions on evictions for non-payment of rent in response to the COVID-19 pandemic. However, even though governments had imposed eviction

Tenant-Organized Eviction Court Watch 109

All Eyes on Evictors by Saiyare Refaei shows the taunting power of the judges and court systems to determine who gets keys to housing.

moratoriums, eviction courts in many jurisdictions in the US were open and operating. How could this be? This contradiction galvanized me to begin observing eviction court. Initially, I was one of three tenants attending and observing Portland's eviction court. We were joined by fellow tenant advocates and neighbours at the beginning of 2021 and eventually formed a tenants' court-watch collective. In our collective learning and praxis, we would take notes, discuss our observations, problem solve how to navigate the courthouse, pose questions about the system, look up answers, and share our experiences and outrage. I have since left that collective but have continued to observe eviction courts across Oregon and have trained new court observers across the state who are starting court-watch programs in their cities. Post-pandemic eviction cases are rising and are higher than pre-pandemic levels in Oregon.[2] Anti-eviction education, advocacy, and organizing will continue to be necessary so long as tenant rights remains precarious.

Court-watching is the act of attending court proceedings that you are not a party to for the purposes of observation and documentation. Court-watching, especially when it is done with other tenants interested in housing justice, can be a tool of class-consciousness raising, collective political education, and skill-building. Notable examples of such knowledge sharing include the 2013 report Tipping the Scales: A Report of Tenant Experiences in Bronx Housing Court, by Community

Action for Safe Apartments, and in 2020, Unequal Burden, Unequal Risk: Households Headed by Black Women Experience Highest Rates of Eviction, by Jane Place Neighborhood Sustainability Initiative in New Orleans.

Eviction-court-watching is often focused on observing and tracking tenants to understand their experiences in eviction court, but witnessing how landlords and judges operate in eviction court is also an important component of court-watching: it helps organizers understand how violence towards tenants is coordinated and enacted.

The first three days I observed eviction court were one of the most radicalizing experiences I have ever had. The repeated, methodical, and ultimately predictable outcomes of all the cases I observed confirmed for me that eviction courts are designed and maintained for the singular purpose of evicting people. This is what activists and academics mean when they call eviction courts an eviction machine. It is formulaic, reliable, and tireless. Experiencing outrage and disillusionment and being moved to action is one of the most useful aspects of building and maintaining a tenant-organized eviction-court-watch program.

We were engaged in a collective practice of "sousveillance," which scholar Steve Mann describes as watching from below: "observation or recording by an entity not in a position of power or authority over the subject of the veillance [seeing]."[3] Sousveillance offers court observers a framework for remembering and embodying our position of power, or restrictions on that power, vis-à-vis the other people in the courtroom. To be subversive, sousveillance requires us to resist the court's terms of engagement. As much as we know the court to be non-neutral, the court is also quick to code us as non-neutral, as interlopers.

Eviction-court sousveillance is about seeing and seeking where the court draws its power from, how it justifies its legitimacy, and how it maintains control. The daily functioning of the court relies on obedience, compliance, deference, and rule-following, and it punishes disobedience, questioning, confrontation. The court's sense of legitimacy is strengthened by procedural repetition. Sousveillance, in contrast to neutral, depoliticized observation, allows for members of the observation collective to disrupt the process and document the results. A few examples we tried included applauding tenants who resisted eviction particularly well in a hearing or trial, shouting suggestions such as "ask for a set-over" during a procedural hearing where a tenant didn't know of an option that was available to them, and — my personal favourite — using the "reaction emojis" embedded in the web video-call platform the court used during COVID. It turns out that it is quite difficult for a landlord's lawyer to concentrate on evicting tenants while poop emojis are popping up all over his screen during his conversation with the judge.

Participating in a tenant-organized eviction-court-watch program can develop strategy and knowledge around how to avoid, or at least reduce the harm of, evictions and illegal lockouts, which can then be shared in collective learning with organizations and other tenants through workshops and educational materials. Observing court changed how I and my co-observers thought about the speed and scale at which evictions take place in our community. Multiple eviction cases are often scheduled together, or on one docket, meaning multiple tenants show up for their hearing at the same time. In the Multnomah County Courthouse, where we were observing, there were on average forty to fifty cases scheduled on a single docket for their first appearance hearing. The whole docket would last from two to two and half hours, with each case allocated only three to five minutes of the judge's time. The court can do this because most cases require very little participation from the tenant. The hearing happens to the tenant more than with them. Most cases end without going to trial, which means tenants rarely get to present their side of the story. Many cases end by default because the tenant couldn't make the hearing, often due to a conflict with work or childcare responsibilities, or with the tenant agreeing to a settlement plan after mere minutes of negotiation. The speed at which tenants are called to the bench and ultimately displaced is breathtaking. In Multnomah County, eviction cases are scheduled five days a week, and the density of each day's docket shows just how intense and frequent eviction is.

All evictions are a process of dispossession and destabilization. Any single eviction is punishment. Collectively, eviction is the vulnerability that all tenants share, at all times, but eviction rates are not evenly distributed across all demographics of tenants: Black women, low-income tenants, and tenants living in sober housing or transitional housing face a greater likelihood of being evicted.

Observing eviction court reveals that the landlord-rentier class fortifies its power through the backing of property managers, judges, lawyers, landlord agents, and sheriffs, who are implicated in a system that reproduces the conditions that make eviction possible. As with many attempts to corral people into neat sets — evictors and evictables in this case — we need to remember that the edges are porous and that degrees of power and participation within and across the border exist. Many eviction workers, including court clerks and residential sober-living-facility employees are themselves tenants. These blurred borders and the existence of malleable membership in multiple classifications are real, but they don't negate the usefulness of being able to analyze amounts of and access to power within the eviction system and process. Court-watching makes visible the nearly absolute advantage the system has cemented for the evictors.

Resist Eviction by Saiyare Refaei depicts a protesting courtroom of community members challenging the hammer of the eviction notice coming down as the judge's gavel.

If you are interested in starting your own court-watch program, Community Justice Exchange has published a useful resource entitled "So You Want to Courtwatch?"[4] Although it is oriented towards court-watching in criminal courts, it is useful for civil courts as well. The tenant sousveillance court-watch style, which we developed, is a combination of what they call a "civic engagement model" and a "system monitor model," but with additional attention to power relationships between landlords and the legal system on one side and tenants on the other, inside and outside the courtroom.

Tenant-organized eviction-court-watching can be incorporated into a tenant union's activities or be developed as its own organization. Tenant union members are sometimes wary of getting involved in organizing at eviction court, because it can pull the union into the world of legal aid.

But introducing sousveillance-focused court-watching into the union's work may balance that tension, making union members more adept at navigating legal processes. As a part of a union or as an independent organization, resist the gravitational pull towards becoming a court-based service provider or navigator. Instead, use your regular presence in that space as a way of connecting with more tenants as an invitation to join the collective struggle.

Notes

1. In this chapter, I focus on the legal eviction process that is defined in the local landlord/tenant law. Many tenants are illegally evicted, meaning the landlord forces them out without going through the local courts.
2. J. Shumway, "Oregon Eviction Filings above Pre-pandemic Levels; Advocates Say More State Aid Needed," OPB, November 10, 2023, https://www.opb.org/article/2023/11/10/oregon-eviction-filing-pandemic-aid/.
3. Steve Mann, "Veillance and Reciprocal Transparency: Surveillance versus Sousveillance, AR Glass, Lifeglogging, and Wearable Computing," In 2013 IEEE International Symposium on Technology and Society (ISTAS): Social Implications of Wearable Computing and Augmediated Reality in Everyday Life (IEEE, 2013), doi.org/10.1109/ISTAS.2013.6613094.
4. Community Justice Exchange, "So You Want to Courtwatch?" static1.squarespace.com/static/5ee39ec764dbd7179cf1243c/t/629034f8e4e22d387c96eab7/1653617912388/Courtwatch.pdf.

LAWYERS IN THE HOUSING JUSTICE MOVEMENT

LOS ANGELES, CALIFORNIA, UNITED STATES

WRITTEN BY
Greg Bonett, Faizah Malik, Katie McKeon & Doug Smith

As the worldwide COVID-19 pandemic deepened the housing affordability crisis in California and across the United States, tenants, tenant organizers, and community-based organizations reconfigured campaigns and revised strategies to respond to the moment of housing precarity. Public interest lawyers — who have historically joined housing justice movement leaders at the front lines by providing eviction defence, rights education, and policy support — also supported these efforts with complementary strategies and tactics.

This chapter reflects on the contemporary framework for "movement lawyering," asking a fundamental question: does this model meet the needs at the intersection of unprecedented housing instability, unaffordability, and health catastrophe? We explore this question from the perspectives of housing justice attorneys with Public Counsel's Community Development Project (CDP).[1]

For decades, legal scholars and practitioners have studied the role of law and lawyers in advancing social justice in the United States. Beginning in the 1930s, civil-rights litigation dominated progressive legal strategy. Carefully planned test cases led to high-profile lawsuits like *Brown v Board of Education*,[2] sparking a widespread embrace of the courtroom as an important arena for social change.[3] The corresponding scholarship emphasized the role of activist lawyers as favoured instruments to advance progressive reform by enforcing legal rights through the courts,[4] often presenting social movements as a backdrop to a high-profile legal-centric strategy.[5]

Beginning in the 1970s, a loose constellation of scholars and practitioners, now referred to as the critical legal studies (CLS) movement, raised concerns about lawyer accountability in civil-rights litigation[6] and argued that some rights-based strategies yielded legal change without meaningful social advancement.[7] CLS challenged the liberal conception of law as rational and apolitical,[8] arguing that some narrow rights-based litigation efforts actually undermined collective action and legitimated inequality by focusing on individual disputes and narrowing the scope of available remedies.[9] Beginning in the 1980s, critical race theory scholars expanded the critique of legal liberalism and elevated a necessary interrogation of law and racial power missing from CLS scholarship.[10]

Acknowledging the limits of litigation alone to dismantle the political and economic conditions that systematically disadvantage poor people and people of colour, legal scholars and practitioners put forth alternative models of lawyering that focus on empowering marginalized communities.[11] In this context, a rich "law and social movement" discipline has emerged, emphasizing the primacy of community organizing and movement activism as the basis for legal and political transformation.[12] This has provided the theoretical basis for a resurgent "movement lawyering" practice model, which focuses on lawyer accountability to social movement organizations.[13]

Our approach to lawyering for housing justice largely follows Scott Cummings' definition of movement lawyering: "the mobilization of law through deliberately planned and interconnected advocacy strategies, inside and outside of formal law-making spaces, by lawyers who are accountable to politically marginalized constituencies to build the power of those constituencies to produce and sustain democratic social change goals that they define."[14] In particular, we draw on litigation, education and policy design, and advocacy to elevate community expertise and shift power towards tenants and community-based organizations.[15]

For over a decade, CDP has supported community-led efforts to combat affordable housing scarcity, extreme rent-burden and displacement pressures, and rising homelessness.[16] This work includes drafting equitable land-use policy to create new affordable housing and preserve existing rent-stabilized and affordable housing,[17] advancing "People's Plan" campaigns to reorient local land-use policies around housing and economic justice,[18] drafting and advocating for local rent-control ordinances,[19] and holding jurisdictions accountable to fair housing and inclusive development standards.[20] Each of these strategies and tactics was put to the test when our housing crisis collided with a public health nightmare in 2020.

The pandemic intensified a deep housing crisis, necessitating new movement formations and grassroots campaigns to respond to imminent eviction risks and exploitative practices in low-income communities. Throughout the pandemic, while tenants and organizers led direct actions and mobilized grassroots advocacy in the foreground, we worked in the background to draft ordinances, model policies, and legal research memos. As the movement responded to emerging needs and shifting political dynamics, these legal instruments provided concrete and detailed demands to which coalitions could tether organizing and direct their actions, communications, and advocacy strategies.

In the first days of the pandemic, tenant and housing justice organizations realized the profound threat of mass displacement as the economy shut down. In response, a new coalition of dozens of organizations — dubbed "Healthy LA" — formed to prevent an impending wave of evictions. In support, we joined eviction-defence attorneys to research and draft legislation to strengthen the City of Los Angeles's proposed emergency eviction protection ordinance. We then drafted and submitted a comprehensive legal analysis and menu of policy options for additional measures, including a rent freeze and a true eviction moratorium, which unlike the city's proposal, would prevent eviction cases from being filed altogether. After rigorous debate during a marathon length council hearing, these stronger proposals fell one vote short of advancing, with a more conservative bloc of council members unwilling to support the stronger protections.[21] Even though Healthy LA did not achieve all its demands, the coalition's advocacy contributed to the City of Los Angeles adopting one of the strongest and longest lasting emergency eviction protection ordinances in the state of California.

The Healthy LA coalition then set to work to advance stronger emergency eviction protections for the other eighty-seven jurisdictions in the County of Los Angeles.[22] In the course of this advocacy, we uncovered an attorney general opinion that interpreted state law to allow counties to apply orders to incorporated cities when emergency conditions crossed municipal boundaries — a unique exception to the traditional limits of county jurisdiction.[23] Using this previously uncovered authority, the county adopted baseline eviction protections for the unincorporated areas and all eighty-eight cities in the county — covering over five million renters — without pre-empting cities' ability to adopt stronger local protections.

Average monthly eviction filings dropped by over 70 percent in the two years following the beginning of emergency measures, compared to the year before the emergency measures.[24] However, even with this impressive reduction in eviction filings, tens of thousands of tenants were evicted during this period. Although LA County adopted a stronger, more protective emergency eviction ordinance, this ordinance (and other state protections) continued to allow landlords to pursue legal actions to collect unpaid rent, often resulting in evictions, whether through official legal channels or through individual campaigns of retaliation, harassment, and intimidation of tenants who were desperately trying to financially recover from the effects of the pandemic.

Although a critical lifeline for thousands of families, the emergency eviction protections were only a stopgap. To address the quickly accumulating unpaid rent, which could become the basis of eviction and long-term economic hardship, tenant organizers and community-based organizations came together to demand that local officials take action to directly "cancel rent" obligations.[25] We reinforced this "cancel rent" demand by developing legal arguments in support of government's power to eliminate rent debt. However, as that proposal began to gain traction, the federal and state governments created the Emergency Rental Assistance Program (ERAP), which provided billions in public funds to create an assistance program for landlords and renters to resolve COVID rent debt. In California, the program paid landlords directly — or, if the landlord refused to participate in the program, the program would pay renters and require that the renter use the funds to pay their landlord. While this public investment in addressing rent debt was welcome news, the ERAP funnelled all the public dollars into a specific government assistance program. Ultimately, the program diverted money we envisioned for a more progressive rent cancellation policy, thus stalling organizing and policy efforts.

In response to ERAP, in the spring of 2021, we connected organizers with the Community Economic Development Clinic at UCLA Law School to help craft new policy responses and solutions to address

COVID rent debt, and the collateral consequences of rent debt such as evictions and harassment, within the constraints of the complicated ERAP legal landscape. The resulting platform of policies — the Debt Free Recovery Plan to Keep LA Housed — served as a critical framework to guide the advocacy of the newly formed collaborative — the Keep LA Housed (KLAH) coalition.[26]

As the pandemic raged on, KLAH became a formidable force, building power and influence through organizing, public pressure campaigns, and legal and policy arguments to prevent the erosion of tenant protections and demand housing justice for those most at risk of eviction and dislocation. The coalition continued to push for the elimination of COVID rent debt,[27] while securing vital extensions of emergency tenant protections at the city and county levels. In late 2022 and early 2023, as local governments began to make plans to phase out their emergency orders, KLAH demanded that the city and county not return to a broken status quo but rather replace emergency protections with a stronger foundation of permanent tenant protections that build on lessons learned from the pandemic. In support, we provided legal research and policy-drafting to help create and publish the LA County Tenant Bill of Rights (TBOR). Like the Debt Free Recovery Plan before it, the TBOR created the foundation for a multidimensional campaign that deployed organizing, mobilizing, communications, direct action, and targeted policy advocacy to secure important new legal protections.

Through KLAH's coordinated efforts, by February 2023, both the city and the county adopted multiple policies from the TBOR, providing greater housing stability for hundreds of thousands of low-income people across the region. Along with other legal-aid lawyers in the KLAH coalition, we drafted a legal memo and provided legal talking points to help secure city council adoption of a package of tenant protection reforms. As a result, landlords may no longer evict tenants for nonpayment of rent unless the tenant owes more than one month of "fair market rent."[28] The Universal Just Cause ordinance now protects nearly every renter household, limiting the grounds for eviction to only certain enumerated reasons. And tenants in non-rent-stabilized units who face large rent increases are now entitled to enhanced relocation assistance.[29] Altogether, this was the most significant expansion of tenant rights in the Los Angeles region in over forty years.

In each of these pivotal moments — the first eviction protection policies, the establishment of new rental assistance programs with federal funds, the recalibration of cancel-rent demands, and the emergence of a framework for stronger post-pandemic tenant protections — we remained accountable to grassroots organizing and movement strategy. The iterative and collaborative process of shaping movement goals into concrete legal and policy instruments helped focus movement strategy and provided the scaffolding to develop clear demands.

As lawyers in this work, we coordinated multiple legal tactics across multiple legal arenas with other lawyers and advocates. Early in 2020, we looked to tenants' and organizers' on-the-ground experiences to shape policy principles, enabling the Healthy LA coalition to collectively design, research, and draft specific legal instruments like policy platforms, memoranda, and white papers.[30] This participatory policy-drafting process was then coordinated with direct-advocacy tactics led by organizers and tenants that persuaded city and county staff to initiate the legislative process to adopt the recommendations. Our legal work to support the direct-action tactics included demystifying the public-hearing process, identifying legally required public-comment opportunities as strategic points of intervention, and working with organizers and residents to draft dozens of individual public comments that gave a full and persuasive narrative arc. Simultaneously, we provided communications support for direct actions, frequently reviewing and editing social-media graphics for legal accuracy, helping prepare scripts for virtual teach-ins and facilitating know-your-rights workshops focused on policy advocacy opportunities.

We also turned to litigation to defend our policy victories and reduce or eliminate the risk of eviction. First, in 2020 and 2021, we joined the city in defending against two federal lawsuits brought by the Apartment Association of Greater Los Angeles (AAGLA) and real estate developer Geoffrey Palmer, challenging the constitutionality of the city's emergency eviction protections.[31] We organized a legal team to intervene in the cases on behalf of tenant-rights groups, the Alliance of Californians for Community Empowerment (ACCE), Strategic Actions for a Just Economy (SAJE), and the Coalition for Economic Survival.[32] Our intervention in the cases focused the court's attention on tenant stories and expert analysis that illuminated the importance of the protections in strengthening public health and keeping people safely housed during the pandemic. Ultimately, the district court judge agreed with us in both cases, denying AAGLA's motion for preliminary injunction and dismissing Geoffrey Palmer's case, preserving hard-fought eviction protections in LA and bolstering other eviction protection ordinances against legal challenge across the state and country.[33]

On the offensive side, in May and June 2022, we filed two affirmative lawsuits on behalf of ACCE and SAJE against the State of California over its inadequate administration of the ERAP, which was denying tenants the full relief they were eligible for, violating their due process rights, and disproportionately discriminating against applicants of colour.[34] Through our lawsuit, we were able to obtain a preliminary injunction in July 2022 to halt further denials of applications, allowing tenants more time to obtain needed rent relief and protect against eviction.[35] We reached a settlement in the case in June 2023, which held the state accountable for its wrongful denials and improved the review process for applicants.[36] This outcome not only keeps many tenants in their homes, it also contributes to the growing momentum behind tenant-led organizing and agitation tactics to advance stronger housing policy.[37]

In coordinating these different legal tactics, we strategically engaged across several levels of government, often integrating analysis and advocacy around interlocking federal, state, and local programs. While fighting for strong local protections, we regularly participated in conversations with a collective of statewide housing justice advocates, lifting up experiences of LA tenants to shape responsive statewide demands. From a policy perspective, state-level advocacy efforts were unsuccessful, as the state legislature ended up adopting statewide policies that pre-empted stronger local protections against evictions for nonpayment of rent.[38] However, engaging in state-level policy discussions helped us develop a deeper understanding of the complicated federal and state legal frameworks that would govern local policies, which enabled us to help the KLAH coalition quickly reconfigure local policy demands into actionable proposals within the constraints of the new laws.

The coordination of multiple tactics at different levels of government has also meant operating simultaneously in multiple legal arenas. This has meant showing up (virtually or physically) in the courtroom, legislative chambers, and the streets — simultaneously operating both inside and outside of formal lawmaking spaces.[39] Cross-discipline collaboration within our organization has been crucial, as we rely on and learn from the eviction-defence and debt-relief legal services provided by other Public Counsel attorneys in order to integrate on-the-ground realities into policy demands.

We consider the legal strategy to be one tool in a vast toolkit to advance social justice,[40] and we try to fashion legal and policy tactics that not only change laws to improve conditions but also help redistribute power away from forces of extraction and exploitation and into the hands of tenants and unhoused community members. For example, while we called out the inadequacy of the rental assistance program, we also decided to seek incremental reform of this program. We did this, however, not just to mitigate the most serious shortcomings but also to build an advantage for future organizing and advocacy efforts. Specifically, we drafted and embedded within the rental assistance program an obligation of the city to collect and publicly report data on access to rental assistance by income, race, gender, age, disability, and neighbourhood. By establishing a new legal requirement for ongoing data analysis of rental assistance, we hoped to spark a flow of information to motivate future organizing and agitation to transcend the limitations of the current rental assistance framework.

We also worked to align temporary policies with widening tenant organizing across the region. For example, when our legal research uncovered the county's authority to extend uniform eviction protections across all the disparate incorporated cities, many tenants suddenly had meaningful eviction protections for the first time ever — conditions ripe for tenant-organizing and power-building. To harness this momentum, we created plain-language documents to break down and explain key tenant protection policies, delivered know-your-rights presentations and teach-ins, and drafted toolkits and model rent-control ordinances. This work is in service not only of greater awareness but also of the creation of new tenant unions and affiliated tenant advocacy organizations and of the widening of the broader tenant-rights movement in Southern California.

Ultimately, the law alone will not bring justice. Our experiences have reinforced a core tenet of movement lawyering — that the law and lawyer alone are incapable of completely dismantling unjust systems of oppression. Throughout the pandemic, we researched, drafted, and advocated for progressive legislation and developed litigation strategies to protect and enhance policy gains. And while this yielded some important wins and critical tenant protections, many righteous demands, like the demand to fully "cancel rent," continue to be rejected by state and local lawmakers. Much work remains to overcome a lack of political will that has continued to stand in the way of fully realizing the movement's vision for housing justice. Thus, the strategy to remake political conditions more favourable to tenants' rights and housing justice have to be accomplished not just through policy advocacy or litigation but also through organizing, narrative change, and electoral strategies.

Effective movement lawyering requires more than simply acknowledging this fact; we need to consistently guard against a legal-centric framing of issues and strategies. We were mindful of this fact but not always successful. As the legal framework for eviction protections and rental assistance became more complicated during the pandemic, it required lawyers to translate the information for organizers and tenants. This had the tendency to centre the lawyers in the work as the "experts." While we have been intentional about centring community expertise and not dictating demands, the work has nevertheless felt very lawyer-led at times.

A hallmark of our practice has been the coordinated deployment of multiple legal tactics in support of movement demands. While beneficial when used for justice, legal tools are mere building blocks that can be assembled and disassembled for different purposes.[41] As such, certain legal tactics we developed in service of movement goals have also been used by others to advance purposes deeply at odds with the housing justice movement. For example, our work to bring attention to the legal authority allowing the county to impose emergency regulations within the territory of cities had the important effect of expanding the reach of the county's eviction protections to cover millions of additional tenants. But weeks later, in response to racial justice uprisings spurred by the murder of George Floyd, county officials used this same authority to impose a countywide curfew — potentially facilitating the arrest of protestors and others in public areas.[42] Movement lawyers must continue to grapple with fundamental questions about the utility of existing legal tools in a project to transform unjust legal systems.

Further, moments of crisis magnify the tension between long-term systems change and immediate direct services, requiring greater reflection and coordination. As we poured our capacity and resources into supporting coalitions seeking broad policy protections, countless individuals needed immediate direct legal representation. Direct representation has not been CDP's lane historically, yet at times we felt helpless and unresponsive. What good is a systems-change analysis when a three-day eviction notice hangs on the door?

Reflecting on our work, we remain confident that legal support for movement-building is necessary, even in moments of intense need for immediate direct representation. But we now feel an even greater commitment to carefully coordinate different modes of lawyering. Our systems-change strategies should not obfuscate or diminish direct services, and direct services should not hinder organizing and power-building. Lawyers engaged at this intersection of movement-building and direct legal service must be mindful of the tensions and pitfalls in each mode. Direct legal services, often overwhelmed by needs that far exceed capacity to assist, can easily become isolated from collective action. Systems-change efforts, on the other hand, carry an inherent risk of being unresponsive to immediate needs, tone-deaf to the urgency of now.[43] We are inspired to improve alignment between direct services and systems change in the housing justice movement.[44] Yet, we recognize the near-impossibility of any one lawyer operating in both dimensions. Public-interest law firms should invest in both direct service and impact work but with intentional coordination at the organizational level to prevent siloing and to maximize a holistic approach that meets injustice at the point and the source of harm.

The last five years have tested our movement-lawyering model, reinforcing our accountability to movement leadership while unearthing areas for improvement and growth. In many ways, the pandemic has shone a spotlight on long-standing systemic failures, underscoring the need for community-led movements for broad systems change. However, the pandemic has also exposed a tension between long-term movement-building and immediate emergency response. Movement lawyering cannot operate apart from direct legal services, and we are eager to design and implement new strategies to align direct services and systems-change work in our organization and across the movement. A common refrain over the past three years has been "we're not going back" — a call to reject a return to the broken status quo. We are inspired to apply this principle to our lawyering model, evolving and adapting in service of a dynamic housing justice movement.

Notes

1. Based in Los Angeles, California, Public Counsel is a non-profit public interest law firm dedicated to advancing civil rights and racial and economic justice, as well as to amplifying the power of our clients through comprehensive legal advocacy. Founded on and strengthened by a pro bono legal service model, our staff and volunteers seek justice through direct legal services, promote healthy and resilient communities through education and outreach, and support community-led efforts to transform unjust systems through litigation and policy advocacy in and beyond Los Angeles. For more information about the Community Development Project, see https://publiccounsel.org/programs/community-development-project/.
2. See Joel F. Handler, Ellen Jane Hollingsworth, and Howard S. Erlanger, *Lawyers and the Pursuit of Legal Rights* (Academic Press, 1978), 22–29.
3. See Joel F. Handler, *Social Movements and the Legal System* (Academic Press, 1978).
4. Handler, *Social Movements*. See also Stuart Scheingold, *The Politics of Rights: Lawyers, Public Policy, and Political Change,* 2nd ed. (University of Michigan Press, 2010), 13–79 (describing a pervasive "myth of rights" that exaggerates the role of lawyers and litigation in social change).
5. See, for example, Richard Kluger, *Simple Justice: The History of Brown v. Board of Education and Black America's Struggle for Equality,* rev. ed. (Knopf, 2004).
6. See, Derrick A. Bell, Jr., "Serving Two Masters: Integration Ideals and Client Interest in School Desegregation Litigation," *Yale Law Journal* 85, 4 (1976).
7. Ann Southworth, "Lawyers and the 'Myth of Rights' in Civil Rights and Poverty Practice, *Boston University Public Interest Law Journal* 8 (1999).
8. Kimberlé Crenshaw, Neil Gotanda, Gary Peller, and Kendall Thomas, eds. *Critical Race Theory* (The New Press, 1996), xviii. See also Richard L. Abel, *Politics by Other Means: Law in the Struggle Against Apartheid, 1980–1994* (Routledge, 1995), 7–21.
9. Scott L. Cummings and Ingrid V. Eagly, "A Critical Reflection on Law and Organizing," *UCLA Law Review* 48, 3 (2001).
10. Crenshaw et al., *Critical Race Theory*, xiii–xxxii. The editors write, "In short, we intend to evoke a particular atmosphere in which progressive scholars of colour struggled to piece together an intellectual identity and a political practice that would take the form both of a left intervention into race discourse and race intervention into left discourse" (xix).
11. Foundational works include Gerald Lopez's *Rebellious Lawyering: One Chicano's Vision of Progressive Law Practice* (Westview Press, 1992), describing how lawyers representing poor communities minimized and undermined community leadership and knowledge, and offering an alternative nonhierarchical model of collaboration between lawyers and communities to contest systemic injustices; and Lucie E. White, "To Learn and Teach," *Wisconsin Law Review* (September–October 1988), describing a "third dimensional" image of lawyering that draws on Paulo Freire's work and is rooted in a collaborative and deliberative process of cogenerating strategies to confront oppression (767). White writes, "Such a practice must seek guidance from the participants' own conversations — their shared deliberations on what they have lived through and how they might now act together — rather than from codes or rules" (768).

12   Scott L. Cummings, "Movement Lawyering," *University of Illinois Law Review* 5 (2017): 1648. Within this broader study of law and social movements, a subdiscipline of "law and organizing" positions the lawyer as a key player in social movements, but subordinate and accountable to grassroots organizing. Foundational law and organizing scholarship presents models of lawyering that prioritize community education, link the provision of direct legal services to participation in organizing activities and provide cautionary guidance against lawyer domination. See Jennifer Gordon, "We Make the Road by Walking: Immigrant Workers, the Workplace Project, and the Struggle for Social Change," *Harvard Civil Rights-Civil Liberties Law Review* 30 (1995); Betty Hung, "Law and Organising from the Perspective of Organizers: Finding a Shared Theory of Social Change," *Los Angeles Public Interest Law Journal* 1 (2008); William P. Quigley, "Reflections of Community Organizers: Lawyering for Empowerment of Community Organizations," *Ohio Northern University Law Review* 21 (1994).

13   There are tensions in the movement lawyering model. For example, the risk of lawyer domination and client coercion, role confusion and legal ethics considerations all arise when putting the movement lawyering theory into practice. See Cummings and Eagly, "Critical Reflection," 479–516. We do not shy away from these and other tensions. In describing "tensions as inevitable and even valuable, a source of insight," Jennifer Gordon affirms that "[conflicts] are part of the work and even sometimes a productive part of the work, and we will do our best to understand and address them and learn from them." Jennifer Gordon, "The Lawyer Is Not the Protagonist: Community Campaigns, Law, and Social Change," *California Law Review* 95, 5 (2007). Our goal for this chapter is to embrace and explore tensions and challenges in movement lawyering during this unprecedented moment, so that progressive lawyering can continue to improve and evolve.

14   Cummings, "Movement Lawyering," 1690. We are also inspired by Betty Hung's description of movement lawyering practice. See, Betty Hung, "Movement Lawyering as Rebellious Lawyering: Advocating with Humility, Love and Courage," *Clinical Law Review* 23 (2017).

15   See Scott L. Cummings and Doug Smith, "Policy by the People, for the People: Designing Responsive Regulation and Building Democratic Power," Fordham Law Review 90 (2022). See also K. Sabeel Rahman, "Policymaking as Power-Building." *Southern California Interdisciplinary Law Journal* 27 (2017–2018).

16   Public Counsel and the UCLA School of Law Community Economic Development Clinic, *Priced Out, Pushed Out, Locked Out: How Permanent Tenant Protections Can Help Communities Prevent Displacement and Resist Displacement in Los Angeles County*, June 2019, publiccounsel.org/issues/community-development/affordable-supportive-housing/publications.

17   See, for example, Measure JJJ, Affordable Housing and Labor Standards Related to City Planning Ordinance, Los Angeles (2016).

18   UNIDAD, "The People's Plan," 2016, unidad-la.org/peoplesplan; *Central City United People's Plan,* centralcityunited.org/about-1.

19   Andrew Khouri, "L.A. County Rent Control and Eviction Rules Advance for Unincorporated Areas," *Los Angeles Times,* September 10, 2019, latimes.com/business/story/2019-09-10/la-county-supes-to-vote-on-permanent-rent-control-for-unincorporated-areas.

20. Emily Alpert Reyes, "LA Will Eliminate 'Veto' Provision for Homeless and Affordable Housing to Keep State Funding," *Los Angeles Times,* October 16, 2018, latimes.com/local/lanow/la-me-ln-homeless-letter-20181017-story.html.
21. Emily Alpert Reyes, "LA Council Members Balk at Broader Ban on Evictions Amid Coronavirus, Citing Legal Worries," *Los Angeles Times,* April 22, 2020, latimes.com/california/story/2020-04-22/la-city-council-balks-at-broader-ban-on-evictions-amid-coronavirus.
22. Los Angeles County comprises eighty-eight incorporated cities, which includes the City of Los Angeles and unincorporated areas.
23. 62 Ops. Cal. Atty. Gen. 701 (Cal.A.G.), 1979 WL 29299. The Attorney General opinion interpreted the California Emergency Service Act to authorize counties across the state to enact emergency regulations in incorporated jurisdictions when emergency conditions extend across municipal boundaries.
24. Eviction filing data from the Los Angeles Superior Court collected and maintained by Kyle Nelson.
25. Healthy LA, "Cancel Rent! Cancel Mortgages!" 2022, healthyla.org.
26. Keep LA Housed, "LA County Tenant Bill of Rights," 2022, keeplahoused.org/la-tbor.
27. Because local officials failed to take action to directly cancel rent debt, advocates proposed using the express power of eminent domain to acquire rent debt from landlords and pay them the fair market value of debt. Advocates successfully persuaded the county to agree to study the feasibility of this proposal, see motion by Hilda L. Solis, County Acquisition of Low-Income Residential Tenant Rental Debt, June 8, 2021, file.lacounty.gov/SDSInter/bos/supdocs/158957.pdf.
28. City of Los Angeles, Ordinance number 187763. This is a remarkable innovation in tenant protection policy and the strongest policy of its kind in the country. "Fair Market Rent" is a standard set by the federal Housing and Urban Development agency as a benchmark for reasonable rents for a variety of housing programs. In 2025, Fair Market Rent for a two-bedroom apartment in Los Angeles County was $2,625 per month. HUD Office of Policy Development and Research, "Fair Market Rents (40th Percentile Rents)," https://www.huduser.gov/portal/datasets/fmr.html.
29. City of Los Angeles, Ordinance number 187737.
30. The work of actually drafting the policy recommendations ended up being mostly lawyer-led, though some non-legal partners with policy-team capacity, such as SAJE, provided significant support. In all policy-development meetings, CDP lawyers sought to ensure active engagement by organizers and tenants, to share their lived experiences. However, because lawyers were often most in the weeds on policy details, lawyers did end up playing a prominent role in those meetings, a fact that CDP lawyers were highly sensitive to but did not have an elegant solution for at the time.
31. Liam Dillon, "Landlord Group Sues City of L.A. Over Coronavirus Anti-Eviction Protections," *Los Angeles Times,* June 11, 2020, latimes.com/homeless-housing/story/2020-06-11/landlord-group-sues-city-of-la-over-eviction-protections; David Zahniser, "Landlord Sued L.A. for $100 Million, Saying Anti-Eviction Law Caused 'Astronomical' Losses," *Los Angeles Times,* August 9, 2021, latimes.com/california/story/2021-08-09/apartment-building-owner-geoffrey-palmer-sues-los-angeles-saying-anti-eviction-law-caused-astronomical-losses.

32 Western Center on Law & Poverty, "Tenants Seek to Join Federal Lawsuit to Defend City of Los Angeles' COVID-19 Tenant Protections," Press Release, July 2, 2020, wclp.org/press-release-tenants-seek-to-join-federal-lawsuit-to-defend-city-of-los-angeless-COVID-19-tenant-protections; Public Counsel, "Thousands of Tenants Seek to Intervene in Real Estate Mogul's Lawsuit Challenging LA Eviction Moratorium," Press Release, October 26, 2021, publiccounsel.org/press-releases/thousands-of-tenants-seek-to-intervene-in-real-estate-moguls-lawsuit-challenging-la-eviction-moratorium; David Wagner, "Housing Groups Join Lawsuit to Defend LA's Eviction Moratorium from Billionaire Developer's Challenge," LAist, November 24, 2021, laist.com/news/housing-homelessness/eviction-moratorium-los-angeles-city-lawsuit-geoffrey-palmer-trump-donor-housing-rent-relief.

33 Apartment Association of Los Angeles County Inc. v. City of Los Angeles, 500 F. Supp. 3d 1088, 1103 (C.D. Cal. 2020), aff'd, 10 F.4th 905 (9th Cir. 2021), cert. denied, 142 S. Ct. 1699 (2022).

34 Western Center on Law & Poverty, "Tenants-Rights Groups Sue CA for Failing to Provide Rental Assistance to Eligible Tenants," Press Release, May 4, 2022, wclp.org/press-release-tenants-rights-groups-sue-ca-for-failing-to-provide-rental-assistance-to-eligible-tenants; Western Center on Law & Poverty, "Lawsuit Filed Against CA HCD for Violating Due Process Rights in Emergency Rental Assistance Program," Press Release, June 6, 2022, wclp.org/press-release-lawsuit-filed-against-ca-hcd-for-violating-due-process-rights-in-emergency-rental-assistance-program/.

35 Western Center on Law & Poverty, "Judge Orders CA Dept of Housing & Community Development To Stop Denying State Rental Assistance Applications Until Further Review," Press Release, July 8, 2022, wclp.org/press-release-judge-orders-ca-dept-of-housing-community-development-to-stop-denying-state-rental-assistance-applications-until-further-review/.

36 Public Counsel, "Tenants' Rights Advocates Reach Landmark Settlement on Behalf of Californians Struggling with Pandemic Rent Debt," Press Release, June 5, 2023, publiccounsel.org/ca-rent-relief.

37 See Eloise Lawrence, "When We Fight, We Win: Eviction Defense as Subversive Lawyering," Fordham Law Review 90, 5 (2022), describing tenant litigation strategies and organizing using the sword-and-shield metaphor, where lawyers "provide the 'shield' (i.e., legal defence), while the organizers and members of grassroots housing justice organizations provide the 'sword' (i.e., public pressure and protest)" (2126).

38 See Hung, "Movement Lawyering."

39 Cummings, "Movement Lawyering," 1648.

40 See Hung, "Movement Lawyering."

41 See Cummings and Smith, "Policy by the People," 2052–54.

42 Supervisor Barger, Ratifying Proclamation of Local Emergency and Executive Order for a Curfew Due to Civil Unrest, June 2, 2020, file.lacounty.gov/SDSInter/bos/supdocs/146291.pdf. Similarly, when advocates proposed that the county use its eminent-domain authority to seize rent debt and pay landlords fair market value using rental assistance funds, it was in the shadow of a long history where eminent domain was used for public-works projects that displaced low-income residents and divided low-income communities and communities of colour. See, for example, Brief for National Association for the Advancement of Colored People et al. as Amici Curiae Supporting Petitioners at 7, in Kelo v.

43 Paul Tremblay presents a "deferral thesis," arguing that "rebellious lawyering constitutes a justifiable, justice-based allocation of resources away from clients' short-term needs and in favor of a community's long-term needs." Paul Tremblay, "Theoretics of Practice: The Integration of Progressive Thought and Action: Rebellious Lawyering, Regnant Lawyering, and Street-Level Bureaucracy," *Hastings Law Journal* 43 (1992): 950.

44 Jennifer Gordon's groundbreaking study of the Workplace Project provides an important starting point for this conversation. See Gordon, "We Make the Road," 437, 446, describing the conflict between individual legal representation and collective action, and offering a model that intentionally integrates direct legal services into organizing strategies and leadership development.

HOUSING JUSTICE IN THE BLUEGRASS STATE

LEXINGTON, KENTUCKY, UNITED STATES

WRITTEN BY
Lukas Bullock

Kentucky has long been considered a conservative state, evidenced by the fact that Donald Trump won 62 percent of the popular vote here in 2020 and 64 percent in 2024, but this is not to say that there is little room for local activism on tenant issues. While Kentucky may seem a surprising location, an emerging housing justice movement in this state has become central to the fight for a better future. The housing justice movement in Kentucky is forwarding anti-racist, anti-capitalist, and pro-social values that seek to bridge the struggles between urban and rural tenants, while pressuring lawmakers to be more attentive to the long-neglected struggle of tenants. Networks of solidarity between urban and rural tenants are pursuing a fight against an exploitative housing system. The movement has achieved several milestones and has made a noticeable impact on local and state politics. Importantly, the tireless work of housing justice organizers has begun to shift political discourse and narratives in new, more radical directions that signal hope for a brighter future for tenants in this state.

I have spent a significant portion of my life in Lexington and attended the University of Kentucky, where I was involved in student activism related to racial justice, environmental justice, and LGBTQ+ rights. My negative personal experiences as a tenant, including living without heat in the middle of winter, fuelled me to talk with other tenants about ways to protest against a system that does not hold absentee landlords accountable. These conversations with fellow renters led to the formation of the Lexington Housing Justice Collective (LHJC), where I have been an active organizer since 2019. In offering this personal reflection, I acknowledge that this work has been a collective effort. Consequently, this chapter includes the words of fellow housing activists in Kentucky. I balance their insights with my own perspective and analysis. I also want to make it clear that this is not an exhaustive overview of the housing justice work that has occurred in Kentucky and that there are several unmentioned organizations, actions, and people here who are doing important work.

As the COVID-19 pandemic hit the United States, LHJC was just emerging from our first concrete action as a young organization. In January 2020, we successfully organized with fifty tenants facing eviction from a sober living facility that was undergoing bankruptcy. We helped ensure that the City of Lexington provided case-work assistance to aid residents in finding alternative living accommodations.[1] With this recent success, LHJC reacted quickly as COVID began to shift our world. We believed in sustaining a localized response that aimed to address gaps in the local government's approach to remedying the economic fallout related to the pandemic. One important harm reduction action that we undertook was monitoring and at times disrupting eviction-court hearings as they transitioned to virtual platforms such as Zoom. We noticed that there was no available data on evictions occurring locally during the pandemic and that tenants were not being informed of basic facts, most crucially that court hearings had moved to virtual platforms; as a consequence, tenants would show up to an empty courtroom while their eviction was finalized in an online hearing without their presence. LHJC informed the city of this problem and later pressured the court into providing tenants with eviction notices that included web links for online court hearings.[2]

Several important themes emerged from our monitoring efforts in local eviction-court hearings. Constance Brown, one of the activists who monitored eviction court, notes:

> Most landlords showed up with lawyers, while most tenants showed up without representation. Large dockets didn't allow for tenants to fully express their side of the story and plead their cases. If a tenant missed their court appearance, even

by five minutes, an eviction order was issued by default. This continued as eviction court moved online to take place over Zoom, while COVID-19 cases continued to rise in Lexington. Many tenants cited code violations, financial exploitation, and harassment from their landlords being met with little to absolutely no accountability when they sought help.[3]

LHJC organizers also found that judges varied significantly in the way they interacted with tenants. One judge in particular, Bruce Bell, was especially unsympathetic in his judgments against tenants during the pandemic. Inspired by the tenant rights organization Kansas City Tenants, who had started staging court disruptions, LHJC decided to disrupt Judge Bell's Zoom courtroom. On December 21, 2020, more than twenty-five protestors joined using the publicly available Zoom link and, when Judge Bell attempted to proceed with an eviction hearing, they read out a script that stated that every eviction is an act of violence. The court was delayed this way for over an hour.[4]

Beau Revlett, one of the co-organizers of the action, explained:

> The best direct actions bring the crisis to its creator. They directly disrupt the mechanisms of our oppression. We gummed up the gears of the eviction machine, and it was directly effective, even if just for a few minutes, at delaying the loss of homes, and it showed the people being evicted, alone facing the power of the state, the courts and their landlord, that they were not alone. We showed that tenants together can wield power.[5]

Speaking about why eviction court was such an important site for resistance, Revlett said:

> We corrected the public narrative on evictions during the pandemic. The city and the local media wanted to claim that evictions were not happening … really nobody was paying attention. We were the only people aside from the tenants, landlords, lawyers, and judges who knew what was happening inside the courtroom. We made sure the rest of the community knew too. This increased pressure on the city to improve protections for tenants.[6]

While the action was small in scale, our efforts did pressure the City of Lexington into action. Almost immediately following the disruption, eviction court summons were changed to include information on resources such as legal aid and rental assistance. Within months, the city had hired outreach workers who would contact people facing evictions to offer them resources face to face. By 2023, as we continued to pressure the city to implement measures to prevent evictions, a right-to-counsel pilot program was funded which ensured that legal counsel was provided to tenants facing eviction, leading to fewer evictions and more cases being settled through mediation. Our goal is for the pilot program to be expanded and permanently funded.

Another instance of disruptive direct action that we engaged in was targeting the residential home of Lexington mayor Linda Gorton in early 2021. With thousands of evictions occurring in Lexington, organized tenants knew that the mayor had the power to ensure greater protections for renters, and members of tenants' movements decided to confront her with the fact that she was not using the tools at her disposal. We formed a caravan of over fifty vehicles that circled her home, honking and chanting as we passed by for nearly an hour. This protest was especially noteworthy in Lexington, where politicians are seldom held to public scrutiny and direct confrontations with marginalized constituents. Disruptive actions such as these were instrumental in politicizing housing issues locally and in making local politicians take the demands of tenants seriously.

After decades of housing policy being largely depoliticized in Lexington, suddenly local officials couldn't maintain the status quo without expecting pressure and resistance from tenant organizations like LHJC. Local city council members started to reach out and engage in dialogue, local city institutions such as the Homelessness Intervention and Prevention Board began to advocate on behalf of our policy proposals, and we began to notice how discourse on housing and eviction began to shift, simply because tenants' rights groups were willing to publicly name, shame, and disrupt the figures and mechanisms of local governance that were complicit in disenfranchising tenants. Within a year of the caravan action, a tenant commission was created to advise local government institutions on housing policy. Of the fifteen members of the commission, LHJC was allowed to recommend eleven tenants, which we viewed as an acknowledgement of the efforts we had engaged in to move city leaders to improve conditions for tenants.

LHJC also raised the issue of gentrification with local lawmakers in response to racial justice protests that were occurring during the summer of 2020. We recognized that the crises of systemic racism and systemic evictions during COVID-19 went hand in hand. As the city set up a racial justice commission to investigate ways that Lexington could minimize racial disparities, LHJC ramped up efforts to address expanding gentrification and the resulting displacement of poor tenants and tenants of colour. We were disappointed to find that the racial justice commission was mostly composed of white real-estate investors whose capital interests in maintaining gentrifying dynamics far outweighed their interest in moving towards transformative forms of racial justice. While monitoring committee meetings, we created and distributed a survey asking residents about their experiences with gentrification. The majority of the several hundred tenants surveyed by LHJC said they faced financial difficulties related to being priced out of their neighbourhoods in addition to COVID-19-related economic hardship.[7] We sent the survey results to the committee, and they invited public comment from impacted tenants at all subsequent meetings. Unsurprisingly, no significant recommendations were made by members of city council to address the concerns of impacted tenants. While it was important for LHJC to make visible the perspectives of tenants affected by gentrification, we realized that much more organizing work was needed before we could effectively contest city officials who enabled gentrification.

Rural tenant activism also made a significant impact in Kentucky during the COVID-19 pandemic. One organization that gained attention was Justice 4 North Fork, a group of tenants who began organizing after they got evicted from their mobile home park in Morehead to make way for a shopping centre. The activism of Justice 4 North Fork exposed the unique issues that rural tenants face and the lack of resources available to those outside of urban spaces. North Fork mobile home park was home to more than a hundred people and one of the few affordable places left to live in Morehead. Many of the residents owned their mobile home and rented a plot of land in the park. In spring 2021, as the pandemic was still in full force, residents learned that they would be evicted and displaced by a strip mall that was scheduled to be built by a prominent Lexington real-estate developer named Patrick Madden. Notably, North Fork was already surrounded by three other shopping centres, many of which had empty storefronts. Despite this, the City of Morehead agreed to provide millions in tax breaks to Madden if he built the shopping mall directly on the footprint of North Fork, and no consultation with the residents was ever held by their landlord, Madden, or the city.[8] The local government institutions that were supposed to protect the tenants of North Fork were instead complicit in their displacement.

Several structural issues are magnified in rural spaces, making tenants especially vulnerable to eviction. On the one hand, lower wages and higher energy, health, and transportation costs, along with the lack of new rental unit development, often makes it difficult for rural tenants to find affordable options and more likely that they will settle for substandard housing. When facing eviction, rural tenants have access to fewer resources and safety nets (however deficient they may be in practice). This means that when evictions occur, rural tenants have little to no recourse. In rural communities across Kentucky, these structural factors are complicit in keeping people in cycles of poverty. Despite this, housing justice movements often fail to account for and organize alongside rural tenants. As Faith Plank, one of the North Fork residents, summarizes:

> Housing justice movements have always been focused on more urban populations historically. It's important to remember that these issues are not unique to cities but are prevalent everywhere. Rural spaces are often left out of housing movements because people aren't aware that they can work together to change their collective position.[9]

Once the planned sale of North Fork was official, residents sprang into action to defend their homes. They wanted to stop the eviction, but if they couldn't avoid displacement, they wanted to secure compensation and be allowed more time to relocate. They collectivized their concerns and began thinking of ways to talk with their landlord, the city, and even Madden himself, in the hopes that it could lead to a less harmful outcome. They were met with apathy, disrespect, and dismissiveness for their legitimate concerns regarding the lack of transparency surrounding their eviction and the lack of compensation being offered for their displacement. Because their eviction was not related to rent payments, they were not covered by the federal moratorium on evictions in place at that time, which demonstrates how loopholes in moratorium policies at both federal and local levels led to many tenants being evicted during the pandemic. Tenants organized rallies and disrupted city meetings in Morehead, demanding a response and an explanation from city officials for approving the tax incentives that enabled the development at their expense.[10] The *New York Times* covered their struggle as well.[11] Residents even filed a lawsuit against the City of Morehead, attempting to block the tax incentives which formed the foundation for the eviction, but the lawsuit was dismissed,[12] repeating a familiar pattern of state complicity in mass evictions that occurred during the pandemic. Despite these setbacks, the community came closer together, and residents leaned on one another in a moment when many of them were losing everything. Plank explained:

> When you're organizing to protect your home it becomes so personal, and all the weight you would've carried alone is taken off your back and shared with your neighbours. Standing with your community is a value I believe everyone should have; it feels extra magical when you're helping your neighbours in the process."[13]

LHJC provided logistical support and aid to Justice 4 North Fork during their campaign, which deepened the ties between urban and rural tenant organizations in Kentucky during the COVID-19 pandemic.

Despite their fight, the North Fork residents were ultimately evicted. However, residents were able to secure much more time to gather their belongings and to find alternative housing. They obtained a small amount of financial compensation for relocation assistance, and all but one of the residents were able to avoid an eviction filing on their record. These concessions would not have occurred had the residents not organized and publicly protested their eviction. In March 2022, residents left the park, and the place where countless memories were created is now occupied by a gas station, a McDonalds, and several other chain restaurants. Meanwhile, former residents are struggling to pay the rent in their new homes, which in many cases is at least three times higher per month than what they were paying at North Fork.[14] What happened at North Fork is not an isolated incident, and similar evictions happened in mobile home parks across America during the pandemic. In Kentucky, where 12 percent of the total population and 20 percent of the rural population lives in a mobile home, cases like North Fork expose the severe lack of protections for rural tenants, who could lose everything based on the whims of real estate developers, landlords, and complicit rural governments. What happened at North Fork is the result of a system designed to exploit the most vulnerable. For Plank, the experience strengthened her resolve to ensure that no more Kentuckians need to face eviction like she did: "I plan to continue building deep relationships with renters in Kentucky and fight for safe, affordable, and high-quality housing for all."[15]

Housing justice organizing has shaped the political landscape in Kentucky since 2019. Housing affordability, tenants' rights, and displacement, previously deprioritized, are now important topics in Kentucky's politics. In mayoral and council elections across the state, candidates have started to address the housing crisis as part of their campaign platforms, and we have begun to put tenants in conversation with elected leaders to start a long-overdue conversation about the changes that tenants are demanding on local and state levels. We also know that we must continue to build tenant power outside of the electoral system and to grow grassroots networks of activists statewide. While LHJC has made important contributions to advancing housing justice in Kentucky, throughout our duration as an organization we have been run by a small group of passionate tenants. We had hoped to evolve into an organization that included a larger base of tenants that would guide and lead our work, but COVID complicated our efforts, and many tenants were unable to participate due to economic stressors and fear of retaliation from their landlords.

Looking to the future, housing activists are becoming more proactive in strategizing a path forward. During the pandemic we were mostly reacting to the inaction of government officials, but we are now taking the lessons we learned and using them to drive demands for fundamental and radical change. We recognize that our activism must win changes that will create more safety nets that will protect tenants from the cycles of precarity that impact tenants across urban and rural contexts. Across the state, tenant unions are springing up in both urban and rural communities, dedicated to base-building and localizing their activism. One key project that has been central to our organizing has been the Kentucky Tenant Listening Project, which has engaged thousands of tenants across the state regarding their perspectives on housing affordability. In this effort, which has been ongoing since August 2021, over five thousand Kentuckians have been surveyed and hundreds of follow-up calls made. To my knowledge, this tenant outreach survey is the first such effort ever to be undertaken in the state, and the preliminary results strongly indicate that many Kentuckians find housing unaffordable and that tenants need more protections at local, state, and federal levels. As we move forward, we aim to continue utilizing projects such as these to expand and inform our work and to connect tenants with movements that work to transform the way housing structures our communities. Our vision and messaging that housing is a human right will remain consistent, and we seek to build on our organizing foundations to achieve our goal of securing safe and affordable housing for all Kentuckians.

Notes

1. Beth Musgrave, "They Were Promised Housing and Drug Treatment. Now They Are Facing Eviction," *Herald Leader,* February 14, 2020, kentucky.com/news/local/counties/fayette-county/article240240966.html.
2. Lexington Housing Justice Collective, "Can't Zoom In? Evicted!" November 10, 2020, lexingtonhousingjusticecollective.org/2020/11/10/november-10-2020.
3. Constance Brown, interview with the author, March 22, 2022.
4. Lexington Housing Justice Collective, "Housing Advocates Disrupt Eviction Court amid Banner Drop," December 21, 2020, lexingtonhousingjusticecollective.org/2020/12/21/december-21-2020.
5. Beau Revlett, interview with the author, March 9, 2022.
6. Revlett, interview.
7. Lexington Housing Justice Collective, "Eviction Data Show Limits of Rental Assistance," February 21, 2021, lexingtonhousingjusticecollective.org/2021/02/24/eviction-data-show-limits-of-rental-assistance.
8. Linda Blackford, "'It's Disgusting.' KY Tax Incentive Used to Evict Mobile Home Park for Shopping Center," *Herald Leader,* April 13, 2021, kentucky.com/opinion/op-ed/article250613164.html.
9. Faith Plank, interview with the author, March 18, 2022.
10. Shelby Lofton, "Rowan County's 'Justice 4 North Fork' Group Rallying to Stop Evictions," *WKYT,* April 20, 2021, wkyt.com/2021/04/20/rowan-countys-justice-4-north-fork-group-rallying-to-stop-evictions.
11. Campbell Robertson, "The Evictions Surprised Trailer Park Residents. The Protest Stunned Officials," *New York Times,* May 20, 2021, nytimes.com/2021/05/20/us/kentucky-trailer-park-protest.html.
12. Bailey Loosemore, "Officials Accused of Breaking State Law When They Displaced Mobile Home Residents," *Courier-Journal,* June 17, 2021, courier-journal.com/story/news/local/2021/06/17/morehead-residents-sue-city-over-mobile-home-park-displacement/7728057002; Chad Hedrick, "Judge Dismisses Lawsuit Filed by Group Displaced from Rowan County Mobile Home Park," *WSAZ,* November 2, 2021, wsaz.com/2021/11/02/judge-dismisses-lawsuit-filed-by-group-displaced-rowan-county-mobile-home-park.
13. Plank, interview.

14 Katie Myers and Liam Niemeyer, "Evictions at a Kentucky Trailer Park Highlight Appalachia's Lack of Affordable Housing," *100 Days in Appalachia,* June 9, 2021, 100daysinappalachia.com/2021/06/evictions-at-a-kentucky-trailer-park-highlight-appalachias-lack-of-affordable-housing/#:~:text=Mobile%20Home%20Challenges.

15 Plank, interview.

ENVISIONING COLLECTIVE BARGAINING RIGHTS FOR RENTERS

VANCOUVER AND VICTORIA, BRITISH COLUMBIA, CANADA

WRITTEN BY
Pierce Nettling, Rebecca Kantwerg, Anna Gabriela Doebeli, Ben Ger, Ryan Hong, Alex J. Kiczales & Alex McLean

People living in so-called British Columbia (BC) live in a housing crisis marked by evictions and ever-increasing rents. From the 2010 Vancouver Olympics to COVID-19, evictions have run rampant, displacing working-class people across the province while wealthier residents take over our cities. Average rents in Vancouver, unceded Musqueam, Squamish, and Tsleil-Waututh territories, and Victoria, unceded Lekwungen territories, increased by 20 percent from September 2021 to March 2022,[1] with Vancouver having the highest rents of any large Canadian city.[2] BC also has the highest eviction rate in Canada, with over 10 percent of renters evicted between 2013 and 2018, and 10.5% of renters being evicted between 2016 to 2021 with immigrant renters experiencing the highest rates of eviction.[3]

This ongoing eviction and affordability crisis in BC must be understood in the context of the capitalist system of settler-colonialism. In BC, the state, developers, and corporate landlords rely on the commodification of property for profit, legitimacy, and power. Real estate is, and has always been, central to BC's economy and colonial existence. Selling land was a key strategy of colonization that justified the theft of Indigenous land and the establishment of BC as a province in the mid- to late 1800s.[4]

Today, real estate and private property interests continue to have significant influence at all levels of government in BC, from guiding policy at the provincial level to supporting the election of municipal government officials. Landlords in BC are well organized and represented by LandlordBC, an association that advocates for the interests of landlords.

Tenants typically do not have the same access to the ear of government. Though tenants have led political campaigns and movements since the 1960s, their demands for social housing and vacancy control have been subordinated to the interests of landlords and developers, who see such measures as a threat to their profit and power. Starting in 1973, tenant associations requested that the BC Law Reform Commission considering the status of landlord and tenant law recommend legislation to facilitate tenant collective bargaining. Opposed by landlords and real estate interests, this effort was rejected.[5] In 2018, tenants asked the BC government's Rental Housing Task Force to recommend vacancy control, but the government declined, parroting the landlords' position that vacancy control would prevent developers from building housing.[6]

Rent Strike Bargain (RSB) — a campaign led by a grassroots group of tenant activists — emerged in 2020 with an idea to enable debates about housing policy to be led by renters, not politicians, specifically at the bargaining table. Inspired by the history of labour organizing in BC, RSB envisioned a means of empowering tenants to have influence over their housing conditions through collective organizing, demands, and actions.

Our chapter outlines RSB's strategic approach to building tenant power for housing justice as a province-wide campaign. Learning from failed pre-COVID organizing strategies, we contend that organizers cannot rely on elections or government lobbying to protect and expand tenant rights. Instead, we learned from the labour movement and suggest that establishing new tenant unions to collectively bargain for tenants is the best path towards a housing system that recognizes housing as a human right.

Tenancy agreements presuppose that landlords and tenants can both freely negotiate terms and decide on whether to enter into a rental contract. The problem is that landlords have much more power than tenants. "Free negotiations" cannot take place when one side, the landlord who owns housing that the tenant needs to survive, can simply walk away. A similar, inherent imbalance exists in the employer-employee relationship. In the labour context, meaningful negotiation is achieved by workers joining together, armed with the power to collectively withdraw their labour, to bargain collective terms of employment. The collective action is what empowers and balances the inequality in bargaining power. In the tenancy context, where a similar (if not even worse) imbalance in negotiating power exists, the lack of protection for tenants who wish to join together and bargain collective terms of housing means that meaningful negotiation is rare (if ever at all).[7]

RSB seeks to address this inherent tenant-landlord power imbalance by promoting organizing, tenant unionism, and collective bargaining. Our work builds upon tenant demands from the 1970s and 1980s, when renters organized in cities and towns across BC. These efforts led to the formation of the BC Tenants Organization and were successful in persuading the BC New Democratic Party (NDP) — the nominally leftwing provincial political party — to adopt collective bargaining rights for renters as a pillar of their 1972 campaign platform.[8] However, once in power, the BC NDP failed to act on that commitment, illustrating the problem of relying on elected parties to secure material gains.

Labour unions provide an example of how recognition of the union can help correct power imbalances. Like in many places, BC's labour unions operated and pushed for recognition through collective action like strikes in the late 1800s to early 1900s,[9] during a time when strikes were illegal and there was no requirement that unions be recognized.[10] It took over a century of collective action by labour unions before the right to meaningful collective bargaining was affirmed as constitutionally guaranteed in the Supreme Court of Canada's Health Services decision in 2007,[11] falling under the Charter right to freedom of association.[12] In Canada and internationally, collective bargaining has been instrumental in securing higher wages and better benefits for workers and has reduced economic inequality,[13] despite the fact that, in Canada at least, state-mandated processes of collective bargaining were introduced with the purpose of controlling and limiting the effect of collective power by strictly limiting how and when workers could collectively bargain and even what terms they could bargain for.[14,15]

RSB's notion of collective bargaining is much broader and not tied to any legal system of regulation. We define collective bargaining, and the collective bargaining process, as including collective negotiation of terms and conditions of tenancy but also as any collective action taken for the purpose of achieving those terms and conditions. Collective bargaining, in order to have any meaning, must include the right to organize and strike. Without tenants' ability to collectively withdraw rent, landlords will either not come to the table or will not meaningfully negotiate once there.

There are legal sources that tenants can use to their advantage as they advance collective bargaining, even if tenant bargaining law isn't yet formalized. The Canadian Charter of Rights and Freedoms (1982) and the United Nations recognize adequate housing as a fundamental human right. We have identified four key legal principles that should be recognized by law and put into provincial and federal practice: 1) the right for tenants to organize; 2) a requirement for landlords to negotiate with tenant unions in good faith; 3) the right to withhold rent (rent strike); and 4) protection against landlord non-compliance or interference, with effective enforcement.

Tenant collective bargaining is already happening across North America, though mostly without state recognition. In places like San Francisco and Washington, DC, tenants have succeeded in confirming legal rights to organize, though the government's interventions are not wholesale endorsements. While DC's Right of Tenants to Organize Act prohibits landlords from interfering with tenant organizing, it does not mandate that landlords respect a collective bargaining process, nor the right to withhold rent.[16] On the other hand, the San Francisco protection adopted in 2022 mandates that landlords meet annually with tenants and bargain in good faith or face monetary penalties.[17] Months before San Francisco tenants achieved this protection, RSB asked the BC government for a similar process; it refused to implement anything. A meaningful model for collective bargaining for tenants must protect organizing, require landlords to meet with tenants to bargain in good faith, and secure protection for tenants during rent strikes. These rights should be standard for tenants in BC and across North America.

Prior to RSB's formation in 2020, some of RSB's organizers were engaged in conversations around fighting for rent-debt forgiveness to reduce evictions and for province-wide rent control tied to the unit rather than the tenancy — known as vacancy control.[18] When the BC government decided against introducing vacancy control, organizers started a campaign that adapts tactics from the labour movement. The idea is to organize and establish new tenant unions, with the purpose of collectively bargaining tenancy rights and conditions. This is an approach based on collective tenant power to negotiate rights rather than relying on government to impose them by statute.

To promote the campaign, RSB relied heavily on virtual organizing. Because people were staying at home in 2020, organizing virtually brought communities together in an accessible way and has been an important tool in our province-wide organizing. Without video conferencing, it would be difficult, perhaps impossible, to foster strong, intra-provincial connections. RSB has also used occasional in-person meetings across BC to solidify the relationships needed for movement-building. Meeting in person also provides more opportunities for "unhoused tenants" to enter the movement, as not everyone has access to the internet. RSB invites unhoused people into the movement, as we see their relationship to the state as parallel to that of tenants and their landlords.

RSB also focused on ensuring our virtual organizing reached tenants across our large province. Building province-wide power is crucial because housing and rent control are regulated by the provincial government, with very little power delegated to municipalities. Individual disputes with landlords or attempts to change the system from within government cannot be relied on to produce the systemic changes we need to secure our homes. In various cities, tenants are facing similar challenges that culminate in provincially regulated disputes, including over rental policy. Landlords have organized provincially, so province-wide solidarity among tenants is essential.

In determining a comprehensive strategy for RSB, our campaign got curious about why previous tenant movements collapsed in cities beyond the lower mainland and Greater Vancouver Area. This research included examining the BC Tenant Organization and its failure to secure collective bargaining rights from the first BC NDP majority government in 1972.[19] This moment, which intersected with a larger, pan-Canadian crackdown on organized renters, taught our campaign two key lessons: first, that reliance on the government, regardless of the party in power, will never result in the change we want without continuous organizing and pressure; and second, that renters, organized in urban and rural settings in solidarity across the province, can build enough power to force societal-scale change. Integrating these lessons, we developed the following four pillars: 1) promoting the establishment of new tenant unions across BC; 2) building tenant-labour solidarity; 3) resurfacing and telling histories of tenant collective action;

and 4) using militant direct action and the law to affirm the right to organize and collectively bargain.

To seed new tenant unions, the RSB Organizing Working Group phone-banked renters, knocked on doors at apartment buildings, and facilitated training and workshops intended to educate and agitate tenants about insufficient legal protections and what tenants can do to support new organizing efforts. These initiatives have allowed RSB to expand our membership across the province, creating regional pods that act as proto-unions and offer a space where tenants can meet regularly to discuss issues in their city. The lead in each pod acts as both the primary driver in pulling a group together and the main liaison between the pod and the campaign. As liaisons, they provide updates, support other regions through sharing information, and make requests for organizing support. Local tenants decide when to shift from a pod to publicly forming a union, while RSB will continue to support a pod or union if it continues to practise the principles of tenant unionism: democracy, autonomy, and organizing.

Our approach to establishing new tenant unions relies on building tenant-labour solidarity and promoting the concept of whole worker organizing within existing labour unions. Whole worker organizing recognizes that workers are also renters and that our shared interests extend beyond the workplace — even if many labour unions are not presently engaged with tenant issues.[20] To address this, we ask endorsing unions — whose reach extends to small towns — to distribute the RSB "Workers Who Rent" survey. The survey collects information about members' housing conditions and identifies local leaders for RSB to contact, connecting us with workers and renters around the province to support them in organizing new tenant unions and building tenant power.

Engaging labour union members who rent is a crucial way tenant movements can apply lessons from the labour movement's experience with collective bargaining to the tenant-landlord relationship. Tenant organizing also has lessons for labour. Framing organizing through tenant-labour solidarity allows tenant workers to critically examine whether labour unions have actively worked against their own interests in supporting developers, real estate, and political parties, and whether union pension funds invest in financialized housing.

Understanding the current relationship between tenants and the state as part of a long history of collective oppression and struggle is fundamental to improving the rights of tenants. RSB has published histories of tenant organizing through blog posts and articles in the press on tenant unions and collective bargaining.[21] RSB's historical research further informed our campaign strategy by learning from the successes and failures of previous organizing efforts. RSB's historical lodestar is the Solidarity Coalition against BC's austerity measures in the 1980s. A democratic grassroots movement of labour, tenant, and community groups, it united to fight the austerity budget and promote economic, democratic, and human rights.[22] It quickly became the largest social movement in the post-sixties period in BC.[23] Like the Solidarity Coalition, our aim is to develop a province-wide consciousness and network of tenant unions to have our demands heard, met, and implemented.

We also recognize how the history of Canadian "housing policy" reflects the struggles of tenants demanding rights, particularly since the 1960s and 1970s, when tenant movements formed associations at municipal, provincial, and national levels to secure the right to housing through legalizing tenant unions and collective bargaining.[24] These tenant-led efforts shaped how the federal government responded during the end of urban renewal in the 1960s, when public housing organizing led to the creation of the 1972 National Housing Act, federally funded tenant associations, and a short-lived national public housing tenants' organization. There are many historical examples across North America of tenants, workers, and organizers realizing that the home is a radical "organizational base" to develop an alternative political horizon.[25]

Canadian law is a blunt tool that is used most often to enforce oppression rather than to empower. It is often used against tenants to support evictions and rent increases. As such, our campaign understands that legal frameworks operate to oppress tenants, and we organize effectively against it. The best pathway to unlocking collective bargaining rights for renters is by building solidarity and tenant unions that can take collective action regardless of express legal recognition.

Like the employer-employee relationship, the tenant-landlord relationship is inherently unequal. Tenants must have control over the terms and conditions of their housing. Tenants organizing, unionizing, collectively bargaining, and striking can ensure tenants have dignity and autonomy in their homes, promote more balance in the tenancy relationship, and make multi-unit living more democratic.[26] Unions at work have brought us a long way; now it's time for a union at home.

Notes

1. CBC News, "Vancouver and Victoria Rents Jump 20% in 6 Months as Thousands Move to BC," March 19, 2022, cbc.ca/news/canada/british-columbia/priced-out-rental-crisis-victoria-1.6390095.
2. Justin McElroy, "Once Again, Vancouver Region Has Highest Rents, Lowest Vacancy Rate of Any Major Metro Area in Canada," CBC/Radio Canada, February 18, 2022, cbc.ca/news/canada/british-columbia/vancouver-rents-cmhc-2022-1.6357136.
3. Silas Xuereb, Andrea Craig, and Craig Jones, *Understanding Evictions in Canada through the Canadian Housing Survey,* Balanced Supply of Housing Research Cluster, University of British Columbia, 2021, housingresearch.ubc.ca/sites/default/files/documents/understanding_evictions_in_canada_2021.pdf; Diary Marif, "B.C.'s new Canadians at Higher risk for Eviction Form Rentals," *New Canadian Media,* 2023, https://www.newcanadianmedia.ca/b-c-s-new-canadians-at-higher-risk-for-eviction-from-rentals/; Craig Jones and Silas Xuereb, *Estimating No-Fault Evictions in Canada (CHS 2021)*, Balanced Supply of Housing, 2021, https://bsh.ubc.ca/research/estimating-no-fault-evictions/#:~:text=We%20find%20that%20British%20Columbia,%2C%20compared%20to%205.9%25%20nationally.
4. Jesse Donaldson, *Land of Destiny: A History of Vancouver Real Estate* (Anvil Press, 2019).
5. Law Reform Commission of British Columbia, *Report on Landlord and Tenant Relationships (Project No. 12) Residential Tenancies,* LRC 13 (1973), https://www.bcli.org/sites/default/files/report13.pdf.
6. British Columbia Rental Housing Task Force, *Rental Housing Review: Recommendations and Findings,* December 2018. https://engage.gov.bc.ca/app/uploads/sites/121/2018/12/RHTF-Recommendations-and-WWH-Report_Dec2018_FINAL.pdf.
7. Paul S. Jon, "Tenant Organising and the Campaign for Collective Bargaining Rights in British Columbia, 1968–75," *BC Studies*, 206 (2020), doi.org/10.14288/bcs.v0i206.192318.
8. Bruce Yorke, "The Tenant Movement in BC from 1968 to 1978," *The Mainlander,* November 9, 2012, themainlander.com/2012/11/09/the-tenant-movement-in-b-c-from-1968-to-1978; Jon, "Tenant Organising."
9. *Health Services and Support — Facilities Subsector Bargaining Assn. v. British Columbia* [2007] 2 SCR 391, 2007 SCC 27, scc-csc.lexum.com/scc-csc/scc-csc/en/item/2366/index.do
10. *Health Services and Support — Facilities Subsector Bargaining Assn. v. British Columbia* [2007] 2 SCR 391, 2007 SCC 27, scc-csc.lexum.com/scc-csc/scc-csc/en/item/2366/index.do.
11. Canadian Charter of Rights and Freedoms, Part I of the Constitution Act, 1982, being Schedule B to the Canada Act 1982 (UK), 1982, c 11, para. 41.
12. Laila Harré, "Unions and Pay Equity in New Zealand: Organisation, Negotiation, Legislation." *Labour and Industry* 18, 2 (2007), doi.org/10.1080/10301763.2007.10669366; Maarten Keune, "Inequality Between Capital and Labour and Among Wage-Earners: The Role of Collective Bargaining and Trade Unions," *Transfer: European Review of Labour and Research* 27, 1 (2021),

doi.org/10.1177/10242589211000588; George I. Long, "Differences in Union and Nonunion Compensation, 2001–2011," *Monthly Labour Review* (April 2013), www.bls.gov/opub/mlr/2013/images/differences-in-union-and-nonunion-compensation-2001-2011.pdf.

13   Judy Fudge and Harry Glasbeek, "The Legacy of PC 1003," *Canadian Labour & Employment Law Journal* 3 (1995).

14   Judy Fudge and Eric Tucker, "The Freedom to Strike in Canada: A Brief Legal History," 2010, CanLIIDocs 542.

15   Council of the District of Columbia, Right of Tenants to Organize, § 42–3505.06 (2006), code.dccouncil.us/us/dc/council/code/sections/42-3505.06.html.

16   City and County of San Francisco Board of Supervisors, Administrative Code — Tenant Organising (2022), sfgov.legistar.com/LegislationDetail.aspx?ID=5191199&GUID=F81B312D-FBF7-4122-BE1C-0313544C15C8.

17   British Columbia Rental Housing Task Force, "Rental Housing Review."

18   Yorke, "Tenant Movement."

19   Jane F. McAlevey, "The Power to Win Is in the Community, Not the Boardroom," In *No Shortcuts: Organising for Power in the New Gilded Age*, (Oxford University Press, 2016), doi.org/10.1093/acprof:oso/9780190624712.003.0002.

20   Ben Ger and Rebecca Kantwerg, "BC Tenants Must Have the Right to Collectively Bargain," *Georgia Straight*, December 8, 2021, straight.com/news/bc-tenants-must-have-right-to-collectively-bargain; Ben Ger, Rebecca Kantwerg, and Steph Langford, "It's Time for BC Renters to Organize a Provincial Movement," *Georgia Straight*, September 12, 2021, straight.com/news/its-time-for-bc-renters-to-organize-a-provincial-movement; Rent Strike Bargain, "The Challenges of Tenant Unionism in British Columbia," *Rank and File*, March 18, 2022, rankandfile.ca/rent-strike-bargain.

21   Ted Richmond and John Shields, "Reflections on Resistance to Neoliberalism: Looking Back on Solidarity in 1983 British Columbia," *Socialist Studies*, vol. 7 (2011).

22   Richmond and Shields, "Reflections on Resistance to Neoliberalism"; BC Labour Heritage Centre, "Solidarity: The Largest Political Protest in British Columbia's History," *Community Stories*, Digital Museums Canada, 2019, communitystories.ca/v2/solidarity-bc-protest_solidarite-protestation-cb.

23   Pierson Nettling, "Tenant Activism and the Demise of Urban Renewal: Tenants, Governance, and the Struggle for Recognition at Habitations Jeanne-Mance in Montreal," *Journal of Urban History* 48, 3 (2022).

24   Rhonda Y. Williams, T*he Politics of Public Housing: Black Women's Struggles against Urban Inequality* (Oxford University Press, 2004); Michael Karp, "The St. Louis Rent Strike of 1969," Journal of Urban History 40, 4 (2014), doi.org/10.1177/0096144213516082.

25   Rent Strike Bargain, "Letter to Minister Eby Regarding Collective Bargaining Rights for Renters," 2021.

THE POLITICAL RENTER CLASS IN SO-CALLED AUSTRALIA

MELBOURNE, VICTORIA, AUSTRALIA

WRITTEN BY
David Kelly, Prashanti Mayfield, Eirene Tsolidis Noyce, Traça DeBarra, Zachary Doney & Jordan Adams

We write this collaborative piece as settlers on stolen land. Our struggle for housing justice is one of dwelling justice — there can be no housing justice that is not in good relation to First Nations' sovereignty, an omnipresent fact that underpins all relations of dwelling here. Our struggle is in constant relation to the dispossession of First Nations Peoples via force and violence that continues today in myriad forms, not least of which the expropriation of land to create property and the regimes of rent and debt that follow.

Birrarung-ga/Naarm, aka Melbourne, is a place that is mediated by settler colonial norms; the logics that drive dispossession and maintain settler futures also envelop the unpropertied settler classes. What we observed and felt in the context of a global pandemic were the wholesale distancing of people and communities from rights and resources needed to dwell safely and securely, a process that has deeply embedded colonial logics.

Australia has been in the midst of a housing crisis for quite a while now,[1] deepening in recent years and expanding to create newly precarious cohorts of renters and unsheltered people. But as Tanganekald scholar Irene Watson points out, the housing crisis in Australia began in 1788 when the British First Fleet invaded.[2] Our experiences during nearly two years of harsh lockdowns in Birrarung-ga/Naarm are imbued with the logics of colonial dispossession that have permeated the Australian housing context for over two hundred years.

The prevailing mythology of the "great Australian dream" of owning a house on a quarter-acre block has rapidly shifted over the past thirty years, becoming increasingly inaccessible to low-income and marginalized groups, resulting in sharper class dichotomies between owner-occupiers, landlords, and renters. The results of these disparities are growing housing unaffordability and inequality, increasing rates of homelessness, and intensely precarious lives for renters in the private sector and in social/public tenures.

Rental insecurity is accompanied by a patchwork of housing policies across state and territory jurisdictions that broadly privilege landlord extractions over renters' housing security and adequate dwelling conditions. When the COVID-19 pandemic hit in early 2020, these unstable housing conditions were exacerbated. In the second-smallest Australian state, Victoria, the state government introduced temporary measures as a public health precaution that promised no household would be evicted, that required landlords and real-estate agents to consider requests for rent reductions, and that created a six-month freeze on rent increases.

In practice, these protections did not provide rental security for many tenants. Vulnerable situations were created for tenants requesting rental reductions, with many refused requests followed by informal evictions. Informal evictions, outside official civil tribunal proceedings, continued to occur throughout 2020. It was in this uncertain environment that the Renters and Housing Union (RAHU) formed, as a means of collectivizing and politicizing the expanding class of precarious renters. RAHU is a renters' union whose membership is made up of people from across the housing-tenure spectrum — including public and private tenants, rooming-house and temporary-accommodation residents, unhoused people, and homeowners. The union works to provide support and advocacy to its members to ensure rights to secure housing and the protection of renters experiencing adverse housing conditions or the threat of eviction. It does this through direct action and collective defence to protect people from eviction and discrimination from landlords, engaging with news media and social media channels, providing reliable information on renters' rights in partnership with housing organizations and experts, and advocating for better housing policies across the political scales of housing governance within so-called Australia.

The following edited transcript is a conversation between RAHU organizers and housing researchers on the genesis of RAHU that took place in July 2020.

Prashanti: How did RAHU start?

Zachary: When all of our incomes evaporated in March and April 2020, a large portion of society learnt what precarity was all at the same time. Everyone in private rental realized that they might get evicted, everyone realized how close to a pretty hard time we were all in…. That moment of realizing the level of instability under which we exist and that we accept as normal was a real eye-opener for a huge section of society. 20,000 people pledged to rent strike. For many people, this was the first time they had ever considered solidarity and the first time they'd ever acted in solidarity — withholding your rent is a big deal. From a series of meetings, rent-strike members voted to form a union. The aim of this union is to organize the renters, the renting class. So, when shit hits the fan in the future and however that comes up, we'll already have a strong, active collective network of people in the same basket.

Prashanti: Are there international connections RAHU drew on?

Reeni: The original rent-strike pledge was started from the Industrial Workers of the World (IWW) here in Kulin nations, in Australia. So, we immediately were able to reach out to other IWW branches nationally and internationally, but a lot of comrades were found outside the normal political organizing space. It was a really incredible moment where there was mass organization, incredibly tight and close engagement globally. Rent strikes look different for different countries and for different reasons, but these are sort of situations that were absolutely ready to go, people who'd lived in precarity and hand to mouth regardless of what country they were in…. People are only one crisis away from homelessness or not being able to pay for food; that's why it was able to happen so quickly.

In the United States, it's been easier, or it's been at least historically more common to have them because there's a hundred, two hundred people living in one building that is owned by one landlord, and that one landlord owns another twenty buildings. Whereas here it looks very different because everything's become so privatized.... mum-and-dad landlords end up owning one investment property, and our ability fight for our local rights in one house is still divided.

During the strike, we asked, how do we give notice to all of these different agencies? How do we collectively negotiate reductions or how do we collectively give notice that we're not paying, because we've been so divided at every step of the way? ... But what's exciting about RAHU is we have this space and it hasn't previously been organized by people affected — there's been advocacy or there's been legal advice, but this new situation can allow for more than just that.

Prashanti: Who is the union is representing — and in what areas?

Zachary: People are confused about what a trade union does. In Australia, union membership has really dropped off since the 1990s. We're trying to educate people about what the role of a community union is: what their rights are in the tenancy, on a lease, or dealing with an estate agent. We are building membership at a moderate pace right now, and currently our capacity is within Melbourne and across a fair spread of different demographics.

Prashanti: Since the rent strike, what reactions have you had from government or on the policy side of things? What's the experience of that been?

Reeni: At one point Prime Minister Scott Morrison was asked about renters, in the first announcements of policy and economic stimulus, and it was completely dismissed. The idea that Morrison can say there needs to be an eviction moratorium, and then offer no policy about that federally, meant that each state government had to come up with something during the height of the pandemic. State legislation was essentially kicking the can down to an arbitrary six-month period without being able to determine what the economy and the pandemic looks like then.

I think the wins that we had were that, while they didn't acknowledge our efforts and the fact that we were striking, they did almost definitely speak about this in their meeting rooms in state and probably federally as well. I think that's what prompted — to be able to even mention in the dialogue that there needs to be a moratorium. In saying that, the wins were triaged measures. They're still significant enough to mean that people weren't going to be chucked out. People still had a home.

David: Who can be a member of the union, and how are they differentiated between tenancy types, e.g.: private renters, public or community renters, mortgage payers? What does that say about class boundaries in Australia at the minute?

Therese: Being an immigrant, I was thinking of that class boundary, where there's a certain group of people who are left out of any kind of assistance at all, and immigrants fall into that category. They're very much vulnerable at the moment, and there is no way out for them. Even with the "working class" of Australia, there's a lower class below that, it's the casual-worker-type class, the immigrant working class, because they are lower than the Australian working class. There's no assistance there whatsoever. They're probably the most vulnerable people that we could incorporate into our union at the moment.

Reeni: That's a really good point. We noticed in the immediate first few months of the strike that we weren't able to create an outreach big enough to contact all of the temporary-visa holders and international students who left en masse because there was absolutely no government support. We managed to still have some engagement, enough that we still currently have members who, like Therese and many others, are migrants or visa holders. But in terms of what RAHU's membership is, it's across the board. It's if you're a renter or if you're in precarious housing, it's a union for you. Precarious housing can be squatting, being homeless — but also if you rent public housing or if you rent directly from a private landlord. We made a definition and a distinction from calling it a tenant union for that reason, because many people don't identify as being a tenant because they have an informal lease agreement; they still are a tenant.

Zachary: Progressive forces in Australia couldn't push our conservative government to extend limited welfare in the middle of a global pandemic to marginalized sections of society. What the government did respond to was lobbying from the property classes of Australia and lobbying from the Real Estate Institute of Australia. They extended welfare packages to existing homeowners, and small business has received a bunch of support, even though these are limited and incomplete supports.

David: On the eviction impetus, of eviction as a process of dispossession, where does that sit within the union movement? Is it something that you will divert a lot of resources to act against? And what do you think it's symbolic of?

Reeni: There was a swath of illegal evictions, in that they were done by slumlord private sublets, illegal sublets, and many, many migrants, like international students, were illegally evicted within a day's notice. There's just no way to police that or catch those who were affected that way. Eviction defence in the initial stages of the strike was very difficult to imagine practically actioning on, because of social distancing and what that would look like for people in that house. We had a bunch of different ideas around how to get past those boundaries: having ropes, having a moving picket, utilizing the media — all sorts of things — but the moratorium came in and it postponed what we feared could be a huge wave of retaliatory evictions in September 2020, when the moratorium expired. What eviction defence would look like in that context (September 2020) is quite concerning because the pandemic will probably still be very much alive and well.

Therese: With the structure of the police, it makes it massively threatening to go up against evictions. They'll get in your face, they'll get your name, they'll know where you live, they know everything about you. It was advised by the government that landlords should compromise with tenants. But what is there to entice landlords to ever negotiate with tenants? Before the pandemic even started, before COVID even came, the housing situation was already competitive and dire. We were in a housing crisis before this coronavirus even came. That's what we're up against already, we're already up against greed, and in the coronavirus times we see that there's very little mercy there anyway.

I suppose the importance of the union is to tackle the issues that were existing before the pandemic even started, because there's plenty of them. We want to start organizing now and get people ready to go for when the moratorium expires in September — we're not alone, which is comforting. We can call upon the support of other people who are organizing in different countries.

Zachary: Organizing during COVID is difficult because we have all lost freedom of assembly. It's a health measure, and it is on one hand correct that it is a health measure, and on the other hand, it is open to and rife with abuse. My opinion, and this may not be a RAHU opinion, is that we are trying to formulate and then advance a series of policy positions to address evictions in the time of COVID-19 and the subsequent economic crisis — or the continuing economic crisis, if we talk about the pre-COVID housing crisis. We would like to have prevention rather than cure, and it remains to be seen how effective that is, and based on how effective that strategy is, we'll start to learn the kind of level of resources that we need to expand on efficient defence.

Reeni: The fight is literally at our doorstep, so if it does come down to an eviction, they've brought the war here, right? They've brought the war to your front door, and they have all the measures and powers on their side in order to move you from your own home, and tenants don't have many rights in terms of how to defend that. In saying that, though, there are many creative ways that people in other countries across the world have managed to triage that. There's a way to change the terrain.

David: September keeps coming up. It's something that a lot of people are talking about. It's not just a month anymore — it's this emotional space that people are already starting to invest in, and so what are your emotional responses to September looming?

Zachary: In September, if the government chooses to allow the concurrent expiry of all the different welfare supports and the eviction moratorium, we're going to have pretty bare-fist class war. People are reluctant to understand that landlords don't provide housing, they gatekeep access to housing. My landlord didn't build this house that I live in, my landlord just owns it, and for the privilege of having a roof over my head I pay the landlord. They're not providing me housing at all. I'm providing me housing and they gatekeep it.

Jordan: September is worrying to me because it's not just going to be a matter of the pandemic ending, and then we have to pick up the pieces and then all the battles that come along with that, we'll still be in the midst of a pandemic that's probably worsening. We'll be fighting these battles under the same conditions, and it's not a light at the end of the tunnel, it's just going to be another front in this continuing thing.

David: This probably invites a romantic answer, and I don't want to over-romanticize anything, but, what's the potential of this moment to re-orientate those relations to property? Do you see this as a moment of potential or a space of hope or anything of that ilk?

Therese: Well, there's a lot of work to be done in order for us to restructure the way housing is provided. We're in such early stages of it at the moment, and resources are scarce, there has to be more education out there about public housing, because people think that private house ownership is the only model at the moment, and we forget that in the past we had a wide and strong public housing structure in this country and in many other countries.

Zachary: In conversations with many people from different walks of life, I'm hearing that people now are feeling that there is uncertainty in their world. Many more people have gone from having a passive experience of the world to suddenly realizing that, wow, history is actually happening now, these are momentous occasions. Now is the time to point out to people why the foundations of the fortress are rotten. We are living the outcomes of 250 years of really bad choices. I think we can point these out, and more and more people can understand what we mean, because at least they've experienced the actual precarity of their existence.

David: What are your thoughts about Indigenous sovereignty and this moment. Is this a moment where we can reorient towards a housing model that is more aligned with First Nations struggle?

Reeni: I think that the overarching thing to start from, as a non-Indigenous person, is mentioning it [housing in Australia] was founded on stolen land. So that's the starting point, and then it's dispossession, and then it's displacement. It's genocide that makes profit off stealing land and making it property. So that's the foundations of this country. That is also completely tied in with capitalism. I can't fathom the effects of that — to go from it being your land to then having to pay money to the government or private landlords. I think there's a bigger discussion to be had about paying rent for that reason, and the concept needs to be mainstreamed that, why are we paying rent to landlords who've benefited from capital and privatization and profiting on the right to a home?

I think the first step is to make sure that we do the work of understanding that, and we do the extra outreach to actively promote and prioritize Indigenous voices to determine what they think would be the best way forward. But it's a huge challenge, and it runs deeper than any of the rest of us. I don't know if [I] can answer that.

Therese: During the rent strike, there was connections made to Warriors of the Aboriginal Resistance, both here and in Meanjin (Brisbane). But, we need to do more. I think the starting point for me has been to work on Pay the Rent and incorporating that into the union.[3] So a portion of our membership dues is going to Pay the Rent, and that's a starting point. Hopefully we end up in a position where we have an Indigenous committee, or we have more active members who can work around that.

Our collective conversation took place less than two months before a looming September when the eviction moratorium was due to end. Despite there being apparent protections against displacement, eviction proceedings continued during the moratorium. Landlords lodged applications to the Victorian Civil and Administrative Tribunal (VCAT) for rent increases, notices to vacate, notices of entry, and breach of duty throughout 2020. In the last week of the moratorium being place, 869 applications were made for notices to vacate (eviction proceedings). In the first week of August, this rose by 55 percent. The moratorium was extended until March 29, 2021, but this did little to stem the rent seeking and applications to VCAT.

RAHU has grown significantly since this time, becoming the largest tenant union in Australia, with branches in almost every state. It has established itself as a reliable and progressive space for collective organizing among the housing precariat in Australia, but especially Victoria. Whilst its base is primarily made up of private renters, it is growing in relevance and appeal to other renters, particularly for residents of public housing. In late 2023, the Victorian government announced that it would be demolishing all forty-four public housing high-rise buildings in the state, displacing over 12,000 households — essentially eradicating inner-city public housing estate communities. How the union responds to this catastrophic housing policy will dictate its own relevance to the struggle and the settler imagination of what is possible for dwelling justice in the colony.

Notes

1. Rae Dufty-Jones, "A Historical Geography of Housing Crisis in Australia," *Australian Geographer* 49, 1 (2018), doi.org/10.1080/00049182.2017.1336968.
2. Irene Watson, "Sovereign Spaces, Caring for Country, and the Homeless Position of Aboriginal Peoples," *South Atlantic Quarterly* 180, 1 (2009), ssrn.com/abstract=2476790.
3. *Pay the Rent,* paytherent.net.au.

MAPPING CONVICTION-BASED HOUSING RESTRICTIONS IN CHICAGO

CHICAGO, ILLINOIS, UNITED STATES

WRITTEN BY
Celia Magnone

Housing banishment laws, formally known as residential restrictions, are an extension of United States sex offender registration policy that prohibits people on a sex offender registry from living between 500 and 2500 feet from certain locations associated with children, such as schools, parks, and daycares. Although they have been discredited as tools of public safety for their reliance on myths around sexual offending and their inability to prevent both new offences and sexual recidivism, residential restrictions remain widespread across the United States, implemented in at least thirty states and thousands of additional counties and municipalities.[1] Residential restrictions effectively regulate the daily lives of people on the registry, representing a significant inequity that excludes them geographically and sociopolitically and ultimately constitutes contemporary banishment. These laws serve to continue punishment for people with past sex convictions who have served their time, producing a range of harmful consequences for those individuals and their families, many directly related to housing access and security.[2]

In Illinois, people with past sex convictions are prohibited from living within 500 feet of schools, playgrounds, and daycare locations (referred to throughout the chapter as prohibited locations). In a dense urban area like Chicago, housing banishment laws legislate people on the sex offender registry into homelessness and housing instability by excluding them from most housing for life. Once homeless, state law requires them to register weekly with police, based only on their lack of a fixed address. This chapter uses GIS mapping to demonstrate the spatial impact of the laws, or the percentage of residential space made illegal for people on the registry by housing banishment, and discusses the social harms of housing banishment and weekly registration laws in Chicago. Findings show that nearly two-thirds (approximately 64 percent) of Chicago's residentially zoned space is rendered off-limits by sex offender laws—a conservative estimation of their true impact due to the shifting nature of the restricted boundaries. The map included with this chapter offers a visual representation of the spatial inequality caused by housing banishment laws to be employed within a broader legislative strategy focused around building collective power between people on the registry, researchers, advocates, and providers across sectors to actively challenge and change the laws.

Rather than framing this examination around communities concerned by the proximity of people with past convictions to their home, my work focuses on the individuals who are themselves banished and aims to consider how banishment is experienced, not merely visualized. Importantly, my research is situated within the existing work of a local campaign to change the Illinois laws using grassroots organizing and legislative strategy. First, I conceptually frame the issue of banishment and discuss the housing outcomes of the laws. Then I focus on policy and procedures in Chicago, and the work to change the laws, before discussing the map as a resource at the intersection of research and activism. I conclude with a brief discussion of how other advocates can confront the issue of housing banishment in their own work to challenge the laws and their impact.

Banishment has a long history as a method of social, political, and spatial expulsion to punish wrongdoing. In its contemporary forms, banishment excludes targeted groups from designated areas for extended periods of time and is characterized by legal hybridity combining civil, administrative, and criminal law. People with past sex convictions are excluded and expelled from legally defined zones, often for life, violation of which is a felony. "Banishment" implies overt, state-sanctioned policy and emphasizes an expansionary logic where overlapping individual zones have a cumulative effect of rendering large areas off-limits.[3] Conceptualizing residential restrictions along the theoretical framework of banishment from housing captures the social and spatial exclusion experienced by people with past sex convictions, as well as the punitive nature of the laws.[4]

What are the direct consequences of housing banishment? Drastically reducing options for legal, secure housing threatens the safety and wellbeing of individuals, families, and communities. People on the sex offender registry are a hidden population highly vulnerable to homelessness and housing instability due to the lack of legally available housing, which presents tremendous obstacles to reintegration.[5] Many people on the registry are forced to move from homes they already have, prevented from going back to their former homes, or prohibited from living with family members who may support or depend on them.[6]

Housing banishment laws have also been linked to homelessness: nationwide, approximately 2–3 percent of people on the registry are homeless, compared to 0.5 percent of the US population. This figure is significantly higher in areas that are dense or have very strict laws.[7] Homelessness in this context includes both its visible (staying outdoors, in shelters, or in encampments) and covert forms (living out of a car, being in one home during the day and another at night, riding public transit overnight, staying with other people on a short-term basis). Although justified as tools of public safety, housing banishment laws legislate people on the sex offender registry into homelessness, which is neither good social policy nor effective public safety.

The impact of these laws falls hardest on already marginalized communities: Black people on the registry are more likely to suffer negative outcomes, and most people who are homeless on the registry are poor Black men, middle-aged and above.[8] These housing-related outcomes continued throughout the coronavirus pandemic, a time when billions of US government dollars were aimed at preventing and mitigating circumstances of housing insecurity. Unfortunately, people with past sex convictions have been routinely excluded from public programs offering housing resources and assistance. Throughout the pandemic, there were no moratoriums on housing banishment — people on the registry continued to be made homeless and forced to move repeatedly because of the laws.

In Illinois, housing banishment laws apply to over 80 percent of people on the Illinois sex offender registry. In Chicago, nearly 20 percent of people on the registry are homeless as a result, 80 percent of whom are Black men between the ages of 30 and 70.[9] Illinois laws not only eliminate housing options, but also force people on the registry out of homes they already have. If a prohibited location opens within 500 feet of a past offender's home, the residence must be vacated in anywhere from one hour to thirty days, depending on the supervision status of the individual with a past conviction.[10] Families are often forced to move or split up, even when the person on the registry is on the lease or owns the home. Parents on the registry may be present at the home during the day but leave the residence overnight to sleep in their car, stay outside, or ride the train to remain in technical compliance with residence restrictions. People are regularly turned away from housing services based on their conviction — and even if they are approved, the residence must be outside of the banishment zone to be legally acceptable.

Once homeless, individuals must register every week, in-person with police — a requirement based only on their lack of a fixed address. Weekly registration represents a significant inequity: people who are homeless must register fifty-two times a year, while people with housing register only quarterly or annually, according to past conviction. Even those on the registry with legal housing remain housing insecure because they can also be forced to move at any time and would be required to register weekly again if unable to find another legal permanent address.

Weekly registration is an untenable and high stakes process. It prevents people on the registry from finding or maintaining employment, attending to family obligations, or dealing with emergencies. There are no exceptions — missing weekly registration for any reason is noncompliance, even under circumstances of illness, hospitalization, or death. Failure to register is a felony offence punishable by reimprisonment or a ten-year extension to the registration duration. Over half of people who are homeless on the Illinois registry have been reincarcerated at least once for an administrative violation,[11] and many have accumulated multiple extensions, adding decades to their registration period. Together, housing banishment and weekly registration criminalize people on the registry by preventing them from finding legal housing and then subjecting them to disproportionately heightened monitoring because they are homeless, essentially setting them up to fail.

The harms of housing banishment were greatly exacerbated by pandemic conditions. People who are homeless on the registry were at a higher risk of exposure, infection, and transmission because of the overlap between at-risk categories: there is an increased chance of severe COVID-related illness for older adults and people with underlying medical conditions, groups that include a large portion of people on the registry. The pandemic disproportionately impacted Black people and communities, relevant to homeless Chicagoans on the registry who are more likely to be Black men, middle-aged and older.[12] Additionally, many people who are homeless on the registry in Chicago have been in and out of homes where they may be taking care of elders, immunocompromised family members, or children, putting themselves and others at a heightened risk of illness.

Housing banishment laws also contribute to ongoing crises of overcrowding in Illinois prisons, which had serious implications for COVID-19 outbreak during early waves of the pandemic. Around 1,400 people are held in prison past their release dates because they lack the legally available housing required for parole. All Illinois prisoners must serve a mandatory supervised release, but release is contingent upon legal housing. For people with sex offence convictions, not being able to secure legal housing means that they are forced to serve their entire sentence, including supervision, in prison. Depending on their supervised release period, people with sex offence convictions will either be held indefinitely or eventually be released into homelessness once their supervision period is complete.[13]

Because housing banishment and weekly registration are state laws, state institutions must follow them, presenting several obstacles for people on the registry beyond concerns for public safety and health. Law enforcement has the power to change practices, but only temporarily without change to the laws themselves. For instance, Chicago police suspended registration in March 2020, eventually reinstating it as a semi-remote process where people register in-person once a month at different locations. Ultimately, remote registration was only temporary: because the law explicitly requires registration for homeless people on the registry to be "weekly, in-person," regular registration had resumed across various Chicago police stations by March 2022.

The administrative requirements of registration also ignore the economic hardships of living and being homeless on the sex offender registry. People on the registry must pay a $100 annual registration fee to police to subsidize law enforcement costs, an extremely high recurring fee for those who are homeless, with dependents, unemployed, or

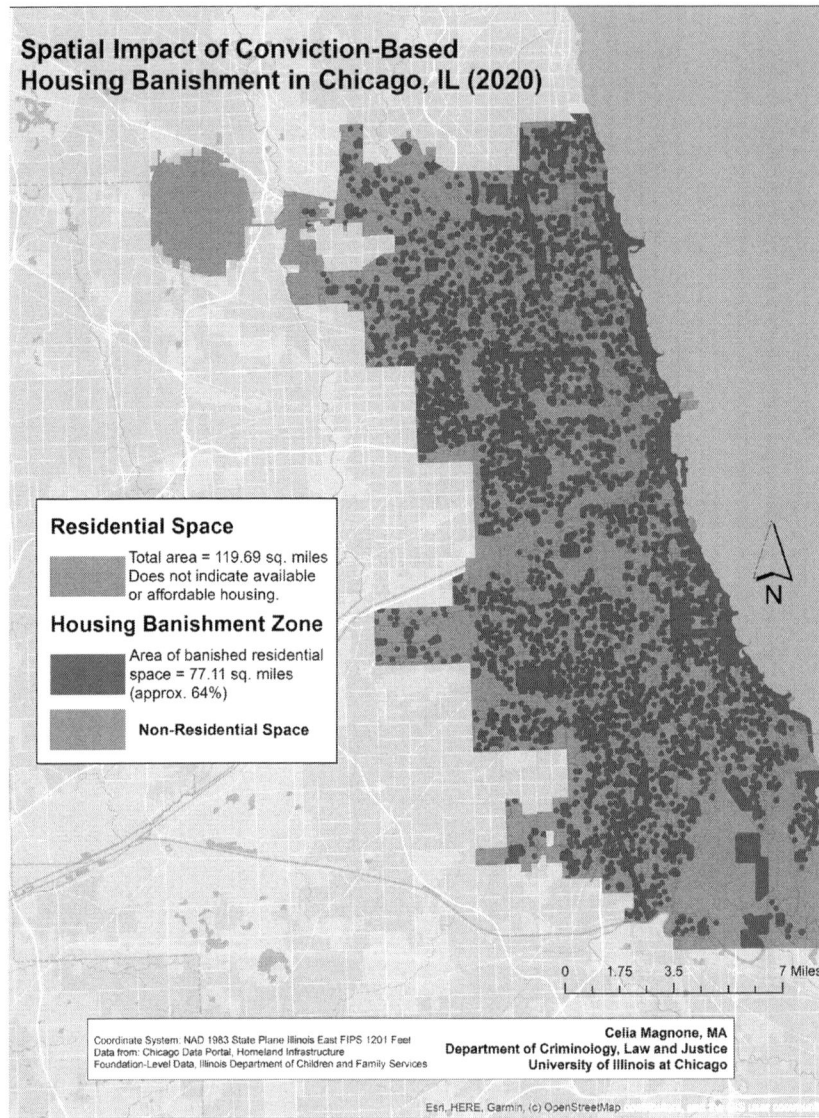

Spatial impact of conviction-based housing banishment in Chicago in 2020.

unable to work. Chicago police waived the fee for 2020 but reinstated it the following year with less than a month's notice. Although registrants are entitled to request a waiver, being granted one requires specific documents showing proof of indigence, which were not easily obtainable while Social Security offices were closed during the pandemic. With some negotiation, police agreed to accept other types of documentation for the waiver, but these alternatives were not necessarily more obtainable, especially to people with no mailing address and limited technological access. Furthermore, the agreement to accept alternative proof was not advertised by police, meaning that many people eligible for a waiver ended up paying to avoid punishment. People who could not afford to pay the fee received a technical violation for noncompliance — some of whom reasoned that being detained for their violation would at least provide them with the basic necessities of food and shelter.

The spatial impact of housing banishment, or how much residential space is made illegal to people on the registry, depends on both the severity of the laws and density of prohibited locations in the area.[14] Chicago is a dense urban area where prohibited locations number well into the thousands. To evaluate the spatial impact of housing banishment laws in Chicago and determine what percentage of residentially zoned space is made legally off-limits to people on the registry by Illinois housing banishment laws, I mapped prohibited locations (schools, parks, daycares) and their restricted zones, and then examined the cumulative effect of those zones in relation to residentially zoned space. I used the areas of the housing banishment zone, land parcels zoned for residential use, and their overlap to calculate the impact. According to this mapping, people on the sex offender registry are banished from almost two-thirds (approximately 64 percent) of residentially zoned space in Chicago.

There are a few important limitations to this research. First, "residentially zoned" does not indicate housing that is affordable, or even available. Second, although the map includes over two thousand daycare facilities, it does not include licence-exempt, private home daycares, which also invoke housing banishment although their locations are not publicly listed. These findings thus likely underestimate the spatial impact of housing banishment in Chicago. Finally, the constantly, unpredictably shifting boundaries of banishment, because of frequent opening of prohibited locations such as home daycares, mean that any such map is subject to some degree of change. The map, while imperfect, is an important visual representation of the spatial inequality experienced by people on the registry in Chicago due to housing banishment.

The Chicago 400 Alliance, a grassroots campaign organized by and with people who are homeless on public conviction registries, has been working to change Illinois laws while advocating to law enforcement for ways to help people navigate them in the short term, such as negotiating with police for procedural changes during the pandemic. In 2021, the campaign introduced state legislation that would alleviate housing banishment and abolish weekly registration and has continued to advocate for policy change using a strategy of collective action and power. However, the original sponsor of the bill in the state house eventually distanced themselves from the legislation. Building campaign power across legislative districts is critical to letting legislators know their constituents are not only harmed by housing banishment and weekly registration but also invested in them opposing the laws — and will stand behind them in doing so. However, there are notable challenges to asking legislators to oppose sex offender registration and housing banishment laws, related to deeply ingrained sociopolitical misconceptions about people with past sex convictions and the value of the laws to reduce or prevent harm. Even though legislators may be sympathetic to the experiences of their constituents on the registry, they are often unwilling to risk political action against the laws out of concern for their own position as elected officials. Convincing legislators to represent and respond to all their constituents, including people with past sex convictions, can only be accomplished by emphasizing the harms that housing banishment produces using a variety of approaches in tandem. It is crucial to present legislators with the direct experiences of the laws by the people subject to them, while researchers and advocates across fields provide empirical evidence of their negative impact to reiterate that housing banishment and weekly registration laws are fundamentally harmful, not helpful.

I worked with the Chicago 400 Alliance for two years, in addition to studying the evolution and impact of sex offender registration laws such as residential restrictions. The map presented here was a project at the intersection between my own research and the work of the campaign to challenge policy in Illinois. Because this map is framed around harm and inequity to people on the registry, rather than their presumed risk to the communities in which they live, it is an important example of counter-mapping in the study of residential restrictions for people on the registry. Maps like this are crucial to visually represent the spatial inequality caused by housing banishment laws. However, mapping the spatial impact of housing banishment alone does not adequately capture the scope of its harm, nor does it inherently stand in opposition to the laws. This image is meant to be situated within a long-term strategy leveraged against state policy that also emphasizes the lived experiences of the people and families who must navigate the laws in their daily lives. The map is a visual tool, demonstrating inequality and harm, that challenges housing banishment by confronting legislators and advocates with its impact and convincing them to act in the interest of true public safety for all the people they represent and serve.

Housing banishment laws put people on the registry in a precarious housing position that keeps them socially and legally vulnerable due to lack of stability. A multidisciplinary approach to examining their impact bridges the gap between areas of scholarship and existing research — an important tool for influencing policy change alongside the experiences and perspectives of people banished by the laws. But there is a greater gap to be bridged between research and action. Because the effects of housing banishment are pervasive, the laws and their impact must be critically engaged with and actively opposed across sectors. Housing banishment for people with past sex convictions is relevant to areas of re-entry, housing, and social services; law; violence prevention; victim advocacy; substance and mental health treatment; and community organizing. Individuals in any of these fields, or others, can take up the issue of housing banishment by learning about local laws and ordinances, how they specifically block people's access to basic needs, and how to effectively help people navigate them. Further, the laws can be challenged directly through the formation and growth of supportive networks of providers, advocates, and researchers willing to speak out against the harms of the laws to legislators and others in their field. Opposing these laws and their exclusionary logics requires active commitment, in both principle and regular practice, to the reality that people with past sex convictions deserve stability and support like all others. True public safety, as a shared goal and responsibility, cannot be conditional or exclusionary. It can only be achieved by investing in strategies and services that provide for and prevent harm against all members of a community.

Notes

1   Grant Duwe, William Donnay, and Richard Tewksbury, "Does Residential Proximity Matter? A Geographic Analysis of Sex Offense Recidivism," *Criminal Justice and Behavior* 35, 4 (April 2008), https://doi.org/10.1177/0093854807313690; R. Karl Hanson, "Long-Term Recidivism Studies Show That Desistance Is the Norm," *Criminal Justice and Behavior* 45, 9 (September 1, 2018), https://doi.org/10.1177/0093854818793382; Jill Levenson, Alissa R. Ackerman, Kelly M. Socia, and Andrew J. Harris, "Where for Art

Thou? Transient Sex Offenders and Residence Restrictions," *Criminal Justice Policy Review* 26, 4 (June 1, 2015), https://doi.org/10.1177/0887403413512326; Jill S. Levenson, "Hidden Challenges: Sex Offenders Legislated into Homelessness," *Journal of Social Work* 18, 3 (May 1, 2018), https://doi.org/10.1177/1468017316654811.

2   Richard Tewksbury, Elizabeth Ehrhardt Mustaine, and Shawn Rolfe, "Sex Offender Residential Mobility and Relegation: The Collateral Consequences Continue," *American Journal of Criminal Justice* 41, 4 (December 2016), https://doi.org/10.1007/s12103-016-9341-y.

3   Katherine Beckett and Steve Herbert, "Penal boundaries: Banishment and the expansion of punishment." *Law & Social Inquiry,* 35 (2010), doi:10.1111/j.1747-4469.2009.01176.x; Elizabeth Ehrhardt Mustaine, "Sex Offender Residency Restrictions, *Criminology & Public Policy,* 13 (2014), https://doi.org/10.1111/1745-9133.12076.

4   Katherine Beckett and Naomi Murakawa, "Mapping the Shadow Carceral State: Toward an Institutionally Capacious Approach to Punishment," *Theoretical Criminology* 16, 2 (May 1, 2012), https://doi.org/10.1177/1362480612442113.

5   Tewksbury, Mustaine, and Rolfe, "Sex Offender Residential Mobility and Relegation"; Lorine A. Hughes and Keri B. Burchfield, "Sex Offender Residence Restrictions in Chicago: An Environmental Injustice?" *Justice Quarterly* 25, 4 (December 2008), https://doi.org/10.1080/07418820802119976; Mustaine, "Sex Offender Residency Restrictions."

6   Jill S. Levenson and Leo P. Cotter, "The Impact of Sex Offender Residence Restrictions: 1,000 Feet from Danger or One Step from Absurd?" *International Journal of Offender Therapy and Comparative Criminology* 49, 2 (2005), https://doi.org/10.1177/0306624X04271304.

7   Jeanna Cann and Deena A. Isom Scott, "Sex Offender Residence Restrictions and Homelessness: A Critical Look at South Carolina," *Criminal Justice Policy Review* 31, 8 (October 1, 2020), https://doi.org/10.1177/0887403419862334.

8   Cann and Isom Scott. "Sex Offender Residence Restrictions and Homelessness"; Tewksbury, Mustaine, and Rolfe, "Sex Offender Residential Mobility and Relegation"; Beth M. Huebner, Andrea Giuffre, Breanne Pleggenkuhle, and Kimberly R. Kras, "The Price of a Sex Offense Conviction: A Comparative Analysis of the Costs of Community Supervision," *Criminology* 60, (2022), https://doi.org/10.1111/1745-9125.12294.

9   The Chicago 400, Residency Restrictions Report, 2020, https://chicago400.net/report.

10 The Chicago 400, Residency Restrictions Report.
11 The Chicago 400, Residency Restrictions Report.
12 The Chicago 400, Residency Restrictions Report.
13 The Chicago 400, Residency Restrictions Report.
14 The Chicago 400, Residency Restrictions Report.

16

ORGANIZING DURING FORCED EVICTION IN KHORI GAON

DELHI, INDIA

WRITTEN BY
Ishita Chatterjee

On June 7, 2021, the Supreme Court of India gave orders to demolish Khori Gaon, a fifty-year-old informal settlement[1] at the border of Delhi and Faridabad, accusing the settlement residents of being "forest encroachers." While informal settlement residents are often labelled as "encroachers," "freeloaders," and "illegal," among other derogatory names, here, the courts framed the issue as a binary conflict, pitting housing against the environment. Calling the community "forest encroachers" effectively condemns them to brutal eviction and dehumanization.[2] In the case of Khori Gaon, the courts also ignored the historical context of the forest and the fact that the land had been mined as a quarry for four decades before the settlement developed. The early inhabitants were quarry workers who had moved here from neighbouring states in search of employment. When mining was banned by the court between 1992 and 2004, many workers remained, trapped by debt. From 2004 onwards, the settlement grew as people displaced from the inner city and job seekers from other areas moved here. By 2021, Khori Gaon had become home to nearly 100,000 residents.

Soon after the Supreme Court order for Khori Gaon's demolition in June 2021, section 144 was declared in the settlement, which prohibits the assembly of five or more people in the area. In the month leading up to the demolition, the settlement was policed heavily and constantly.

Electricity and water supply were disrupted. Community leaders and activists were arrested and often locked up in undisclosed locations for attempting to organize. The media was barred from entering the settlement to cover the developments.

This chapter contains a conversation between the activists Vimal Bhai[3] and Neelesh Kumar, community members Rekha, Arshad Ali, and Arvind Kumar, and the author, who played roles in strategizing and organizing with residents of Khori Gaon. It covers the period when the individuals in this conversation came together and started their intense collaboration to fight for justice for Khori Gaon. We focus on the challenges we faced due to the pandemic-related restrictions and the heavy-handed approach of the police.

Ishita: What did you do after hearing about the June 7, 2021, court order?

Rekha: Eviction notices were put up in a few places on 8 June. However, it had no signature or stamp; hence, we were unsure if this was an official order. That same night, police started patrolling and making announcements to vacate within a day. How does one pack their lives and leave in one day? The police did not tell us where to go. No alternate accommodation was provided to us. So, we stay put.

Ishita: After the eviction order, the police disconnected your electricity supply and stopped the water tankers from entering. That created another set of problems. Since Khori Gaon is built on a post-quarry landscape, its ground is filled with deep craters and steep slopes.

Rekha: This made our lives miserable. Moving around at night became extremely risky. We had to buy water from outside at a very high price and travel two to four kilometres through the rugged terrain. We were tortured so that people would leave out of desperation. We have seen multiple demolitions in the last two years. Earlier, in September 2020, they had broken down around 200 houses.

When they returned in April 2021, that time there was no eviction notice; the bulldozer showed up unannounced. I asked the police, would you demolish the entire settlement this time? The inspector informed me that they were here to clear the area visible from the main road as the state was under immense pressure to get rid of the "slum" from the rich people and groups who advocate for saving forests and the environment.

Ishita: Were you aware that the final demolition was carried out by calling you forest encroachers?

Arshad: We came to know we were being called forest encroachers only through the media articles and the public hearing. When we purchased our plots, there was no forest here. So, it really puzzled us that we were being criminalized for something we hadn't done. While most of us did not have knowledge of legal processes or urban policies, we understood our civil rights. But nothing was communicated to us; hence, we couldn't organize.

Vimal: Yes, there was no public consultation process or even communication from the state. That also made it challenging for us. In the one month between the order and demolition, we had to reach out to the community and explain what was going on under heavy surveillance.

Ishita: One of the initial steps you took was to organize a public hearing though demolitions had already started, there seemed to be no relief from the courts, and resident protests were met with severe force and violence. Could you elaborate on how organizing a public hearing in such circumstances serves as a powerful tool in community mobilization?

Vimal: Public hearing is a form of collective action where the citizens who have been denied their rights or have been otherwise wronged are given the space to share their grievances and ask questions. It can also lead to corrective action against injustice. Typically, public hearings are conducted at the site of evictions, but because of the pandemic-related restrictions and section 144, we conducted it online. It was broadcast and recorded to reach a larger audience. The public hearing for Khori Gaon aimed to inform the affected community about ongoing developments and to spark a broader conversation on forced evictions under the guise of forest conservation. Experts from various fields were invited to contribute to the discussion.

Ishita: Did the public hearing have its intended impact?

Arvind: It was the first time we realized there was support for us. We were treated as criminals by the police and state officials, not even knowing where we had gone so wrong that we deserved to be made houseless during a pandemic. Due to the multiple demolitions last year, we knew further demolitions were likely on the horizon. We had the power of attorney papers and other documents with our proof of address, but from 2016 onwards, government officials from various departments have come to us saying we have settled on government land. Previously they would demolish a small area and then leave us alone. However, this time they came back with a court order.

Ishita: What happened just after you received the court order for demolition? Were the community leaders and various groups able to come together and develop a collective strategy?

Rekha: At first, we hoped they would come to demolish a few houses and leave just like the previous times. Those of us who would be on the path of bulldozers would have to endure. But the community will help rebuild their lives as we have done previously. Hence, the first two days were quiet. But when around 2000 police personnel entered Khori Gaon, we realized this was different. Most people started gathering in smaller groups to discuss. I was informed about a team of lawyers and an activist who had defended our case in court. I requested more information about the petition, the petitioners, and an explanation of the court order. But I did not get answers from the community leaders. The other leaders — mostly men — also kept their plans to themselves, leaving me and other women in the dark. For women, this struggle goes beyond eviction; it is a constant fight to be included and considered an equal among the sea of men.

Arshad: In Khori Gaon, there was a leader in every lane. Leadership depended on networks with the local service providers, links with urban local bodies as well as relationships with the land mafia.

[In South Asia, the term "mafia" is used for groups that can range from local gangs to extensive networks involving politicians, business people, and the underworld, who exploit the failure of formal systems. They use illegal or criminal tactics and can operate covertly or function openly with political backing. They are often named after the domain they control, such as real estate mafia, water mafia, sand mafia, land mafia etc. Electricity and water provision for the vast settlement was a challenge; hence each area had to compete with the other. These local leaders, while often corrupt, also filled a gap. They engaged in civic processes and represented the residents. However, often, the residents would be exploited during these negotiations for access to services from the government or private providers which is further described in the interview transcript that follows.]

When the eviction order came, these leaders were out of their depth to handle this situation. Throughout Khori Gaon's growth, leadership took the form of clientelism. However, most politicians remained silent and refused to show their support after the court order. So, the local leaders were also in a fix. Recognizing this gap, many social workers, youth group leaders, and NGOs came to us within the first month, claiming they would find lawyers to fight on our behalf. Multiple groups started forming in different parts of Khori Gaon.

There was utter confusion in the community. Even though many local leaders were corrupt, they were also the only ones the community knew well. It was not easy to trust someone new, especially during a demolition. However, as it became apparent that the local leaders were clueless, we also wanted to engage with the outsiders.

Ishita: Neelesh, you have been working for housing rights of Delhi settlements for the past eight years, and Vimal Bhai, you have spent a big part of your life, thirty-eight years, in environmental forced eviction and land acquisition cases. Both of you joined the community relatively late. What were your challenges? And how did you get involved?

Neelesh: I worked in Khori Gaon during the September 2020 eviction while distributing aid and running a community kitchen. I faced communication problems with the local leaders and the other activists during that time. However, the collaboration was short, so it did not lead to significant issues. But I was aware of the group dynamics.

Once the Supreme Court order came out, the same group of local leaders and activists reached out to those of us who work in the housing and environmental rights field. However, they were not sharing information with the community. This created panic and led to rumours, which was dangerous in this sensitive situation. It is wrong to keep the community in the dark about the court case details being fought in their name, even if the discussion is difficult. Hence, I decided to distance myself from them and reach out to the residents directly.

Vimal: The deterioration of housing rights in environment-related forced evictions has been a worrying development, and we all seem to have very few answers. But we still have to engage, tell the community what is going on and their options and not make false promises.

The lack of information can disconnect the ground reality and legal processes.

I faced similar issues as described by Neelesh. Meetings were held in big offices, not in Khori Gaon with the community. There was a lack of transparency; I realized decisions were made about the community by those who hadn't engaged with them. Hence, I did not want to get involved at first as I knew little about Khori Gaon. But I took the initiative after the violent and inhumane behaviour of the police. This was one of the most violent evictions I have encountered, and I could not just watch from the fence. I contacted housing rights academics, environmental policy researchers, lawyers, activists, and others with shared values. That is how I connected with you, Neelesh, Manju Menon, and our lawyers.

Ishita: Many small-scale and individual efforts were made before we came together. They were impactful and contributed to the bigger movement. We initiated meetings with the urban local bodies and sent letters to the chief ministers of Delhi and Haryana. Some of us used Twitter and other social media platforms to highlight the case. We wrote newspaper articles to start conversations around social justice in environmental conservation arguments. At the same time, small demonstrations were taking place on the ground. One event stood out because of the number of women involved, the absence of prominent community leaders, and it was youth-led. Neelesh, you played a significant role in organizing this. How did you facilitate this?

Neelesh: The youth from the community had started standing up to the older leaders and activists, so there was momentum and enthusiasm among this group. I visited Khori Gaon daily, alone and engaged with them. When they questioned my motives, I informed them that I had come to them in my individual capacity. I patiently listened to their complaints and demands, even when they were confrontational. Gradually, we started a conversation regarding the documents they had and how we could use them to demand rehabilitation and compensation. I informed them that they had legal rights even if they were called encroachers by the government and the court. Since the youth were keen on re-appealing the court order, they found this helpful, and I was able to gain their trust.

Preparation for the gathering happened in a self-organized manner. We reached out to everyone. Since we provided information and engaged in a dialogue with the community, many people joined us, especially women. Those of us who could mobilize and were ready to take responsibility quickly built a network. One pattern we noticed was that youth from all genders and women got along well.

Ishita: How were you able to organize under surveillance? When did the state declare section 144?

Neelesh: After the court order, the police patrolled the area in smaller numbers; they came regularly to intimidate the residents. Their primary strategy was to arrest the prominent leaders who they thought could create a problem for them. They knew about the power dynamics in Khori Gaon and probably did not think the community could organize without the leaders so quickly.

Our gathering was planned in one of the broader streets of Khori Gaon. It was summer; hence we created a shade that could accommodate a big crowd. The conversations during the gathering were empowering. People realized they had to raise their voices now, or Khori Gaon would be erased. There was an urgency and purpose. Most people stayed back even at night and vowed not to leave the tent until alternative accommodation was provided. Our demands were not irrational. While demolition cannot be justified in any situation, most people accepted the Supreme Court's decision. All they wanted was a place to move into.

Demonstration to oppose the order to demolition Khori Gaon, held on 14 June 2021. Photo by Neelesh Kumar.

However, that night, the police came and arrested a few youths. They broke the tent, demolished the lights and electricity connections, and section 144 was imposed immediately. This law provides police with absolute power and infringes individual or community rights.

Ishita: Additionally, the media was barred from covering the news. What did the community do?

Arshad: We are not allowed to gather inside the settlement, so different groups and social workers affiliated with political parties approached us and organized protests outside Khori Gaon. Many of us joined them as visibility was necessary, and we were running out of options. We moved to the designated protest space outside Khori Gaon in small, carefully managed groups. By maintaining the size of each group at three or fewer, we aimed to avoid arrest and comply with the law while moving within the settlement. Once the state realized this, they started arresting community leaders again, fabricating false cases and keeping them behind bars for multiple days till they were bailed. In one of the protests, the police arrested 300 people. These incidents made it to the news, and there was uproar for a few days. However, most social workers and political parties disappeared soon after. They never even came to enquire what had happened to us once the demolition started.

Ishita: Media coverage during this period was critical. You had to come up with tactics to counter the media ban. What were the steps you took?

Neelesh: Even though the police stopped media from entering, a few reporters continued covering the news by entering the settlement through routes where they were not patrolling. The community helped them in this process. Their challenge was quickly figuring out what was happening as they could not spend more time in the settlement due to heavy surveillance. So, we provided the material and all other details necessary to write the articles. The residents even collected news and shared voice notes, videos, and images with them. We created new communication channels. There was also good camaraderie among the journalists. The unfolding events shocked everyone; they felt a sense of responsibility. Whenever we wanted to highlight some development, I would inform them, and they often responded.

Vimal: Media reports helped, but they were still unable to provide an in-depth discussion of the developments. Hence, we started writing the press notes. This helped expand public awareness and knowledge about the issues and aided in wide dissemination. We were able to share ground realities of the atrocities without the details getting filtered in editing. These press notes were often republished by social media and internet journals focusing on social justice.

Ishita: When the clampdown on media intensified, we could not capture great visuals and had to rely mostly on text. During this time, some of the individual residents' role in creating visibility was important. Arvind, what was your strategy?

Arvind: I had been following the news about evictions and demolitions in the name of forest conservation for some time. I felt the previous evictions made our chances of getting a stay almost negligible. Hence, I wanted to reveal to the world that the Khori Gaon community has been wronged; the forest officials, the politicians, and the police exploited us. They forced us to give bribes if we wanted to live in this settlement and made false promises. However, I was also scared they would harm us further. They arrested people without reason and inflicted violence on us; even women and children were beaten mercilessly. But I had to try. I reached out to journalists writing about Khori Gaon on Facebook. Not everyone responded, but a few did. After explaining the situation and providing them with details and photos, some agreed to publish an article or show the images and videos I had captured. I shared whatever I could to make a strong case. But I requested not to be named, fearing my family's safety.

Ishita: Just as media articles can amplify your voices, they can also report incorrectly. This happened many times.

Arvind: Yes. I understand it is not easy to write about such a complex situation in such a short time, but some of the statements can cause irreparable harm to the community. Journalists who hadn't engaged with the topic enough, often incorrectly analyzed the case. Others were state mouthpieces; they published twisted facts and lies. For example, due to pressure from grassroots collectives like ours, civil society, and a few journalists, when the state finalized the rehabilitation policy and a list of eligible residents were shared, the news was celebrated as a victory. But the reality is that out of 10,000 or so families who resided in Khori Gaon, only 1,009 families were on that list. Hence, I started commenting on articles online and social media posts to highlight the reality.

Ishita: Despite the limited legal protection for informal settlement dwellers in India, regulations mandate due process during evictions, including conducting surveys, providing temporary shelter, and ensuring proper rehabilitation of residents. However, the state disregarded these legal requirements, and the court failed to enforce them, resulting in an unjust process. On July 14, the day demolitions began in Khori Gaon, the government presented a draft rehabilitation policy, offering no time for Khori Gaon residents to respond as required by the policy. The policy was restrictive, failing to address ground realities, and would leave over 90 percent of residents ineligible for rehabilitation. We submitted comments on behalf of the residents, but these were ignored. We subsequently petitioned the court to demand revisions to the policy, and while the court ordered the Haryana government to seek suggestions, our comments were still disregarded. The restrictive policy was finalized on August 20, just three days after Khori Gaon was completely demolished.

As media coverage about Khori Gaon dwindled and the court proceedings dragged on, it became evident to us that this neighbourhood and the community were being slowly erased from public memory. The blog[4] has been one of our methods to record and archive. Arvind, even before we started the blog, you have also been capturing photos and videos, though you had no prior experience with documenting and creating records.

Arvind: When the evictions started, I realized there would be no sign left of this settlement that I called home. On the one hand, I wanted to capture the destruction and violence, and on the other hand, I also wanted to remember Khori Gaon's happy moments. I started capturing photos and uploading them to Google after each day's demolition drive ended. But I also captured smaller celebrations and everyday life.

Images of the demolition captured between July and August 2021. Photo by Arvind Kumar.

Epilogue

Using the colonial-era Epidemic Diseases Act of 1897, the state governments during the COVID-19 pandemic provided municipal corporations with the power to restrict movement, conduct surveillance, and barricade localities. Even aid and food distribution were blocked in Khori Gaon during the demolition, citing contamination excuses. The discussants of this chapter, along with other community members, academics, and lawyers, filed two cases in the Supreme Court, one challenging the demolition of the settlement without any due process, and the second challenging the restrictive rehabilitation policy.

After the demolition, the lawyers representing Khori Gaon argued in court that there were more developments on forest land, most of them belonging to the middle-class and rich people, and yet they were not treated the same way as the urban poor settlement. In response, the court passed an order to demolish all that didn't fall under forest activity. This would mean the state would have to demolish farmhouses, hotels, government buildings, police stations, gated colonies, and private institutions. The state, however, immediately proposed amendments to forest law allowing construction, claiming that the enormous socioeconomic cost of demolition was unsustainable. The court case pertaining to this matter dragged on for a year, eventually concluding with a ruling that allowed non-forest activities, provided they received prior government approval.

As of September 2, 2024, more than three years after the Supreme Court gave the demolition order, 88 percent of the displaced population remains ineligible for rehabilitation flats due to the restrictive policy. Further, the rehabilitation flats are uninhabitable, and bulldozers have been sent regularly to raze the homes of those who continue to live in Khori Gaon under tarpaulin sheets as they have no place to go.

The team lost Vimal Bhai on August 15, 2022, due to his deteriorating health; however, the struggle continues. We continue to document the struggle in our blog — https://khorigaon.in/.

Notes

1. Informal settlements are the neighbourhoods built by the urban poor, which are often in tension with the law and possess insecure tenure. While often called "slums," I deliberately stay away from the word since slums, and by extension their residents, are stigmatized. Some of the vernacular terms for informal settlements are *basti, favela, villa, barrios, asentamientos, and kampung*. For more details, read K. Dovey, T. Shafique, M. van Oostrum, and I. Chatterjee, "Informal Settlement Is Not a Euphemism for 'Slum': What's at Stake beyond the Language?" *International Development Planning Review* 43, 2 (2021).
2. I. Chatterjee, "No City for Khori Gaon Residents: Forced Eviction during a Pandemic in the Name of Forest Conservation," *Radical Housing Journal* 4, 2 (2022), DOI: 10.54825/JALK6985.
3. Vimal Bhai passed away on August 15, 2022. Though the community deeply feels his absence, his leadership and dedication during challenging times continue to sustain and inspire the movement he helped build.
4. https://khorigaon.in/

THE PUBLIC PARK AS A COMMONS

TORONTO, ONTARIO, CANADA

WRITTEN BY
Anna Kramer & Jesse Upton Crowe

This chapter[1] draws from the voices of past and present Encampment Support Network (Parkdale neighbourhood committee) members to describe the struggle for a radically humane approach to housing justice during the pandemic. In it, we trace the exceptional moment of visibility in central spaces created by the pandemic, the activism that emerged from this moment, and the action taken by the City of Toronto in response.

When the first wave of COVID-19 swept through Toronto/Tkaronto, at a time when parks were one of the few places for people to gather, shelters for unhoused people were reduced to one third of their capacity. Doctors prescribed tents to homeless patients as a way to avoid congregate indoor settings, and the city temporarily suspended enforcement of the camping ban in public parks. People who had previously been warehoused out of sight in shelters joined those who had been camping in hidden locations — like under expressways or in ravines — and set up large encampments in several neighbourhood parks across the city. In the late-capitalist norm for cities in the Global North, the unhoused are scattered in interstitial and forgotten spaces, banned from central public space like parks and sidewalks. For example, Chapters 608.13 and 608.14 of the Toronto Municipal Code states that no one is allowed to install tents or permanent structures in city parks and that no person is allowed to sleep in a public park, even when they have nowhere else to go. This is an alienating and individualizing experience.

The tent of a resident in Dufferin Grove Park. Photo by Anna Kramer.

This exceptional moment when the global pandemic intersected with the ongoing housing crisis created the opportunity for more frequent encounters between the unhoused and housed in public space. For more than a year, between the summers of 2020 and 2021, large encampments inhabited at least five neighbourhood parks in Toronto, existing side by side with picnickers, playgrounds, and outdoor music events, in some of the only spaces that were possible for people to gather without fear of COVID-19 transmission. Encampments became an increasingly common part of the city's daily public life, and the people living in them mixed with others. It was a chance to form solidarities across spatial boundaries and connect across divides that often keep people from seeing each other as part of the collective working class. But as the pandemic pulled housed residents out of their homes and into parks and other outdoor recreational spaces, something far from solidarity took shape: housed neighbours called the city and police to remove encampment residents and their tents.

The presence of unhoused people, despite policing, despite anti-camping bylaws, despite discouragement from city officials and hostility from some neighbourhood associations, was a spatial claim and a survival tactic. This chapter follows this spatial claim, witnessing the agency and bravery of the unhoused and the organizing of solidarity networks that arose in response, in the context of continuing state violence. We are writing from Tkaronto/Toronto about our experiences as part of the Encampment Support Network (Parkdale neighbourhood committee), with insights from several unhoused and formerly unhoused comrades.

The Encampment Support Network (ESN) was one of the grassroots organizations that sprang up in Toronto in response to the increased visibility of urban encampments and the violent ways in which they are displaced. Our response, along with those of groups like the Bike Brigade, ALAB Resource Clinic, and Toronto Tiny Shelters, brought together activists from parallel struggles, including rent strikes and Black Lives Matter. Started by artists, service workers, and activists — many of whom were laid off and on temporary pandemic payments — ESN quickly found a place for itself through its political activism by not just providing provisions but also by demanding access to public infrastructure, such as water, toilets, showers, and public housing.[2] Neighbourhood committees formed around encampment locations, including Moss Park, Trinity Bellwoods, Alexandra Park, Cherry Beach, Lamport Stadium, and Dufferin Grove. ESN organized daily outreach to encampments, which included handing out survival supplies, such as tents, drug harm reduction kits, sleeping bags, ice, Gatorade, and coffee. Through the work of artists in the group, the activism took on a creative quality, including a podcast, sign painting, a memorial tent, and a website.[3]

It was a discursive battle in public space to cast a net of protection around highly visible and vulnerable unhoused communities, to try and diffuse the accusatory stigma around drug use, sex work, and other underground economies. ESN advocated on two fronts — towards the city, to point out all the ways that it was hostile to, and failing, unhoused people; and towards housed urban citizens, to foster a sense of shared neighbourhood networks and solidarity rather than division and expulsion as a way to counter the normalized hostility and fear, often under the guise of concern for public health and safety, that the unhoused regularly experience. These spatial solidarities were based on an understanding that housed and unhoused people are all a part of the public and can share spaces like parks. Working in solidarity with those who are occupying parks as living spaces is part of what it means to be a constituent or citizen of the city.

ESN recognized encampments as a radical move in the context of a settler colonial state, where land is assigned separated uses, where land is private property that, by definition, creates exclusion, where housing is inaccessible to those who cannot buy into the market, and where the police maintain spatial control and enforce policy and regulation.

The visibility of encampments and support from neighbours was very different from the usual attempted erasure, banishment, and invisibility experienced by the unhoused.[4] One of the residents of Trinity Bellwoods Park, Hawk, speaking to the city's ombudsperson, compared the difference of living in a public park during COVID-19 with his seventeen years of unhoused experience living in all kinds of camps. When he set up in Trinity Bellwoods, "It was like summer camp." The support and atmosphere of harm reduction available in parks, with meals being handed out by local organizations and open city washrooms, contrasted starkly with the "deep dark places," like hidden encampments. "I've had to hide in the ravines, gangrene on my scrotum, frostbite hands, almost lost feeling." In all his years on the street, he'd never seen anything like the encampments in parks during the pandemic. Hawk would always leave ahead of park evictions to avoid triggering his post-traumatic stress disorder. As the city moved people out, he worried that people newly homeless during COVID-19 would be "tricked into being swept away again." As a veteran of being unhoused, he felt a responsibility to others: "I think about them all the time. The city needs to change things because the people pushed into the ravines, under highways, are the city. They are the city." The unhoused not only belong to the city but define the city. The continued presence of the homeless is an existential question for the city that delegitimizes exclusionary property and housing systems.

Hagbard is a former ESN (Parkdale neighbourhood committee) member who now lives in city social housing. During the first summer of the pandemic, he was staying at a temporary shelter hotel near a highway, a long bus ride from downtown. The Comfort Inn is surrounded by parking lots and plazas with ubiquitous car dealerships, restaurants run by newcomers, and Tim Hortons chain coffee shops. Nearby is a hydro corridor where the Ontario premier, Doug Ford, was known to sell hash in his youth.

As a way of coping with this "lonely hell," Hagbard improvised a private beach from discarded construction materials he found beside dumpsters, near a 6-foot grass median between the parking lot and the hotel. He used bags of sand, left over from tiling, and laid down some tiles and concrete for a little seat. "I could just sit there, take off my shoes, and run my toes through the sand." In his beach in the parking lot, Hagbard was improvising placemaking and shaping the city into something more humane, an act reminiscent of the Paris uprisings of 1968, when students ripped up paving stones for barricades to resist police and found sand underneath. *Sous les pavés, la plage!* (Beneath the paving stones, the beach!) This became a symbol of the movement's desire to disrupt capitalist urbanization and find a connection to a different life underneath — the right to the city being the right to shape the urban environment collectively.[5] Hagbard claimed his humanity by taking off his shoes and relaxing in an alienating automobile-dominated landscape.

Hagbard's beach was an individual act, but it was part of a collective effort to re-imagine community and the city as not defined by property relations and land-use bylaws but instead by alternatives that hold possibility for decolonial and non-capitalist relations to land.[6] The encampments in public parks speak to the innate organizational potential of enlisting networks of support and solidarity as social infrastructure to counter an alienating housing system, showing how home and community can be imagined differently. They give us a glimpse of a different city, where land is accessible to the unhoused, fit with infrastructure, until everyone has a home. Hagbard's political vision imagines mobile infrastructures of care networked with people, extending across all types of spaces, whether inside shelters, outside in encampments, or in permanent affordable housing.

At first, ESN outreach volunteers were unsure of how to show up in these improvised spaces. The creation of real trusting relationships required continually overcoming the deep skepticism of people used to living invisibly in the margins. We struggled to extend our praxis of outreach with survival supplies beyond material goods to building solidarities. Tents were peoples' homes, albeit in public space, and so, forming networks required a constant balance between sharing space and maintaining boundaries, between not wanting to interrupt peoples' homes and personal dynamics, and spending real time laughing, drinking, and meeting inside the encampment space.

Jesse remembers the awkwardness of attempting to forge solidarities across this social divide — across differences in politics, culture, values, methods, perspectives, and understandings of the world. As Hagbard described it, "Sometimes, I would just sit with you for the length of a cigarette and be on my way. I never knew how long I was really allowed to hang out [laughter]." Eventually, formal meetings happened more within the camp and were sometimes difficult, lengthy, and unpredictable as people wandered in and out. We tried to collectively navigate a variety of challenges, from meal delivery to providing survival supplies to addressing NIMBYism. Although these networks were not easy to create, these tenuous solidarities were a profound yet incomplete shift in the power imbalances and relationality between housed and unhoused members of the network.

After a year of tolerating or ignoring these camps or attempting to clear them by moving people into shelters, the mayor of Toronto initiated a massive police action to clear encampments over several weeks in the summer of 2021. The city posted notices of their intention to clear the parks. When the looming threat of police action necessitated early morning scouting shifts, some of the remaining barriers between housed activists and unhoused park residents were dismantled. Activists showed up at the encampment daily at 6 a.m., watching out for signs of an impending eviction. Park residents camping in tents beside the St. Felix respite centre would often be up already, as they were required to check in to the shelter four times a day to maintain access to meals and washrooms. One of those times was four in the morning, so people would be awake and hanging out as dawn came. A member of the scout team reflected: "We'd show up before dawn, and they'd be like, 'they're the Gatorade people and why are they here this early?' So they'd come over and talk to us. And some of them would be, 'yeah, that's badass, come and chill with us. Why are you sitting across the street? Come and hang out with us.' This was what broke the ice." Eventually, encampment residents themselves would join us on scouting shifts, and this led to us meeting in encampments to plan our resistance tactics directly with residents.

Approximately two months into our scouting efforts, the City of Toronto brutally and violently evicted encampment residents in a series of escalating shows of force. The first attempt, at Lamport Stadium, was successfully resisted. In one dramatic instance on June 22, 2020, one hundred and fifty police and private security arrived in Trinity Bellwoods Park to fence in encampment residents' belongings and push people out. They were met by a counterforce of many activists, witnesses, and encampment residents who stood their ground and made clear their demands. It took an entire day for the police to clear the park. Displaced residents scattered to various places, some to shelter hotels, others to remaining encampments.

After the public outcry following the evictions, city officials quietly offered affordable housing to some people living in another city park, Dufferin Grove, where many people from other parks had re-gathered after being forced from encampments police had evicted, while at the same time pressuring people to accept shelter spaces and actively preventing more people from setting up camp.

Encampments continue in some parks and in other spaces along highways, on church land, and in boulevard medians, despite Toronto continuing to enforce bylaws and evicting encampments, moving people most often to congregate shelter space. The police, along with private security hired by the city, continue to surveil urban spaces and move people along. After the summer 2021 encampment evictions, many of the ESN committees disbanded, but the Parkdale neighbourhood committee continues to organize with unhoused and formerly unhoused residents in encampments, social housing, and shelters.

Small numbers of supportive and affordable housing are built as a concession to the public good within major private for-profit developments but not nearly enough to match the rapid loss of existing affordable rents through evictions and financialization. At the same time, the large publicly owned Port Lands are being planned for mainly private condo redevelopment. The rental market is increasingly competitive, and inflation has made food costlier, so people are horribly squeezed and feel like there is nowhere else to go and cannot fathom a way to change it. The city still has no plans to offer necessary infrastructure such as water, toilets, and places to camp for the unhoused in the city.

The system has broken open, and the public has seen inside the violence and oppression hammered down on unhoused and underhoused people.[7] This visibility itself is not enough to create movements; in fact, as we see in the continued policing and banishment of the unhoused across Turtle Island and with the US Supreme Court Grants Pass decision, homelessness is more intensively criminalized and scapegoated for urban problems in tandem with its visibility.

Solidarity cannot be taken for granted and needs to be intentionally built. In this experience of collective precarity, we have begun to grasp how to, tenuously and provisionally, create networks of resilience through resistance. Our experience shows that solidarities formed outside of the government can be transformational. Our work remains incomplete but the revolutionary potential for activism and collective action in moments like these must be strengthened by connections to other movements.

Notes

1. Interviews informing this research follow a university ethics protocol, which includes ongoing consent, the use of pseudonyms where necessary to ensure non-identifiability of participants and honoraria for time. We write from our own perspectives while remaining accountable to our collective. Thanks to Hagbard for your insight, which structures this chapter.
2. Jessie Speer, "The Right to Infrastructure: A Struggle for Sanitation in Fresno, California Homeless Encampments," *Urban Geography* 37, 7 (October 2, 2016), https://doi.org/10.1080/02723638.2016.1142150.
3. "We Are Not the Virus," podcast interviewed unhoused residents as they struggled to access water and shelter from strong winds; Signs said, "We Need Permanent Housing Now" and "The Housing Crisis Is a Real Estate Game"; A tent on the sidewalk with the names of over 500 unhoused community members who had lost their lives during the mayor's term; The website can be found at https://www.encampmentsupportnetwork.com/
4. Nazanin Zarepour, "Encampment Evictions: Toronto's Attack on Class Consciousness," *The Maple*, August 17, 2021, https://www.readthemaple.com/encampment-evictions-and-torontos-attack-on-class-consciousness/.
5. Ruth Wilson Gilmore, *Abolition Geography: Essays towards Liberation,* edited by Brenna Bhandar and Alberto Toscano, (Verso, 2022).
6. Robyn Maynard, Leanne Betasamosake Simpson, Robin D.G. Kelley, and Ruth Wilson Gilmore, *Rehearsals for Living, (*Haymarket Books, 2022).
7. Echo Park Lake Research Collective, Ananya Roy, Ashley Bennett, Jennifer Blake, Jonny Coleman, Hannah Cornfield, La Donna Harrell, et al., (*Dis)Placement: The Fight for Housing and Community after Echo Park Lake,* 2022, https://escholarship.org/uc/item/70r0p7q4.

ENCAMPMENT EVICTIONS IN WASHINGTON, DC

WASHINGTON, DC, UNITED STATES

WRITTEN BY
Aaron Howe & Shannon Clark

Unhoused people spend a lot of time outside. Not only outdoors, but outside of normative understandings of work and home, which create the conditions for dehumanization and stigmatization that reproduce individualized narratives of homelessness. At Remora House, a mutual aid collective in Washington, DC, that provides material aid and advocacy for people living outside, we try to rewrite normative narratives, redirecting the blame from individuals onto unequal housing and wage systems. However, the professionalization of homelessness services co-opts the radical potential of mutual aid groups, adding a "reflection of state power in the same organizations that originally emerged to resist the very same state."[1] While the non-profit industrial complex continues to dominate the redistribution of resources, mutual aid organizations, which have drastically expanded following the outbreak of the COVID-19 pandemic, are making impressive strides in improving the material conditions of daily life.

At Remora House we attempt to build mutual relationships with the unhoused people we work with. This perspective often pits us against non-profits and "experts" who seek top-down understandings of the world that fit with their funding models.[2] For example, because living in a tent is illegal in DC, non-profits receiving city money are not allowed to distribute tents. To the contrary, at Remora House we not only provide tents to unhoused people, but we also advocate for the rights of people to live in tents when no safe and humane alternatives exist. While encampments are not ideal living situations, they provide alternatives to the institutional spaces, such as homeless shelters, that currently dominate the lives of unhoused people.[3] Tents provide people with a space they can call their own, offering privacy, safety, and comfort in otherwise hostile anti-homeless landscapes.

Decades of neoliberal economic restructuring have decreased the profitability of manufacturing and industrial production in the US. These changes have left behind a wake of vacant warehouses and factories in predominantly low-income neighbourhoods. The redevelopment of these vacant properties into luxury apartments and boutiques has become a prime source of capital accumulation in the neoliberal era. Cities engage in "zero-sum inter-urban competition" against other cities to "appear as innovative, exciting, creative, and safe places to live and consume in" to attract higher-income residents, investments, and development.[4] Encampments break the image cities are trying to achieve, disrupting gentrification and placing unhoused people as obstacles to capital accumulation.

Anti-homeless laws are used to deter unhoused people from occupying space in gentrifying areas to create the image of a clean and safe neighbourhood that appeals to higher-income residents. While the local and federal government in DC followed the guidance of the Centers for Disease Control and Prevention to not evict encampments at the beginning of the pandemic, starting in the summer of 2021 encampment evictions escalated to a historic high. In this chapter, we explore how non-profits were used in DC to implement an anti-homeless Housing First (HF) policy, centring the escalation of state-sponsored violence against unhoused people following the COVID-19 pandemic and how mutual aid groups create alternatives beyond the state.

Throughout the 1980s and 90s professionals and hired experts replaced volunteers and activists, institutionalizing responses to homelessness within the non-profit industrial complex and stripping the movement of its radical potential. In 1994, as homelessness in the US drastically grew, the Clinton administration introduced the Continuum of Care (CoC) plan. The CoC plan attempted to place multiple homelessness services under a single umbrella that moved unhoused clients through a series of stages, such as drug or mental health rehabilitation, to become "housing ready."[5] Grant-minded "experts" and professionals responded to different CoC stages, creating the contemporary homelessness institutional landscape that "resulted in a narrower, more specialized organization" that often "fueled misconceptions about the causes of homelessness as providers moved in the direction of treating individual problems."[6] This created a narrative that homelessness was caused by individual failures, such as addiction, laziness, and criminal behaviour, rather than by inadequate housing systems, low wages, and failures in government policy to keep people housed.

This is the political-economic milieu in which HF was initiated in the US when George Bush signed it into federal policy in 2002. Unlike CoC "housing ready" processes, HF prioritizes "housing first," followed by needed wraparound services such as mental health and addiction treatment.[7] While the shift is indeed progressive, many argue that HF policy fits with neoliberal processes of redirecting state welfare to the private sector, such as non-profits. Moreover, HF redefined who is "deserving" of federal assistance by prioritizing housing the "chronically homeless," defined as those who have been homeless for a year or more or have been homeless at least four times in the past three years. While CoC policies required unhoused people to engage in addiction and mental health services before becoming "housing ready," HF policy emphasized removing these people from public spaces. While HF policy successfully housed some "chronically homeless" people, those who remained on the streets faced increased criminalization and encampment evictions.

Prior to the COVID-19 pandemic, "standard dispositions" were the routine way the Office of the Deputy Mayor of Health and Human Services (DMHHS) handled encampment "cleanups." These required a two-week warning, and unlike permanent evictions, which were used less frequently, residents were allowed to re-establish their encampment after "wet and soiled items including wet or soiled bedding, clothing, or tents"[8] were thrown in the garbage. City workers had the power to determine what items were and were not "wet and soiled" and often used this policy to justify the removal of tents and other property from public spaces. For a few months following the CDC's guidelines to not evict encampments, DC stopped all standard dispositions and evictions. However, throughout the pandemic, unhoused people logically chose to avoid congregate shelters, and encampments grew around the city. By April 2021, not only did full standard dispositions resume, but the permanent eviction of encampments escalated dramatically.

The coupling of standard dispositions with the permanent eviction of unhoused spaces has been a primary force of Mayor Bowser's anti-homeless policies since she took office in 2015. In 2015, the DMHHS conducted 29 standard dispositions, and in 2019, they conducted 119.[9] Moreover, months after taking office, Mayor Bowser spent nearly $100,000 to fence off a historically popular camp in Foggy Bottom. Then, in January 2020, following an intense lobbying campaign by the NoMA Business Improvement District, the K Street NE underpass was designated as a "pedestrian passageway." These pedestrian passageways were, on paper, created to ensure sidewalks were clear and provided adequate space for pedestrians to traverse. In reality, pedestrian passageways became a justification for overriding the standard disposition policy to create anti-camping zones. Just months before the COVID-19 pandemic, at least forty unhoused people were displaced and forced to relocate to NoMA's two other underpasses, on M and L Street.

"No-tent zones," like DC's "pedestrian passageways," "have become prime tactics used by the state to create the consumption spaces necessary for neoliberal capital accumulation"[10] aiding in the gentrification of certain city areas. While city leaders promised the "pedestrian passageway" would not be used in other parts of the city, by the fall of 2021 the L and M Street underpasses were also established as "pedestrian passageways." Hints of these forthcoming no-tent zones surfaced in May 2021; when we were distributing supplies to encampments in NoMA's underpasses, unhoused residents told us that their encampment was going to be evicted. During a three-day blitz, city employees and non-profit workers created a list of all unhoused people, known as a "by name list" (BNL), living in the M and L Street underpasses. Many unhoused people we worked with, who had lived in these underpasses for years, were not included on the BNL because they were not around when the list was created.

Months passed with no further information, until finally in August 2021, the DMHHS announced the forthcoming the Coordinated Assistance and Resources for Encampments (CARE) Pilot Program, which targeted encampments in NoMA, Foggy Bottom, and Shaw. CARE attempted to temporarily house people on the BNL, which in NoMA had been created almost four months prior, in one-year bridge housing as they waited for a permanent supportive housing voucher, which provides permanent rent support from the federal government. The BNL included 111 people: 45 from NoMA, 34 from Foggy Bottom, and 32 from Shaw, which were drastically lower than the numbers of people who actually lived at these camps.[11]

While this experimental housing program could have been a progressive step towards housing for all who want it, CARE was coupled with the permanent eviction of each of these camps. Mutual aid groups immediately protested the creation of no-tent zones, as officials from the DMHHS weaponized HF to say these groups were against housing. However, as one unhoused resident who was evicted from NoMA before going to the Shaw camp noted, "The pilot program only selected a few people from down here. The same way we didn't make it on the list down there [on L Street], probably won't make it down here either."[12] Once again, we see the precarity of state-sponsored housing services and how they are doled out unsystematically in ways that justify state-sanctioned violence.

After a series of delays, the eviction of the M and L Street camps was set for October 4, 2021. At that time at least thirty unhoused people still lived in NoMA's underpasses, including many on the BNL who were not yet in bridge housing as well as those who never made the list. On the day of the evictions, mutual aid volunteers responded to the needs of residents, bringing gloves, trash bags, water, and extra hands to help pack and move. As the DMHHS cleared the M Street underpass, they ran into resistance when one unhoused resident, who was just days away from getting his apartment keys, refused to move.[13] Mutual aid volunteers locked arms and created a perimeter around his tent, prompting more unhoused neighbours to stop packing. After a tense standoff, the DMHHS backed off and placed traffic cones around the tents that were not moving. As word of this action spread, ten unhoused people on L Street similarly refused to move.

The DMHHS used a Bobcat 272D3 skid-steer loader to clear the remaining tents, crushing and lifting them over the short guardrail and into the back of a garbage truck. We watched as the Bobcat grabbed a tent which was clearly coned off. "Somebody's in there!" an unhoused person yelled as the skid loader lifted the tent and moved to drop it into the trash compactor. Mutual aid volunteers and medics rushed to free the man trapped in his tent in the bucket of the Bobcat several feet off the ground. Dozens of cops aggressively established a police line, blocking anyone from helping, talking to, or comforting the man, whom many of us knew, as we waited nearly fifteen minutes for an ambulance. While the man could have been seriously injured or killed, he was luckily released from hospital that night with only minor injuries.[14] Following this incident, the eviction was temporarily called off. Many tents remained in the M and L Street underpasses, yet the city installed large concrete barriers on the north side of M Street, which was fully cleared. That night mutual aid groups served food outside the camp, checking in with those who remained and talked about next steps.

The Bobcat incident and concrete barriers stirred a lot of negative attention surrounding CARE. Yet, on October 28, the DMHHS brought the same Bobcat back to L Street, supported by dozens of cops, including the bomb squad and K-9 tactical units. The cops created a hard blockade and only let "professional" outreach workers enter the underpasses. Overcome by the police presence and being in a better situation to relocate, none of the remaining unhoused residents resisted the eviction. Within twenty-four hours, the two underpasses were cleared of tents and replaced with concrete barriers that left a four-foot "pedestrian passageway." Today, dozens of "pedestrian passageways" are located around DC, reflecting the entrenchment of post-COVID homelessness policy.

Intense conversations followed, and many charged that the DMHHS moved so quickly with the CARE program that they almost killed a man. Mutual aid volunteers, non-profits, and some DC council members called on the DMHHS to pause the CARE program until everyone on the BNL was in housing.[15] Yet on December 2, 2021, the Shaw camp was evicted. Days before the eviction, the city installed a fence around the park, leaving only a small exit for the remaining unhoused people. Pressure from DC's council pushed the DMHHS to create a dashboard, which on December 2 showed that, of the thirty-two people on the BNL at the Shaw camp, only thirteen were in bridge housing.[16] On the day of the eviction, dozens of mutual aid volunteers beat the cops to the site and entered the fenced area before the police line formed. Tensions were high and the police outnumbered volunteers. A bigger Bobcat was brought to clear the camp. While the eviction was not stopped, mutual aid groups were able to help unhoused people relocate and bring attention to the criminalization of homelessness intrinsic to HF policy.

The NoMA Bobcat incident, concrete barriers, and the Shaw stand-off provoked a lot of community discussion, and the eviction of the Foggy Bottom camp was indefinitely delayed. The negative attention put

Wayne Turnage, deputy mayor of the DMHHS, on the defensive: "Mutual aid volunteers are using unhoused people for their own ends, such as bolstering their social media followings."[17] However, unlike the unpaid volunteers who had worked at these camps for over a year, Turnage was a well-paid ($230k/year) mayoral appointee with little knowledge of the daily struggles of unhoused people. To justify the DMHHS's heavy-handed approach, Turnage defended the concrete barriers as a way to stop "backfill," meaning unhoused people returning to the site. He said: "The housing first model has created a moral hazard by incentivizing residents in shelters and other areas to migrate to the [encampments] in an effort to secure immediate housing."[18]

Housing, we know, ends homelessness. However, HF policies further veil the class divisions that produce homelessness in the first place and do little to address larger contradictions within our housing systems. The failures of HF are directly related to its implementation by state actors and the non-profit industrial complex, which ignore the real issues unhoused people face. In particular, we worry about the "structural kinship" between HF policies and the removal of "chronically homeless" people from public space.[19] As Craig Willse notes, "Chronic homelessness programs serve the economy twice over: first by removing an economic obstacle and then by investing in a growing non-profit industry of population management."[20]

Non-profits helped create and implement DC's CARE program, offering "expert" justification for increased criminalization. However, mutual aid groups saw through the façade, highlighting CARE as a criminalization campaign with some housing added. The evictions of DC's largest encampments occurred before many on the BNL were in bridge housing. While many people were housed through the program, some of those on the BNL have only recently received housing, while others remain living on the streets. Moreover, dozens of unhoused people who were never included on the BNL were displaced from their tent homes and communities and remain unhoused. Yet, Turnage declared the CARE program a success, threatening to expand it to other camps around the city.

COVID-19 both increased the number of encampments in US cities and reduced the profitability of urban consumption as people stayed home. The centrality of urban capital accumulation is directly related to the escalation of encampment evictions, highlighting the political-economic context of contemporary poverty governance. While CARE was only partially successful in providing housing, it was successful in clearing unhoused people from gentrifying urban spaces that state actors and developers marked as sites for economic growth.

Although we were not able to get more people on the BNL or save all the camps from being evicted, we were able to indefinitely delay one eviction and temporarily delay the others, buying time for unhoused residents to strategize and organize for future resistance. This fight is internally tied to struggles being waged against high rents and evictions that force people to live in public spaces and the battle for higher wages and better working conditions that allow people to stay put. We have a long way to go. But by walking away from the state and non-profit actors who reproduce the state's control over housing and homelessness policy, we believe we are one step closer to obtaining housing for all who want it. Until the day comes that everyone has safe, humane, and accessible housing, we will continue to fight for the rights of people to occupy public spaces.

Notes

1   Dylan Rodriguez, "The Political Logic of the Non-Profit Industrial Complex," In *The Revolution Will Not Be Funded: Beyond the Non-Profit Industrial Complex*, edited by INCITE! Women of Colour Against Violence, (Duke University Press, 2017).
2   Vincent Lyon-Callo, *Inequality, Poverty, and Neoliberal Governance: Activist Ethnography in the Homeless Sheltering Industry*, 3rd edition (University of Toronto Press, Higher Education Division, 2004).
3   Aaron Howe, The City and the City: Tent Camps and Luxury Development in the NoMA Business Improvement District (BID) in Washington, D.C.," *International Journal of Historical Archaeology* 28 (January 18, 2023), https://doi.org/10.1007/s10761-022-00691-2.
4   David Harvey, "From Managerialism to Entrepreneurialism: The Transformation in Urban Governance in Late Capitalism," Geografiska Annaler, Series B, *Human Geography* 71, 1 (1989), https://doi.org/10.2307/490503.
5   Lyon-Callo, *Inequality, Poverty, and Neoliberal Governance*, p. 12.
6   Christina Marie Elwell, "From Political Protest to Bureaucratic Service: The Transformation of Homeless Advocacy in the Nation's Capital and the Eclipse of Political Discourse," PhD dissertation, *American University*, Washington DC ProQuest Dissertations, 2008, p. 95.
7   Lyon-Callo, *Inequality, Poverty, and Neoliberal Governance*.
8   Office of the Deputy Mayor of Health and Human Services, "Protocol for the Disposition of Property Found on Public Spaces and the Outreach to Disabled People," https://dmhhs.dc.gov/page/encampments.
9   Howe, "The City and the City."

10 Harvey, "From Managerialism to Entrepreneurialism."
11 DMHHS/DHS, "Encampment CARES Dashboard," 2021, https://tcp.maps.arcgis.com/apps/dashboards/ec20f8ce7b6a480a923dcb272f80197c.
12 Hannah Schoenbaum, "Homeless Truxton Circle Residents Brace for Early December Eviction amid Pleas to Halt Encampment Clearings," *Street Sense Media*, November 17, 2021, https://streetsensemedia.org/article/dc-care-dmhhs-tents-truxton-circle/.
13 Maydeen Merino and Spencer Donovan, "DC Government Removes Tents, Injures One Resident, Houses Others, and Deploys Concrete Barriers to Enforce a 'Pedestrian Passageway,'" *Street Sense Media*, October 6, 2021, https://streetsensemedia.org/article/dc-tents-encampment-eviction-injures-one-houses-others/.
14 Marissa J. Lang, "Calls to Halt District Program Meant to Move Homeless out of Tents into Housing Intensify," *Washington Post*, October 8, 2021, https://www.washingtonpost.com/dc-md-va/2021/10/07/dc-homeless-pilot-criticisms-grow/.
15 Lang, "Calls to Halt District Program.
16 DMHHS/DHS, "Encampment CARES Dashboard"
17 Marissa J. Lang, "Mutual Aid Groups Formed amid the Pandemic Have Turned Their Focus to the Homeless." *Washington Post*, December 30, 2021, https://www.washingtonpost.com/dc-md-va/2021/12/30/mutual-aid-homeless-response/.
18 Franzi Wild, "Planned Truxton Circle Encampment Evictions Delayed," *Georgetown Voice*, November 27, 2021, https://georgetownvoice.com/2021/11/27/truxton-circle-eviction-delayed/.
19 Tom Baker, and Joshua Evans, "'Housing First' and the Changing Terrains of Homeless Governance," *Geography Compass* 10, 1 (2016), p. 32, https://doi.org/10.1111/gec3.12257.
20 Craig Willse, *The Value of Homelessness: Managing Surplus Life in the United States* (University of Minnesota Press, 2015), p 30.

19

UNHOUSED TENANTS AND THE STRUGGLE FOR HOUSING LIBERATION

LOS ANGELES, CALIFORNIA, UNITED STATES

WRITTEN BY
Annie Powers & Ashley Bennett

On March 24 and 25, 2021, an organized encampment at Echo Park Lake, a public park in Los Angeles close to downtown, was evicted by a mass militarized police force. That police force was preceded with a campaign by the City of Los Angeles — and the council district governing the gentrifying neighbourhood of Echo Park — to offer people living at the park a variety of so-called "housing solutions." Far from actual housing, these offers were most often to emergency shelter programs, and although touted as the path to permanent housing, they were scarce, temporary, and isolating. The park was then enclosed by a fence that caged the public space where tents once stood and a community had thrived for more than a year after the encampment's violent eviction.

Although this mass displacement was characterized by press and politicians as a "clean-up," better known as a "sweep," we argue that Echo Park Lake constitutes an eviction — as do all sweeps.[1] By deploying the language of cleaning to justify evictions, the people experiencing eviction are deliberately dehumanized and placed far outside the category of "tenant." However, just as a sweep is an eviction, so too is an unhoused person a tenant. Taking a cue from the Los Angeles Tenants Union (LATU), which characterizes a tenant as anyone who does not control their own housing, we conceptualize unhoused people as tenants. At a time of renewed and urgently needed tenant struggles, it is crucial to think about organizing amongst and with unhoused people as a key part of those tenants' movements. Indeed, with this framing, the ways in which unhoused people's experiences are on a continuum of housing precarity that includes all tenants becomes clear — and also clear is that it will take all tenants together to imagine and build a world of housing liberation. This analysis stems directly from the organizing of unhoused tenants at Echo Park Lake — and the continued work of those same tenants after their eviction — and demonstrates that the false division between housed and unhoused must end in favour of an understanding of tenancy that includes all who do not control their own housing.

We write on behalf of the After Echo Park Lake Research Collective, which published a monograph, *(Dis)Placement: The Fight For Housing and Community After Echo Park Lake*,[2] based on a year of ethnographic interviews and data analysis. We were on-the-ground organizers with the Echo Park Lake encampment from 2019 to 2021, and this article draws in part on that firsthand experience.

In late 2019, an encampment community began to grow at Echo Park Lake, and it quickly became targeted by the Los Angeles Police Department and park rangers. Like police, park rangers, who are mandated to enforce park rules and laws and respond to emergencies, have become increasingly militarized over the past several decades: they are able to make arrests and carry gear almost identical to that of LAPD officers, with the exception of firearms, although rangers themselves have demanded that they be equipped with guns for the past twenty-five years. Black unhoused leaders at Echo Park Lake were eager to fight back, and community organizations Street Watch LA and Ground Game LA supported the unhoused community in resisting and demanding real housing. After a series of successful sweep blockades in early 2020, in which housed and unhoused alike defended the camp's right to exist while no housing was available for them, COVID-19 hit — and sweeps were halted under the Safer at Home order issued across LA County. Safer at Home also led to the city's abandonment of the Echo Park Lake community. Shower services were halted. Bathrooms were locked overnight. People long struggling with mental and physical disability hoped to enter Project Roomkey (PRK), a statewide emergency shelter program to provide hotel rooms to unhoused people particularly vulnerable to COVID-19. Despite demands made by the encampment — in the form of signs asking Mayor Eric Garcetti for a hotel room and even a day-long occupation of an empty Ritz Carlton room — PRK remained inaccessible to most in the camp, as the program offered a tiny number of slots compared to the overwhelming numbers of unhoused people in LA. Meanwhile, the city left people to die outside. In the case of Andrew Kettle, an Echo Park Lake resident, a 911 call hurt more than it helped. When emergency medical responders arrived on scene by ambulance to respond to Kettle's illness, they dismissed his symptoms as something he just needed to sleep off in his tent. He was left there and tragically never woke up.

In these conditions of systematic abandonment, the Echo Park Lake community came together to create infrastructure to keep each other safe and well. The encampment began holding collective meetings to discuss conditions and needs, and out of this organizing emerged a constellation of community programs and resources. A kitchen was conceived and developed to combat food scarcity and communalize the donations offered by housed community members. A garden created a space for peace and healing. Organizers built showers and politicized them with a sign explaining that "Mayor Eric Garcetti took our showers." In collaboration with Street Watch LA, the "Power Up!" mutual aid table became a fixture, where members of the encampment could charge their phones, pick up or drop off clothes, share food, and build relationships with unhoused and housed people alike. Indeed, the encampment began to organize as Echo Park Rise Up, generating a jobs program to help keep the park clean and people fed. Along with these demonstrations of collectivization and the social economy in practice, Echo Park Lake became an example of abolition in practice. The unhoused community created a set of agreements — keep your area clean, keep drug use inside tents, do not steal — that were by and large enforced by the community rather than involving police or park rangers. In all these ways, Echo Park Lake built as much a vision of tenant-controlled housing as is possible given the conditions of state abandonment, private property relations, and the ever-looming threat of the militarized LAPD. The park became a home. One member of Echo Park Rise Up draped a banner over their RV that put it best: "Affordable housing is community self-determination." Such world-building was possible in the opening offered by COVID-19: Safer at Home meant cruel state abandonment, but it also gave the unhoused community of Echo Park Lake the opportunity to imagine and create without the daily threat of sweeps and police enforcement.

The imagination and analysis behind these practices and infrastructures of collective care were about more than just survival. Although there were powerful forces of gentrification in the neighbourhood, there were also housed tenants and community members involved in organizations like Street Watch LA, LATU, and Ground Game LA who materially and spiritually supported Echo Park Rise Up. All these organizations understand housing insecurity as a continuum enforced by state violence, situating housed tenants within that continuum. In the true spirit of radical mutual aid, housed and unhoused alike learned from one another, shared with each other, and broke bread together. Contrary to a charity model, the encampment encouraged collective learning about the conditions of racial capitalism and ways of being in community to contest and resist those conditions. In a GoFundMe set up to generate monetary support for the camp, leader Ayman Ahmed characterized this mutual aid as a type of world-building:

> Imagine a world where there was no "bottom." One where your neighbor was your neighbor because they're your neighbor not because of tax brackets or real estate. A world where good is done for the sake of good not gain. In the past few months, we the unhoused community at Echo Park Lake, have been creating the groundwork for this world.[3]

The Echo Park Lake community could imagine, and even generate in microcosm, the world that the tenants' movement hopes to see: one that is not determined by access to commodified private property. This does not mean that conflict and tension did not abound — after all, the park still existed within the system of racial capitalism and could not avoid the harassment of entities like police, whose duty is to enforce the reproduction of that system. Nevertheless, the community-building at Echo Park Lake pointed to the possibility of a better world — not just for unhoused people, but for all tenants.

Echo Park Rise Up continued to emphasize that the Echo Park Lake community was not just the unhoused camping at the park but included the housed participating in this world-building project as well. In August 2020, the Echo Park Rise Up Instagram account posted an image of the park's garden with the caption:

> This community garden is part in memorial for Brianna and Andrew who both left this world too soon, Rest In Peace and part for all of us. Not just us "unhoused" but for all of you in homes as well. We are all members of the same community and not doing things together makes no sense at all. Please come and plant with us, grow life with us where life was taken, let's show the city that love really does break down all barriers by building something together, regardless of economic positions and the labels that come with them. No more "homeless." No more "homeowner/renter." No more labels. Just people living together in community growing some plants.[4]

Embedded in this description of the garden is an understanding that unhoused and housed are arbitrary divisions that should be abolished — in favour of a category, like tenant, that encompasses all of us in the fight for a better world. Indeed, this post indicates the way that the Echo Park Lake community functioned as a radical critique of capitalism that manifested in material ways. The resources in the kitchen, showers, community garden, and more were available to all. This socialization of resources generated a commons through the dissolution of economic status in the public space of the park. Denying capitalism's attempts to divide us, refusing capitalism's privatization of public space, the Echo Park Lake community imagined housing liberation for everyone — housed and unhoused.

During the Echo Park Lake eviction, residents of the encampment were pressured to leave not just by the imminent threat of a militarized police force, but by offers to join the temporary program Project Roomkey (PRK) — with the false promise of permanent housing thereafter. Although Echo Park Lake tenants had demanded PRK rooms for months, the program only became an option once the encampment was targeted for eviction. This "carrot and stick" strategy, conjoining enforcement and services, is now deployed across Los Angeles — testament to the state's use of co-optation and contortion of radical demands as a tactic of counter-insurgency, breaking up communities like the one at Echo Park Lake with the promise of programs like PRK. But those who enter PRK find that it, too, is a stick, operating as a publicly funded suspension of civil, human, and housing rights. It is out of this experience that the category of "unhoused tenant" emerges as an urgent call to the tenants' movement.

PRK systematically strips those in it of agency, autonomy, and basic rights. Upon entry to PRK, residents must sign a contract that revokes their status as tenants, instead consigning them to the category of "participant" in an emergency program. In direct contradiction to LA's Residential Hotel Ordinance, fought for by skid row residents to restrict the renovation and conversion of residential hotels, people who stay in a PRK hotel for thirty days or more are not considered tenants because they have signed away that right in their contract. Conditions in PRK underscore this rightless status, demonstrating how the program strips away not just tenant rights — but along with them, civil and human rights. Unhoused people staying in PRK are subject to restrictive curfews, spoiled food, random room searches, hostility and harassment from staff, and around-the-clock closed-circuit surveillance. Staff can enter rooms at any time — just one knock is considered sufficient notice — and residents have reported intrusion during private moments like showering or using the toilet. Often far from their communities, residents are required to be alone in those rooms — no visitors, not family nor friends, not even neighbours inside the hotel. These prison-like conditions are catastrophic for residents' physical and mental health, neither of which are supported on-site. Indeed, people are fighting in these hotels to survive: deaths run so rampant and are so unacknowledged that La Donna Harrell, an unhoused member of the After Echo Park Lake research collective, characterized PRK as "death jail." Those that do survive are subject to eviction — termed "exit" — at any time for alleged violation of any of these rules.[5]

Out of these desperate conditions has arisen Unhoused Tenants Against Carceral Housing (UTACH), whose very name places unhoused people inside the category of tenant. Refuting their contractual status as "participants," members of UTACH demand the same rights afforded tenants under the law — rights like a written notice for entry or a legal process for an eviction, both of which are deliberately stripped away in PRK. Moreover, the grievances articulated by members of UTACH address the dehumanization and destabilization caused by rules that systematically deny tenancy rights to those living inside PRK. In early 2021, organized residents living in the Airtel Plaza Motel, then closing ("demobilizing"), laid claim to their rights as tenants by insisting that the COVID-19 eviction moratorium also applied to them. While these PRK sites still closed down, many of those that organized were moved to different hotels, where they shared lessons from their fight to stay. Indeed, this anti-eviction organizing points to the fact that the long forewarned COVID-19 mass evictions have already begun — from PRK sites. But they have been hidden from view by both the dehumanization of the unhoused and the systemic attempts to obfuscate their rightful claims to tenancy.[6]

Despite the promise of permanent housing made by PRK, even those who manage to stay have found their future options for housed tenancy to be extremely limited — a precarity shared by all poor tenants. For many in PRK, the best-case onramp to so-called "permanent housing" is an Emergency Housing Voucher (EHV), a subset of section 8, federal low-income housing access vouchers that exist solely for unhoused individuals — but are far from a guarantee of housing access. Finding a landlord who will accept a housing voucher, passing a background and credit check, proving income or employment, and paying an enormous deposit all make it extremely difficult (if not impossible) for the unhoused to make use of these vouchers. Indeed, some vouchers only offer rental assistance for a set length of time — often twelve or eighteen months — a reminder that so-called "permanent housing" still requires an individual to pay market rate rent in desperately unaffordable Los Angeles. This echoes the experience of low-income, long-term tenants now paying far below market rates — many of whom become targeted by landlords eager to evict them in favour of wealthier tenants paying higher rents. When pushed out of their homes, these low-income tenants face the same obstacles to renting that unhoused PRK tenants do — and for both, not finding a place to stay means homelessness. Unhoused and housed tenants alike experience this constant precarity in navigating a housing market designed to maximize real estate profits at the expense of the poor.[7]

Those profits — and the precarity of tenants — are enforced by police. As UTACH's name points out, unhoused tenants experience the housing system in Los Angeles as tied up with criminalization and carcerality. Indeed, evictions from PRK continue even as the familiar places where the unhoused have long eked out survival are now subject to new iterations of criminalization — this time, through a new version of LA Municipal Code 41.18, which targets the poor by banning sitting, sleeping, or lying in what have become hundreds of zones across the city. UTACH's hard-earned and collectivized knowledge of this system, which criminalizes anyone who can't afford the rent, is key to their self-definition as unhoused tenants. Particularly for low-income people, carcerality is a universal quality of the experience of all tenancy — if not now, then in a future housing experience. The example of the 2013 Echo Park gang injunction, deployed in the neighbourhood to pave a path for real estate capital and to accelerate gentrification, demonstrates the way that state violence is wielded against housed tenants just as it is unhoused. The gang injunction banished poor people, regardless of housing status, from their homes and communities by giving police carte blanche to arrest and incarcerate poor, Black, and brown people for engaging in basic human activities like hanging out or standing in public. Indeed, the experience of the unhoused is a bellwether for our collective future. Police use unhoused tenants as a sinister testing ground to develop counter-insurgency tactics, data collection, and surveillance technology they will then deploy against housed tenants. Just as housing and policing are linked for the poor, so too must the tenants' struggle be linked: it is one system that evicts, criminalizes, and banishes anyone not in control of their own housing. The carceral conditions of unhoused lives are not merely a window into the future for all tenants unless we organize — but also the key battleground in the ongoing class war on the poor. Unhoused tenants show us that the fight for housing and the fight for abolition must be one and the same.

In order to preserve its supremacy, the regime of racial capitalism to which we are all subject operates in a variety of ways to engineer divisions — especially along lines of race and class. What the organizing of unhoused people in PRK and at Echo Park Lake demonstrates is that housing status is yet another of these divisions, intended to segregate and weaken our collective fight for housing liberation. The fight for tenants to stay in their homes and the fight against sweeps are not always seen as the same terrain of struggle, and yet they must be. The threat of becoming homeless is a cudgel often used to cow precarious tenants into submission to unjust, unhealthy, and in many cases, carceral conditions. The neoliberal city — the system of capitalism itself — benefits from the tenants' fights remaining divided, our power remaining scattered.

And indeed, in many ways, the power of UTACH has scattered. The first months of organizing led to press conferences, meetings with city agencies like the Los Angeles Homeless Services Authority and the

Mayor's Office, and ultimately the easing of the curfew from 7 p.m. to 10 p.m. and the provision of overdose-reversing Narcan at PRK sites. In response to UTACH's assertion of tenants' rights, however, the state has responded with ever-greater repression and co-optation. As a COVID-19 mitigation rule, tenants in PRK were forced into isolation and prohibited from visiting or speaking to one another inside the hotel. When UTACH organizers attempted to reach their neighbours anyway, PRK staff cut phone lines, systematically tore down flyers, broke up conversations, placed unhoused tenants in quarantine, harassed tenants, and targeted organizers for eviction from PRK. And eviction sweeps of encampments across the city have resumed in force — and in some places, never stopped. Not dissimilar from the 2013 Echo Park gang injunction that effectively criminalized standing and hanging out, the recently revised version of LA Municipal Code 41.18 bans sitting, sleeping, and lying on the sidewalk. While 41.18 went into effect in 2021, the "anti-camping" sentiment of the code was previously rendered unconstitutional in court because criminalizing someone for survival is cruel and unusual punishment when there is nowhere else to go. Now, by yoking sweeps to the carceral offer of moving into PRK properties, police can resume targeting people who are simply trying to rest. With the inauguration of LA mayor Karen Bass in 2023, "Inside Safe" applies the Echo Park Lake model citywide, conjoining eviction sweeps with offers to carceral shelters or motel rooms for as short a stay as a single night. Most return to the street but find the places where they previously encamped now subject to 41.18 enforcement.

These attempts to disorganize UTACH have succeeded, particularly as the homeless services system individualizes the fight for housing, siloes unhoused people into a tangle of bureaucracy, and churns people through endless carceral placement that they must endure and survive. The struggle of unhoused tenants for some modicum of stability in the face of constant evictions points to the importance of uniting the tenants' movement. Bringing together housed and unhoused tenants enables the tenants' movement to fight for and support the struggle of the poorest among us.

For the tenants' struggle to unite housed and unhoused, the tenants' movement must understand that sweeps are evictions, unhoused people are tenants, and organized unhoused communities must be in control of the terms of their housing. Indeed, with the expiration of eviction (and sweep) moratoriums that allowed precarious tenants — both housed and unhoused — to eke out spaces of survival, even more housed tenants will face homelessness. But more than simply linking our organizing, Echo Park Lake and UTACH both demand that we consider unhoused tenants as a priority in the tenants' movement: their experience is our collective future, particularly as ending COVID-19 protections push more and more tenants to the streets. As demonstrated here, that future might be bleak — like it is in PRK or on the street — but if the people organize collectively, it could be beautiful. Like the Echo Park Lake community argued, a different world — without private property, without class hierarchy — is possible. But to get there, the tenants' movement must abolish the borders between housed and unhoused to fight for all tenants, everywhere. When we do, taking seriously the theorizing of unhoused tenants, we can not only imagine the world we want to see — a world of tenant power, where housing is for everyone, where criminalization does not exist — we can create it. Unhoused tenants demonstrate that the path forward is a unified tenants' movement.

Notes

1 We write on behalf of the After Echo Park Lake (After EPL) Research Collective, inaugurated after the mass eviction of the unhoused community at Echo Park Lake, which brings together university and movement-based scholars with unhoused comrades to study displacement in Los Angeles. The collective works in solidarity with Unhoused Tenants Against Carceral Housing (UTACH) and has overlapping membership. Both authors of this chapter, Ashley Bennett and Annie Powers, were on-the-ground organizers with the Echo Park Lake encampment from 2019 to 2021 and in solidarity with UTACH beginning in 2021, and this article draws in part on that firsthand experience.
2 Ananya Roy, Ashley Bennett, Jennifer Blake, Jonny Coleman, Hannah Cornfield, La Donna Harrell, Terrie Klein et al., *(Dis) Placement: The Fight for Housing and Community after Echo Park Lake*, 2022.
3 Roy et al., *(Dis)Placement*, p. 92.
4 Ayman Ahmed, "Echo Park Lake: A Vision of Love and Community" (2020), https://www.gofundme.com/f/echo-park-rise-up-a-vision-or-love-amp-community.
5 Roy et al., *(Dis)Placement*, pp. 54-65.
6 Roy et al., *(Dis)Placement*, p. 62.
7 Roy et al., *(Dis)Placement*, pp. 144-45.

HOUSING SHOULD NOT BE A LUXURY

VANCOUVER, BRITISH COLUMBIA, CANADA

WRITTEN BY
Marena Skinner

Art activism plays an important role in most social movements, and tenant organizing and housing justice movements are no exception. This image, which has been turned into posters and stickers and shared widely on social media, was created by print and multimedia artist Marena Skinner, who is now based in Edmonton. This is one of many images that circulated throughout Vancouver, Marena's former home in pre-pandemic days in response to the city's rising housing costs. As pandemic housing challenges set in, Marena's posters and stickers adorned lampposts and surfaces throughout the city, just as fellow artists and activists creatively spread their demands for housing where they live. The art created within housing justice movements and by tenants lends itself to be taped to street-facing windows in apartment buildings, hung from the balconies of rental units, and posted outside of tents at encampment sites, declaring as Marena's image powerfully does, that housing should not be a luxury.

Artwork by Marena Skinner.

AFTERWORD

OURS TO SHAPE

LOS ANGELES, CALIFORNIA, UNITED STATES

WRITTEN BY
Alexander Ferrer

A crisis is often an acute condition. Yet, as we have noted throughout this volume, the housing crisis is a permanent condition for many, tenants and owners, housed and unhoused, who stand constantly at the threshold of displacement. The reality of this permanent crisis, however, does not negate the importance of its punctuation by the acute moments its "catastrophic convergence" (to borrow a phrase from Christian Parenti)[1] with generalized social disruption generates. Compounded crises are also an opportunity for insurgency, the opening of possibilities for new forms of struggle, and the development of alternative paradigms of governance and building power.

The housing question, now like in many periods before, has re-entered public discussion as this ever-present crisis has begun to claw at middle-class pockets (and consciousness). While we welcome the renewed attention to housing, we worry that a decidedly middle-class concern once again dominates the debate. Despite the global emergence of a re-energized and militant housing justice movement, the housing question of popular discourse remains resolutely pre-political, dominated by ideological promises of a quick fix through liberalization schemes and the general reduction of the housing question to a problem of market management and supply. Housing, they assure us, is a commodity like any other and, with the right set of policy tools, the market can be brought to balance to the satisfaction of all parties.

The heightened visibility of the capitalist housing market's immiserative tendencies in the form of mass houselessness has also awoken in the middle-class public a visceral and reactionary demand for immediate solution. Currently, this crisis is dually managed through a framework of paternalistic service provision and outright violence.

In our volume, we challenge the assumption that people in housing crisis are passive and centre the analysis that shows how the housing system experienced at the margins is organized according to logics of power and difference. Thinking with and within movements at a moment of compounded crisis, we bring attention to the inherently political nature of housing and think through the multifaceted dynamics of re-posing the housing question politically in a manner which prefigures a radical transformation of what it means to be home. These chapters demonstrate the urgency, vibrancy, and originality of the movement for housing justice under the conditions of compounded crisis and assert that, far from being passive objects of intervention, tenants, the poor, the unhoused are and have always been protagonists in resolving housing crises. We trace through our chapters how popular mobilizations have imagined, contested, struggled for, and struggled to defend the answers posed to contemporary housing questions.

Of course, if response to the housing crisis has not been solely the product of top-down interventions of government, neither has the housing justice movement prevailed in impressing its visions uniformly. The claims of housing justice movements have too often been dismissed as utopian, parochial, misguided, or worse, at the whim of public-private partners and non-profit managers tasked with urban rule. In contrast to the potential for rupture embedded in moments of crisis, the overarching response of this constellation of crisis managers has been to produce a governance apparatus that seeks to facilitate a return to the violence of normalcy.

Responses to the COVID-19 pandemic illustrate the dialectic between the new possibilities opened up by struggle and the drive to preserve and restore the existing order of social relations. The explosion of tenant unionism and direct confrontational struggle and the proliferation of mutual aid efforts in cities everywhere reflect the promise of these moments and the galvanizing nature of the conjuncture of crisis and a rising social movement. The rollout of social protections which appear state initiated are actually, as we show, conditioned by the mobilization of those affected.

The moratoriums on evictions in many places around the world in the initial months of the latest pandemic ended not with a surge of evictions, as many activists feared, but instead with a gradually cresting wave. In the main, the promised eviction moratoriums merely deferred evictions until the point at which they could again be carried out without damaging the legitimacy of the rentier system. Rental assistance, paid directly to landlords rather than to tenants, preserved the evictability and displaceability of tenant "beneficiaries" of these funds. In Canada and the United States, federal funding for local programs was unevenly and incompletely spent, whether due to administrative sclerosis or disciplinary malice. Funding which promised potentially unlimited spending on the purchase of houses and hotel units for emergency housing was barely used.[2]

In many respects, this absence of a surge in evictions is a testament to the success of organized tenants and advocates who were able to push governments across the globe to adopt eviction protections, often because of protracted contestation. It is also a testament to the inadequacy of the protections that were ultimately extended, which were temporary, contingent, and partial, and whose withdrawal has manifested in the resurgence of eviction rather than its enduring defeat. In many respects, the nature of pandemic eviction protections reflects an orientation of governance not towards the prevention of harm but towards its manageable dispensation. Legislative protections "flattened the curve" of eviction, preventing collapse but not cruelty. As we move further past the moment of rupture, the picture darkens. The language of crisis is increasingly redeployed to justify the violent displacement and (always temporary) disappearance of the encampments which grew rapidly during the pandemic — a project which not even the declaration of public health emergency predicated on sheltering in place could halt entirely.

What all too often follows moments of intensive organizing is immense exhaustion and burnout. Much of the activist energy that rapidly appeared in the early 2020s around racial justice, police abolition, and housing justice dissipated, with organizations disbanding, institutionalizing, re-forming, and splitting. And many participants in tenant struggle, particularly the established non-profit advocacy and community organizing outfits which in many places were instrumental in the extraction of protections from the state, have increasingly turned to defending, extending, and administering the insufficient policies that were won. The collective insurgency of occupation gave way to the business of forming community land trusts and the individualization of navigating rental assistance applications. Tremendous promises won through confrontation, like the promise of tenancy-preserving eminent domain, are now held up by the recalcitrance of elected officials.[3]

Ultimately, the possible rupture we imagined might come from the flurry of pandemic tenant organizing never materialized quite as we hoped it would. Does this mean we "let a good crisis go to waste," as the perhaps apocryphal saying goes? The housing justice movement did not fail to make its mark during the crisis, as our contributors demonstrate. The answers to the questions at the heart of this volume — what kind of infrastructures, what kind of solidarities, and what kind of politics will be the legacy of the mobilizations of this and future crises — are still being crystallized. As the continued risk and severity of COVID-19 is increasingly downplayed and ignored even while people continue to get and stay sick unabated, the legacy of this struggle at the junction of housing, racial, and health justice is ours to shape.

Let's get at it.

Notes

1   Ashley Dawson, "Tropic of Chaos: Christian Parenti Interviewed," *Social Text Online,* October 7, 2011, https://socialtextjournal.org/tropic_of_chaos_christian_parenti_interviewed/
2   Ananya Roy, "Emergency Urbanism," in *The Long Year: A 2020 Reader,* edited by *Thomas J. Sugrue and Caitlin Zaloom* (Columbia University Press, 2022).
3   Milly Chi, "LA City Council Leverages Eminent Domain to Buy Hillside Villa Apartment Building on Behalf of Tenants," *PBS of Southern California,* August 31, 2022, https://www.pbssocal.org/news-community/l-a-city-council-leverages-eminent-domain-to-buy-hillside-villa-apartment-building-on-behalf-of-tenants.

INDEX

ableism, tenant struggles amid, 3–4
abolition,
    growing movement for, 8, 10, 90, 104
    housing politics and, 83, 92, 104, 203, 209
    organizing frameworks incorporating, 49–50, 55, 60, 85, 198
addiction, 189
    amid COVID-19: 5, 39
    housing while recovering from, 34, 38–41
advocacy, 82, 158
    campaigns, 163–5, 168
    housing policy, 19–20, 42, 47, 118–22, 132
    legal, 115–16, 118–22, 124n1, 126n27
    organizations, 85, 118, 140, 187–8, 209
    tenant-led, 56, 83, 102–3, 109, 149–51, 181
affordability, housing, 163, 183
    COVID-19 and, 25, 114
    decrease in/need for, 31, 91, 96, 149
    government (inadequate) provision of, 39–40, 47, 51, 185
    historical, 9, 16, 25, 27, 133–4
    lack of, 11–12, 29, 58, 139, 202
    struggles to preserve/demand, 22, 51, 93, 115, 136–7, 198
Ahmed, Ayman, 199
Airbnb, 96, 98, 104
anarchism, 9, 60
Anti-Eviction Mapping Project (AEMP), 95, 100–2, 104
anti-eviction organizing, 83, 92, 109, 202
    in Serbia, 73–80
anti-racist struggles, 104
    housing movement incorporation of, 51, 55, 83, 85–6, 129
    reawakening, 4–6, 10–11, 64–6, 48, 92
    see also Black Lives Matter movement
apartments, 58, 119, 206
    disrepair in, 25, 36–8
    luxury, 34, 98, 188
    surveillance in, 34–5, 40–1, 88–91, 99
    tenant organizing in, 25–6, 67, 88–9, 110, 144
Armour (property management), 35–6
art activism, 206
Atlanta, 71–2
    eviction crisis in, 65–7
    Peoplestown, 64, 72n2
austerity measures, 3, 12, 17, 20–1, 145
autonomous cooperative living, 60–2
autonomy,
    encampment practising of, 55–6, 60–2
    infringement on, 47, 201
    value/principle of, 55, 60, 144–5
Australia, 150–1
    housing crisis in, 148–9, 152–4
    housing narratives in, 149, 155
    post-pandemic policing/surveillance, 6, 153
    see also Renters and Housing Union (RAHU)

bailiffs,
    evictions by, 86, 91
    Serbian public-private, 74–6, 79–80
banishment laws, housing,
    amid COVID-19: 159–64
    impacts of, 157–60, 162–5
    homelessness and weekly registration, 160–2, 164
banks, 1, 58
Belgrade, anti-eviction organizing in, 73, 79–80

Bell, Bruce, 131
biopolitics, 36–7
Black Lives Matter movement, 45–7, 51, 83, 97, 181; see also anti-racist struggles
Black people,
    historical communities of, 24–6, 64, 67–71, 82–3, 97
    homeownership, 25, 59, 82–3
    housing segregation/displacement, 25, 47, 82–3, 85, 91–2
    poverty/homelessness and, 10, 54, 110–11, 159–61
    self-determination struggles, 24–8, 30, 61, 67–71, 197
    value of organizing history/experiences, 69–71
    violence/surveillance against, 5–8, 82, 86–90, 97, 102, 203
Black Power Movement, 24, 27, 30
Brown, Constance, 130–1
Bush, George H.W., 6
Bush, George W., 189

Canada,
    eviction crises in, 139–42, 209
    housing initiatives/strategies, 39–40
    housing policy, 15, 39–40, 140, 145
    Indigenous people, treatment of, 16, 38
    post-pandemic policing/surveillance, 6–7, 42, 89
    public housing, 15–16, 36
capital,
    accumulation, 1, 39, 58, 99, 188–90, 193
    social, 69
    tenant struggles versus, 3–4, 58, 133, 155
capitalism,
    alienation under, 7, 179
    anti-, 9, 129
    inequities under, 10, 139, 203
    racial, 24, 42, 104, 199–200, 203
    rehabilitative, 37, 39, 41–2
    settler-colonial, 139, 155, 183
capitalist state,
    free-market policies and, 30–2, 207–8
    housing struggles versus, 1, 9–10, 58, 80, 183, 200–1

carcerality,
    rehabilitative housing and, 37–8, 40–1, 43
    surveillance technologies and, 97, 102, 104
    tenancy and, 201–4
Castells, Manuel (The City and the Grassroots), 8–9
Center City (Philadelphia), 45, 47, 49
Centers for Disease Control (CDC) guidance, 45, 48, 55, 189
Chicago, 47
    housing banishment law impacts, 157–64
Child and Family Services, see foster care system
Chinese immigrants, 15, 57
Chua, Charmaine, 55
civil rights,
    housing policies/litigation, 97, 114–15, 124n1
    movement, 5, 59
class,
    consciousness, 11, 64, 67–9, 93, 109, 180
    disparities, 47, 76–7, 111, 149–52
    divisions in organizing, 65, 69–71, 152, 193, 205
    Marxist analysis of, 9–11, 61
    middle, 59, 61, 77, 177, 207–8
    public housing and, 36, 58
    renter/precarious, 148–52, 154
    war, 61, 154, 203
    working, see working class
classism,
    housing policies and, 58–9, 139
    tenant struggles versus, 3–4, 7, 61
collective bargaining, 143, 145
    concepts of tenant, 140–2, 144
    utility of, 140–1, 145
colonization, 10, 139; see also settler colonialism
Comerford, Thomas, 28, 32
commoning,
    emergence of new forms of, 76, 78
    infra-/urban, see infra-commoning
Community Development Project (CDP), Public Counsel, 114–16, 123, 126n30

Index 213

condo developments, 11, 34–5, 185
connection,
   building, 75, 143, 155, 186
   importance for movements, 3, 7–8, 150, 183
Continuum of Care (CoC) plan, 188–9
cooperation, practising value of, 45, 60–2
court-watching,
   concept and functions of, 109–10, 112
   collectives/programs/resources, 108–12
   experiences of, 130–1
   sousveillance, 110, 112–13
COVID-19 pandemic,
   activism pivoting focus of, 73, 76, 79, 84–5, 92–3
   Downtown Eastside (Vancouver) amid, 14, 16–21
   emergency relief programs/withdrawal, 20–1, 57–8, 92, 117–20
   evictions moratoriums, 56–7, 86–90, 108–9, 116–17, 134, 151–6, 209
   exacerbation of precarity, 5, 16–22, 24, 31, 70, 79, 150
   government responses to, 15–20, 57–8, 76–80, 85–90, 149–51
   health care measures, 4–5, 14, 17–21, 80, 116–19, 149
   homelessness amid, 37–40, 48, 54, 66, 179–82
   housing banishment laws, 159–64
   housing crisis elements from, 1–2, 5, 17–21, 116
   landlords in, 1–2, 4–5, 38–41, 117
   municipal responses to, 14, 17, 20–21, 92, 130, 177, 179, 182
   mutual aid organizing, 17–20, 23n16, 54–6, 65, 72, 198–9
   rent debt in, 66, 70
   rent payment struggles in, 1, 57, 85, 99, 108, 117, 134
   shelter-in-place restrictions, *see* shelter-in-place orders
   shelter services, 7, 48, 55, 179, 184–5, 197–8
   tenant organizing, 5, 65–70, 90, 114–17, 135, 210
   wage loss, 4–5, 85, 99
   workplace closures, 3–5

COVID Emergency Tenant Response (CETR) initiative, 18–21
criminalization, 75, 205
   of homelessness, 10–11, 185, 189, 192–3, 203–4
   housing banishment and, 158, 160
   of poverty, 7, 10–11, 169
   surveillance technology and, 96–7
critical legal studies (CLS), 115
Cummings, Scott, 115

death, 87, 160
   Black folks', 5–6, 66, 86–7, 104, 122
   COVID-19 and, 1, 56
   Indigenous premature, 42
   by police, 5–6, 11, 35, 66, 86–7, 104
   tenant, 5, 49, 201
debt strike, 103
dehumanization, 11
   homelessness and, 167, 187, 196
   resisting, 7–8, 201–2
Detroit,
   Buildings, Safety Engineering, and Environmental Department (BSEED), 82, 84–5, 88–9
   rental property ordinance enforcement, 84–5, 89–91, 93, 94n6
Detroit Police Department (DPD), 86
   tenant surveillance by, 89–91
Detroit Renter City (DRC),
   anti-surveillance campaign, 89–90
   COVID-19 pivoting focus of, 84–5, 92–3
   formation and disbanding of, 82–3, 91–3
   rental ordinance/eviction activism, 84–91
   see also The Barbara
Detroit Will Breathe (DWB), 87–8, 92
developers, real estate,
   interests of, 11, 58, 139–40, 144
   tenant displacement by, 119, 133, 136, 194
disabled people,
   housing precarity faced by, 5, 58, 121
   poverty and, 10, 197–8
disinvestment, social/neighbourhood, 7, 12, 15, 26, 37, 46, 64

displacement, 79, 116, 205n1, 207
  activism to counter, 25–7, 47, 82–3, 95, 115, 134–6
  encampments and, 54, 167, 181, 185, 190–3, 209
  policies/processes for, 108, 111, 155–6, 177, 196, 209
  racialized resident, 25–7, 47, 64, 82–3, 91, 133–5
  working class, 91, 139
  see also gentrification
dispossession, 104
  eviction as process of, 111, 152
  of housing, 10, 12, 58, 61, 98, 111
  policy impacts and, 12, 15, 82
  racism and, 10, 15, 59, 82, 91–3
  settler-colonial, 15, 59, 61, 148–9, 155
Downtown Eastside (DTES, Vancouver)
  COVID-19 impacts/response, 14, 16–21
  government policymaking and, 14–15, 17–21
  Residents Association, 17
  single room occupancy hotels in, 14–18, 20–2, 23n16
  SRO Collaborative Society, *see* SRO Collaborative Society
  tenant networks, importance of, 16–22
drugs, 188
  narratives on use of, 36–7, 56, 181
  poisoning risks, 17–19
  supplies of, 16, 18–22, 49
  tenant use of, 34, 38–40, 198
  treatment programming, 36, 165
  see also methamphetamines
Dufferin Grove Park (Toronto), 180–1, 185
Duggan, Mike, 84

Efficiency Lodge (Atlanta), 69–70
Echo Park,
  city abandonment of residents, 197–9
  collective care/Rise Up organizing in, 198–200
  eviction by police, 196–8, 200–5
encampments,
  CDC guidance against evictions, 45, 48, 55, 189
  in COVID-19: 48, 86, 182, 209
  displacement of, 54, 167, 181, 185, 190–3, 209
  eviction, 182, 184–5, 188–92, 194, 196–8, 200–5
  experiences in, 49–50, 54–6, 60–2
  gentrification versus, 50–1, 188, 190, 194
  municipal hostility to, 7, 55–6, 61–2, 179–85, 189–92, 202–4
  networks for support, 179, 181–3, 185, 187, 191–3
  organizational support, 190–4, 197, 199
  policing of, 1, 48–51, 55–6, 168–75, 180–5, 197
  policymaking on, 7, 10, 46, 179, 185
  in public spaces, 55, 59–61, 179–83, 189, 194, 196
  sweeps of, 6–7, 45, 196–9, 203–5
Encampment Support Network (ESN, Toronto), 179, 185
  formation and outreach, 181–4
Engels, Friedrich (The Housing Question), 9–11
Epperson, Louise, 25
Eubanks, Virginia, 98
Europe, 4, 6, 80
  Serbian housing/income disparities versus, 74, 76–7
eviction, 196–8, 200–5
  court watch, 110–12
  crisis of, 65–7, 139–42, 209
  encampment, 182, 184–5, 188–92, 194, 196–8, 200–5
  families', 29, 48, 50–1, 78, 117, 175
  gentrification and, 47–8, 50–1, 188, 190, 194
  hotel, 59, 70, 201–2, 204
  illegal, 22, 86, 89, 111, 113n1, 153
  infrastructure, 74–5, 79, 85–90, 131, 135, 188–91
  landlords in proceedings, 110–12, 118, 130–1, 156
  mass, 5, 35, 135, 202, 205n1
  migrant vulnerability, 79, 139, 152–3
  moratoriums, 56–7, 86–90, 108–9, 116–17, 134, 151–6, 209
  organizing against, 65–7, 72–80, 83–92, 109, 202

police assistance in, 48, 86–7, 55, 74, 196–205
as process, not event, 108, 110–12, 152
protection ordinance, 116–17, 120–2
Zoom use in court cases, 130–1

facial recognition technology, 89, 98, 102–4
fair market rent, 118, 126n28, 127n42
families, 67, 108
    eviction of, 29, 48, 50–1, 78, 117, 175
    nuclear/patriarchal notions of, 37, 57–9, 61
    public housing for, 29, 73
    separation of, 16, 46–7, 157, 159–61, 165, 201
    vacant housing occupation, 45, 48–50
family reunification housing, 39–41
fascism, 1, 8, 74
feminism, 61, 83
financial crisis (2007–2008): 66, 83, 96–8
financialization, housing, 58, 185
    responses to, 12, 144
Floyd, George, 5, 86–7
    uprisings from police murder of, 48, 54, 66, 104, 122
food, 198
    access/scarcity, 6, 60, 78, 150, 163, 185
    distribution, 18, 54, 73–8, 177
    encampment/public, 60, 192, 201
foreclosures, 58, 96
    legal defence of, 4–5
    mortgage, 4–5, 82–3
    tax, 4–5, 82–3
foster care system, 39–41, 47
Foucault, Michel, 36

Garcetti, Eric, 198
gender, 121
    housing conditions/poverty and, 10, 36, 41, 59
    surveillance/screening by, 96, 98
    tenant struggles and, 3–4, 16, 173
gentrification,
    acceleration of, 46–7, 79, 91, 196, 203
    COVID-19 amid, 34, 51
    encampments/homelessness versus, 50–1, 188, 190, 194
    funding for, 34–5
    landlord technology and, 95–6, 98, 104
    police role in, 47–8, 50–1
    struggles against, 46–7, 79, 82, 92, 133, 199
Geoffrey's Garden, 40–1
Gibson, Kenneth A., 24
Great Recession (2007–09), 83
    housing struggles after, 4–5, 31–2
Grenfell Tower, 5

Hagbard (former Encampment Support Network member), 182–4, 186n1
harm reduction,
    amid COVID-19: 18, 54–5, 65, 130, 181–2
    housing/buildings, 34, 39, 49
    peer-led, 17–19, 23n13
Harper, Karin, 35, 37–41
health care,
    mental, *see* mental health care
    provision, *see* public health care
Healthy LA, 116, 119
Heningburg, Gus, 28
Henry, Toby, 28
home,
    amid COVID-19: 1, 5, 24, 57, 66, 143, 193
    creating spaces of, 15, 24, 80, 151, 167, 183
    Indigenous versus settler concepts of, 7
    struggles' shifting notions of, 1, 58–60, 145, 187, 208
homelessness,
    banishment laws and, *see* banishment laws, housing
    COVID-19 impacts, 37–40, 48, 54, 66, 179–82
    criminalization of, 7, 10–11, 185, 189, 192–3, 203–4
    family, 45–6, 50–1
    health impacts of, 11, 160–1, 179
    initiatives to address, 37, 39–40, 47, 62, 132
    mass, 207–8
    rising, 16, 57, 149, 205
    threat/risk of, 16, 29, 150, 203–5
    see also encampments
homeless people, 102, 207–8

activism of, 45–9, 54–6, 143, 149–52, 163, 199–200
as defining cities, 2, 182
policies against/denying rights of, 46, 188–94
racism/stigmatization facing, 7, 58, 67, 159–60, 187–94, 201–4
support for, 50–2, 76–8, 121, 169, 179–85, 198
as tenants, 196–7, 202–5
Hôpital Général, 36
hotels, 177
  emergency/short-stay rooms, 3, 15, 58–9, 182, 201–2, 209
  eviction from, 59, 70, 201–2, 204
  extended-stay/residential, 66, 69–71, 201
  mutual aid hubs in, 54–6
  shelter, 185, 197–8
  single-room occupancy, *see* single-room occupancy hotels
housing crisis, 79
  assumptions of people in, 208
  capitalism and, 4, 9, 32
  COVID-19 impacts, 1–2, 5, 116
  mobilizing to address, 68, 136
  as permanent/long-term, 11, 139, 148, 153–4, 180, 207
"housing first" policies, 39, 42, 188–9, 193
housing justice, 206
  concepts of, 56–7, 60–1, 148
  creating spaces for, 56, 60–2, 85, 179
  frameworks for, 93, 103–4, 118, 148
  lawyering for, 114–15, 120, 122, 127n37
  lessons about, 56–7, 60, 62, 136, 140
  mass crisis and, 4–5, 26, 116, 122–3, 208–10
  movements for, 8, 56–8, 122–3, 129, 134,
  narratives, 50, 60, 129
  networks for, 95, 118, 120
  personal draw to, 12, 60, 66, 69, 109, 129–30
Housing Justice League (HJL, Atlanta), 64
  Eviction Defense Manual, 65–7, 72
  Tenant Power Hotline, 65–8, 70–2
  working groups, 65, 71
housing policy,
  advocacy, 19–20, 42, 47, 118–22, 132
  Australian, 149–50, 156
  Canadian, 39–40, 140, 145
  civil rights and, 97, 114–15, 124n1
  classist, 58–9, 139
  organizing to strengthen, 120, 140, 149–50
  racist, 14–15, 25, 37, 57–9
  US, 57, 59, 120, 132
Housing and Urban Development (US federal department; HUD), 27, 29–30

Illinois, 164
  housing banishment law impacts, 157–61, 163
India, 167
  rehabilitation policy, 172, 175–7
  see also Khori Gaon
Indigenous people,
  homelessness experiences, 7, 16, 54, 62
  leadership in struggles, 42, 61–2, 155–6
  settler state relations with, 11, 38–9, 42, 59, 139
  sovereignty struggles, 7, 13n6, 148, 155
  see also settler colonialism
im/migrants, 41, 57
  eviction vulnerability, 79, 139, 152–3
infra-commoning, 76
  analysis of, 74–5, 78, 80
  concept and rise of, 73–5
infrastructure, 181
  eviction, 74–5, 79, 85–90, 131, 135, 188–91
  health care, 14, 17, 21
  lack of, 71, 73, 75–6, 185
  social, 14, 71, 73, 76–9, 183
  solidarity/informal, 73–7, 79, 183, 198–9, 210
insecurity, housing, 11
  marginalizing issue of, 31, 58, 160
  organizing to counter, 8, 76, 78, 199
  policymaking and, 149, 159, 178n1
institutions, 101, 209
  financial, 12
  government, 132, 134, 161
  incarceration in, 38, 47, 188–9
  power inequities in, 8, 23n16, 61, 75–6, 96–7
  racism embedded in, 27, 36, 59, 69

settler colonial, 13n6, 177
intermediary lease occupancies (ILOs), 96, 98–9, 102

Joint Action Roof Over Head, *see* Roof, the

Keep LA Housed (KLAH) coalition, 118, 120
Kentucky, 87, 129–30
  rural tenant activism in, 133–6
Khori Gaon (India),
  court-ordered demolition impacts, 167–70
  forest encroachment narratives about, 167, 169, 172
  leadership clientelism and secrecy, 170–2, 174
  media coverage/bans, 168–9, 174–6
  police violence/surveillance, 167–75
  public hearing organizing, 169–70
  youth mobilizing in, 171–4

Laberge, Corey, 42
Land Back movement, 7–8, 13n6
landlords, 209
  abuse/exploitation by, 16, 34–5, 37–41, 84–7, 94n6
  COVID-19 and, 1–2, 4–5, 38–40, 117
  in eviction proceedings, 110–12, 118, 130–1, 156
  interests/lobbying of, 36, 57, 79–80, 139, 153–5
  lack of maintenance by, 15, 25, 84
  mobilizing to challenge, 47, 50, 67–70, 88–90, 134, 141–2
  price fixing, 96, 100, 104
  relationship with tenants, 4, 70, 85–8, 144–5, 202
  surveillance/screening by, 38, 40; *see also* landlord technology
  unaccountable, 15, 25, 89–93, 129–30, 150–2
  see also recovery landlordism
landlord technology,
  companies, 99–101, 104
  concept and industry of, 95–8, 102–3
  digital doormen, 96, 98, 100–1
  gentrification and, 98–9, 102
  organizing against, 95–6, 102–4
  virtual rent and management systems, 100, 104
land trusts, community, 51–2, 210
lawsuits, 94n6, 104, 114, 119
  dismissal of, 29, 135
  tenant filing of, 120, 135
lawyers,
  landlords', 111, 130–1
  public interest, 114, 118, 122, 126n30, 170–2
  social justice role, 114–15, 120–3, 124n11
  tactical coordination, 119–23, 127n37, 177
  see also movement lawyering
legal aid, 112
  connecting tenants to, 70, 92, 132
  inability to provide, 67
  workers, 4, 9, 118
Lexington, 131
  pressure on city officials, 130, 132–3
Lexington Housing Justice Collective (LHJC), 130–3, 135–6
liberalism, critiques of, 46, 82, 115
living, encampment practising of, 61–2
Living Recovery Foundation (LRF, Winnipeg),
  COVID-19 approaches, 39–41
  recovery landlordism of, 35–8, 40–2
lockouts, 101, 108, 111
Los Angeles, 6, 31
  encampment support organizations, 197, 199
  housing struggles in, 4, 196–8, 200–5
  legal and tenant support groups in, 95, 103, 119–20, 126n30
  Project Roomkey (PRK), 197–8, 200–5
  Safer at Home, 197–8
  Tenant Bill of Rights (TBOR), 118
  tenant protection ordinances, 103, 116, 118–20
  see also Healthy LA; Keep LA Housed coalition; Los Angeles Tenants Union
Los Angeles Tenants Union (LATU), iv, 199
  concept of tenant, 3, 196–7

low-income housing,
    activism, 51, 68, 118
    gentrification versus, 47, 127n42
    privatization of, 31-2, 188
low-income tenants, 149
    Downtown Eastside, 14-15, 18, 20
    eviction of, 88, 111, 116
    subsidies/vouchers, 30, 202-3
Lossin, R.H. ("In Defense of Destroying Property"), 6

Madden, Patrick (Lexington developer), 133-4
Makoon Transition, 40-1
Manitoba, 39-41; see also Winnipeg
Mann, Steve, 110
mental health care, 16, 19, 47, 165, 188-9, 201
methamphetamines,
    recovery landlordism and, 35-6, 39-40
    Winnipeg crisis, 34-5, 39-40
Michigan, 89
    housing justice organizing in, 85-6, 90, 92
    see also Detroit Renter City; No Rent MI
migrants, see im/migrants
Minneapolis,
    encampments in, 54-6, 60-2
    Park Board, 55-6
    police violence in, 5, 86
mobile home residents, 133-5
moral imperatives, 32, 193
    rehabilitative housing and, 34, 36-9
mortgage payments,
    delayed, 1, 74
    tenancy and, 3, 152
    see also foreclosures
movement lawyering, 114-15, 121-3, 125n13
municipalities, 6, 93, 121
    community surveillance and, 15, 97, 102, 157
    COVID-19 and, 14, 17, 20-21, 92, 130, 177
    encampments, hostility to, 7, 55-6, 61-2, 179-85, 189-92, 202-4
    lack of tenant support, 15, 84, 131-3, 140, 143
    landlord/developer support, 11, 34-5
    public/affordable housing struggles and, 15, 27-31, 39, 50-1, 130-5, 196-8
    rental property ordinances, 82-4, 87-91, 103, 116-19
mutual aid,
    building networks of, 16-22, 65, 72
    collectives, 187-8, 191
    concept and importance of, 60, 65, 75, 199
    resource/support hubs, 54-6, 198-9, 208
    volunteers, 17, 19, 191-3

neighbourhoods, 121
    Black, 24-6, 64, 67-71, 82-3, 97
    committee/network formation, 179, 181-3, 185
    connection through, 7, 21, 60-1, 87
    COVID-19 impacts on, 17-20, 37-8, 73
    gentrification of, 25, 46-50, 91, 196, 199, 203
    low-income, 14, 47, 50, 88-9, 188
    organizing of, 7, 25-6, 54-5, 60-1, 92-3
neighbours, 201
    canvassing/conversations with, 65, 87-8, 133, 204
    displacement of, 54-5, 64, 176, 178n1
    solidarity with houseless, 48-50, 73, 182, 191
    surveillance of, 102, 180
    tenant/community defence of, 4-6, 12, 20, 87, 109, 135
neoliberalism, 56
    policy reforms, 20, 30, 39, 188-90
    state retrenchment, 21, 23n16, 203
networks, 165, 170
    care, 76-7, 80, 183
    encampment support, 179, 181-3, 185
    housing referral, 38-40
    mutual aid, 16-22, 54, 65, 71-2
    organizational, 29, 95, 145, 150
    resource distribution, 27, 77-80
    social, 17, 25, 31, 74-6, 173
    solidarity, 129, 136, 181-5
    surveillance, 97, 101-4
Newark (New Jersey), 28-9, 31
    Central Ward, 25-6

Black Power movement tenant
    organizing, 24, 27, 30
Newark Housing Authority, 25, 27–31
NIMBYism, 7, 184
non-Indigenous people, 42–3, 155
non-profit industrial complex, 187–8, 193
non-profits, 52, 190
    advocacy, 16, 18, 64, 124n1, 192, 209
    housing, 16, 22, 37, 40
    limitations of, 23n16, 50, 187–8, 193
    tenant power inequities with, 11–12,
        16, 47, 82, 194, 208
No Rent MI (NRM), 85–6, 88
North Fork (Kentucky), 133–6
nuclear families, *see* single-family homes

occupation, 188, 198
    defence of, 5, 54, 56, 58, 194, 210
    land/vacant housing, 45–6, 48–50, 54,
        181
    settler colonial/violent, 10–11, 42
Occupy movement, 64, 83
organizing, tenant, *see* tenant organizing
overdose prevention, 17–19, 204

Parenti, Christian, 207
Parkdale neighbourhood committee, 179,
    181–2, 185
Penner, Patrick, 34–5, 37
[people.power.media] (PPM, San
    Francisco), 95, 102
Peoplestown, 64, 72n2
Philadelphia,
    COVID-19 impacts, 48
    gentrification in, 46–9, 51
    housing/land occupation in, 45–50
Philadelphia Housing Action (PHAct),
    land trust action, 51–2
    protest encampments, 49–50
    vacant housing occupation, 47–51
Philadelphia Housing Authority (PHA),
    gentrifying role, 47–9, 51
    private police violence, 47–51
Plank, Faith, 134–6
police, 35
    aiding landlords with evictions, 48,
        86–7, 55, 74, 199–200
    brutality, 5–6, 10, 26, 54, 86–7, 184

    encampments versus, 1, 48–51, 55–6,
        168–75, 180–5, 197
    gentrification role, 47–8, 50–1
    homeless folks versus, 80, 180, 185,
        191–2, 202–4
    killing by, 5, 11, 35, 54, 86
    station destruction, 54, 177
    surveillance, 89–91, 97, 101, 104, 153,
        158–64, 185
    tenant struggles versus, 3–4, 61, 85, 90,
        167, 203
    violence of, 35–6, 45–51, 54, 191–2
    see also abolition
policing, 76
    bloated budgets of, 6, 31–2, 161
    calls to defund, 5–6, 92
    militarized, 49, 196
politicization, tenant, 5, 20, 77–8, 132, 149,
    198
Portland, 108–9
poverty,
    criminalization of, 7, 10, 102, 202–3
    efforts to reduce, 37, 193–4
    housing conditions and, 31, 41, 56,
        134, 202
    marginalization and, 10, 28, 115, 133,
        159, 202
    narratives/stigmatization of, 35, 37,
        77–8, 177, 178n1
    organizing despite, 28, 30, 124n11,
        204
precarity, housing, 165, 205
    COVID-19 exacerbation of, 5, 16–22,
        24, 31, 70, 79, 150
    historical, 25, 148–9
    landlord surveillance and, 98, 104
    mobilizing amid, 52, 76–80, 114,
        148–52, 197
    structural causes of, 52, 56–7, 67, 136,
        202–3
    tenancy and, 16–22, 66, 108–9, 156
    vacant housing occupation and, 45, 52
prison industrial complex, 101, 104
prisons, 160
    in COVID-19: 41, 161
    housing conditions akin to, 36–8, 101,
        201
private property, 139

challenging structures of, 52, 56, 104, 198–9, 205
settler colonial/liberal relations of, 7, 46, 59–60, 99, 182
profitability, housing, goal of maximizing, 1, 38, 40
property management,
   deflecting blame,
   in eviction court, 84, 111
   failures of, 49, 89, 101
   neglecting maintenance, 35, 98–9
   tenant-run, 24–5, 29–31
   virtual, 96, 100–1, 104
proptech, *see* landlord technology
Public Counsel, 114, 121, 124n1
public good, housing as, 4, 24, 58, 83, 185
public health care, 83, 201
   COVID-19 measures, 4–5, 14, 17–21, 80, 116–19, 149
   crisis, 14, 21–2, 57, 92, 153, 209
   (lack of) access to services, 6, 18, 20, 54–5, 75–6
   provision, 17–22, 55, 161
   rental housing and, 15–21, 48, 114–20, 149, 203
   struggles for, 14, 27, 80, 119, 181
   systemic racism in, 15, 48, 59
   see also mental health care
public housing,
   activism for, 58, 145, 152, 155–6, 181
   community importance of stable, 24–5
   control/surveillance through, 36, 97
   funding for, 30–2, 39
   government disinvestment from, 16, 26, 31, 47–8
   racist narratives about, 25–6
   tenant management of, 24, 26–9
public spaces, 97
   encampments/unhoused people in, 55, 59–61, 179–83, 189, 194, 196
   policymaking on, 179–83, 189, 193
   shared use of, 5, 182–3, 200
   see also encampments
race,
   housing/rental conditions and, 10, 54, 121
   gentrification/dispossession and, 67, 91–3, 127n42, 133, 203

movement divisions, based on, 7, 61, 65–6, 115, 124n10, 203
racial capitalism, 24, 42, 104, 199–200, 203
racialized communities,
   exclusion from movements, 7, 65, 69–71, 77
   narratives about, 26, 57, 77, 96–8, 102
   segregation of, 15, 25, 47, 59
   surveillance of, 96–8, 102, 104
   white folks' privilege versus, 32, 69–71, 77, 91
racial justice demands, 66, 87, 122, 129, 133, 209
racism,
   anti-Black, 5–6, 8, 82, 86–7, 97, 102
   in housing policies, 14–15, 25, 37, 57–9
   police, 5–6, 8, 47, 54, 86–7, 97
   structural impacts of, 5, 74, 120
   systemic, 26–7, 76–7, 115, 133
   tenant struggles amid, 3–5
   see also anti-racist struggles
radicalization, tenant, 5, 78, 110
Razack, Sherene, 42
real estate, 199
   developers, *see* developers, real estate
   government support for, 34, 49, 152, 170
   investment interests, 12, 58, 133, 139–40, 149, 202–3
   platform technology use, 95–6, 99, 104
real estate state, 2, 8
recovery landlordism, 35–8, 40–2
redlining, 25, 59
Refaei, Saiyare (All Eyes on Evictors / Resist Eviction), 109, 112
rehabilitation policy, India, 172, 175–7
rehabilitative capitalism, 37
   as settler colonial strategy, 39, 41–2
rehabilitative housing, 188
   history of surveillance through, 34–7
Remora House (Washington, DC), 187–8
rent control, 2, 41, 58, 79–80, 121, 142–3
rent debt, 127n42
   COVID-19 exacerbating, 66, 70
   mobilizing to cancel, 103, 117–18, 126n27, 142
Renters and Housing Union (RAHU)
   formation and functions of, 149–50, 154, 156

rent strike organizing, 150–3, 155–6
rent increases, 16, 41, 139
  organizing to counter, 22, 35, 103, 118, 149
  policy support for, 27, 145, 156
  tracking of, 35, 100, 156
rent payments, 41, 84, 156
  COVID-19 impacts, 1, 57, 85, 99, 108, 117, 134
  struggles to make, 57, 67, 108, 135
  virtual platforms for, 96, 100
Rent Strike Bargain (RSB), 142
  campaign formation and focus, 140–1, 143–5
rent strikes, 86, 103, 181
  Australia, 150–6
  campaigns for using, 140–2
  Newark tenants', 24–5, 28–32
reparations, 8, 11, 57
residential restrictions, *see* banishment laws, housing
Revlett, Beau, 131
Right to Remain (R2R) research collective, 18, 21–2
  support for DTES SRO-C, 16–17, 19
Roberts, Dorothy, 37
Roof, the (Joint Action Roof Over Head), 74
  COVID-19 response, 73, 76, 79
  see also infra-commoning
Roy, Ananya, 58
rural communities, 134, 136, 143
rural tenants, 12, 129, 133–5

San Francisco,
  CCTV surveillance in, 96–7, 104
  corporate landlord practices in, 99–101, 103–4
  gentrification in, 95–8, 104
  short-term rental shifts in, 98, 102
San Francisco Police Department (SFPD), 97, 101, 104
screening, tenant, 38, 96–8, 100, 104
Scudder Homes (Newark), 26, 28
securitization,
  evictions and, 70, 74
  financial, 12
  landlord measures of, 36, 38–40, 101–2, 149
  post-9/11: 89, 96–8
  surveillance and, 36, 101–2, 104, 184–5
  tenant measures of, 29–30, 50, 80, 157
segregation, housing, 15, 25, 47, 58, 96
self-determination,
  Black struggles for, 27, 30
  community struggles for, 30, 37, 56, 198
  Indigenous struggles for, 7, 13n6
self-reliance, tenant,
  COVID-19 and, 20–1, 37–8, 55–7
  informal networks, 25–31, 75, 143, 172
  learning, 30, 140, 198, 203
Serbia,
  EU-mandated reforms, 74–5
  housing/rental crisis response in, 73, 76, 79–80
  informal economy/rental sector in, 75–7, 79
  see also infra-commoning
settler colonialism, 177
  capitalism and, 139, 155, 183
  dispossession and, 15, 59, 61, 148–9, 155
  Indigenous people and, 7, 13n6, 16, 39–42, 59–60
  poverty and, 10, 14–15
  private property ownership and, 7, 46, 52, 99, 139, 182–3
  recovery landlordism and, 41–2
  tenant struggles amid, 3–4, 148–9
sex offender laws, *see* banishment laws, housing
sex work, 18, 56, 181
Share-A-Ton Sanctuary Hotel, 54–5, 62
shelter-in-place (COVID-19) orders,
  financial impacts of, 5, 85
  homelessness/encampments and, 48, 86, 209
shelter services, 176, 204
  amid COVID-19: 7, 48, 55, 179, 184–5, 197–8
  lack of adequate, 62, 75–6, 163, 179, 193, 196
  user experiences, 11, 55–6, 182, 188–9
short-term rentals (STRs), 96, 98–9, 102
single-family homes, 36, 58, 61, 96
single-room occupancy hotels (SROs),
  conditions in, 14–16, 19–20, 23n16

COVID-19 impacts on, 17–21
Downtown Eastside (DTES, Vancouver), 14–17, 19–20
proliferation of, 14–15
Skinner, Marena, 206
"slum" clearance, narratives of, 25, 36–7, 57–8, 168, 178n1
slumlords, 14, 153
Smith, John, 26
Smith, Mary, 26
Smith, Neil, 35
sober/recovery housing, 34, 37, 39, 111–12, 130
social assistance, 15–16, 57, 152–4, 189
social housing, 2, 57, 73, 140, 182, 185; see also supportive housing
social media,
   art/graphics on, 88, 119, 199–200, 206
   awareness campaigns on, 70, 85–6, 172, 175
   tenant organizing on, 35, 66, 76, 149, 192–3
social reproduction, 61, 75–6, 78, 80
solidarity, 86
   organizing ethos of, 43, 74–9, 181–3, 186
   rent strike, 28, 30, 150
   with tenants, 78, 129, 143–5
sousveillance, court, 110, 112–13
Spade, Dean, 60
squatting,
   concepts and purpose of, 3, 46, 152
   state/private responses to, 50, 74
   support for, 45, 51–2
SRO Collaborative Society (SRO-C),
   COVID-19 organizing, 17–20, 23n16
   work with R2R, 16–17, 21–2
state, the,
   abandonment by, 15–21, 25, 32, 54, 58, 197–9
   capitalism and, see capitalist state
   COVID-19 responses, 15–20, 57–8, 76–80, 85–90, 149–51
   ignoring tenant needs, 12, 151, 168–74, 176
   racist policies of, 6, 16, 57–9
   recovery landlordism and, 36–7, 42, 189
   tenant organizing versus, 28, 60–1, 85–92, 135–7, 151, 208–9

tenant unions versus, 141–5, 156
violence/surveillance (sanctioned) by, 6, 46–52, 62, 99–100, 181, 203–4
see also real estate state
state governments (in United States), 103
   eviction infrastructure and, 74–5, 79, 85–90, 131, 135, 188–91
   eviction protection, 116–17, 120–2
   housing banishment registration and, 158, 161, 164–5
   police/surveillance use by, 74, 168–74, 177
Stella Wright Homes,
   conditions in, 26, 28–9
   funding for, 31–2
   tenant organizing/management of, 24, 27–9
Stella Wright Tenant Association (SWTA), 28–9
   Management Corporation (SWTAMC), 29–31
Stewart, Michelle, 42
supply,
   drug, 16, 18–22
   housing, 11, 201
supportive housing, 22, 37, 42, 190; see also social housing
surveillance technology,
   companies, 99–101, 104
   gentrification and, 98–9, 102
   housing and, 36–8, 40, 96, 98, 100–1
   industry of, 95–8, 102–3
   organizing against, 95–6, 102–4
   "post-pandemic," 101–2
   racism and, 5–8, 82, 86–90, 96–8, 102, 203

Taylor, Breonna, 5, 66, 86–7
Taylor, Keeanga-Yamahtta, 5
tenant,
   concepts of, 3–4, 196–7
   organizing, see tenant organizing
tenant organizations,
   activism of, 30–1, 102, 132, 136, 140–3
   experiences in, 26, 28, 92, 119, 121, 145
   formation/rapid growth of, 27, 71, 103, 145
   see also tenant unions

tenant organizing,
    concepts/lessons of, 91, 93, 103, 144–5, 206
    COVID-19 and: 5, 65–70, 90, 114–17, 135, 210
    digital, 35, 65–70, 87–8
    eviction court watch, 110–12
    knowledge sharing in, 67, 86, 92–3, 95
    need to focus on urgent/reactive, 64–71, 117, 121
    outreach, 16–17, 65–6, 83–8, 91–3, 136–7, 181–3
    racial and class tensions in, 69–71
    rent strikes, 24–5, 28–32, 140–2
    single-room occupancy, 17, 21
    see also tenant organizations
Tenant Overdose Response Organizers (TORO), 17, 19, 23n16
tenant power, 31
    demonstrations of, 7, 55–7, 103, 118
    focus on building, 64–7, 71–2, 121, 207
    importance of, 11–12, 14, 205
    processes of, 3–4, 92–3, 136, 140, 143–4
tenants' rights, 7, 93, 201
    education about, 88, 92–3, 109
    to housing/to occupy space, 9, 46, 49, 56, 79–80, 145, 197
    legal eviction proceedings, 70, 132
    organizing for, 118–19, 121, 131, 140
    property owners/landlords versus, 42, 61, 93, 155
tenant unions,
    collective bargaining by, see collective bargaining
    concepts of, 152, 196–7
    formation of, 121, 136, 140–4, 149–51, 208
    organizing of, 3, 85–6, 112, 145, 156
    proposed principles of, 142, 144
    utility of, 112–13, 140–2, 145, 151–3
tenement housing, 38, 58
The Barbara (Detroit rental building), surveillance of, 88–90
Toronto,
    COVID-19 responses, 179, 182
    encampment clearance, 182, 184–5
    legislation on encampments, 179, 185
    police violence/surveillance in, 180, 182, 184–5
trans people, poverty and, 10
Trinity Bellwoods Park, 181–2, 184–5
Trinity Properties, 99, 101
Trump, Donald, 6, 129
Turnage, Wayne, 193

Unhoused Tenants Against Carceral Housing (UTACH), 201–5
unions,
    labour, 141, 144–5, 151
    tenant, see tenant unions
    see also collective bargaining
United Kingdom, 15, 97
United States, 15, 32, 46, 109
    encampment/homelessness policies, 7, 10, 46, 185
    foreclosures across, 4, 188
    housing/property policies, 52, 58–60, 96–100, 159, 189, 209
    Housing and Urban Development (department), 27, 29–30
    post-pandemic policing/surveillance, 6, 89, 97, 101–2
urban commoning, see infra-commoning
urban renewal, narratives of, 25–6, 145

vacancies, 100
    COVID-19 and, 37–8
    policies to control, 140, 142
    rates of, 30, 35, 37–8, 47
vacant buildings/land, 88, 188
    occupation of, 30–1, 45–8
    organizing to secure, 27, 51
Vancouver, 206
    COVID-19 response, 14, 17, 20–21
    Health Department, 15, 17
    policymaking by, 14–15, 17–22
    racialized displacement in, 14–16, 22
    rent increases in, 16, 22, 139
    single-room occupancy hotels in, 14–17, 19–20
    tenant movement collapse in, 143
    see also Downtown Eastside
Veritas, 99–100
    mobilizing against, 103–4
Victorian housing, 36, 38

vouchers, housing, 12, 30, 190, 202

wages,
    COVID-19 loss of, 4–5, 85, 99
    low, 88, 134, 189
    rent outpacing, 2, 10, 139
    struggles for higher, 141, 187, 194
Washington, DC, 187
    bridge housing, lack of, 190–3
    "by name list" (BNL), 190–4
    Coordinated Assistance and Resources for Encampments (CARE) program, 190–4
    Deputy Mayor of Health and Human Services (DMHHS), 189–93
    encampment evictions, 188–92, 194
    mutual aid group encampment support in, 187, 191–3
    police presence in, 191–2
wellbeing, resident, 59
    collective, 78
    post-pandemic, 6, 42
    threats to, 42, 93, 159
wellness checks, 38–40
whiteness, 59, 69, 71
white people,
    activism involvement, 65, 69–71, 82
    gentrification and, 25, 57–9, 61, 82, 98, 133
    property ownership, 25, 32, 58–9
    racist policies favouring, 57–9, 98
Willse, Craig, 193
Winnipeg, 42
    meth crisis in, 34–5, 39
    neglected and vacant buildings in, 37–8
women, 10, 175
    Black, 69, 71, 110–11
    community organizing of, 170–3
working class,
    Black tenants, 24–5, 28–32
    housing conditions, 36, 58–9, 102
    immigrant, 149, 152
    organizing, 9, 24–5, 28, 54, 180